Scratching Out a Living

CALIFORNIA SERIES IN PUBLIC ANTHROPOLOGY

The California Series in Public Anthropology emphasizes the anthropologist's role as an engaged intellectual. It continues anthropology's commitment to being an ethnographic witness, to describing, in human terms, how life is lived beyond the borders of many readers' experiences. But it also adds a commitment, through ethnography, to reframing the terms of public debate—transforming received, accepted understandings of social issues with new insights, new framings.

Series Editor: Robert Borofsky (Hawaii Pacific University)

Contributing Editors: Philippe Bourgois (University of Pennsylvania), Paul Farmer (Partners in Health), Alex Hinton (Rutgers University), Carolyn Nordstrom (University of Notre Dame), and Nancy Scheper-Hughes (UC Berkeley)

University of California Press Editor: Naomi Schneider

Scratching Out a Living

LATINOS, RACE, AND WORK IN
THE DEEP SOUTH

Angela Stuesse

UNIVERSITY OF CALIFORNIA PRESS

University of California Press, one of the most distinguished university presses in the United States, enriches lives around the world by advancing scholarship in the humanities, social sciences, and natural sciences. Its activities are supported by the UC Press Foundation and by philanthropic contributions from individuals and institutions. For more information, visit www.ucpress.edu.

University of California Press
Oakland, California

Portions of chapter 3 and chapter 4 originally appeared in "Low-Wage Legacies, Race, and the Golden Chicken in Mississippi: Where Contemporary Immigration Meets African American Labor History," *Southern Spaces*, 2013, http://southernspaces.org/2013/low-wage-legacies-race-and-golden-chicken-mississippi.

Portions of chapter 7 appeared in an earlier form in "Race, Migration, and Labor Control: Neoliberal Challenges to Organizing Mississippi's Poultry Workers," in *Latino Immigrants and the Transformation of the U.S. South*, edited by Mary Odem and Elaine Lacy, 91–111 (Athens: University of Georgia Press, 2009); reprinted with permission of the University of Georgia Press.

An earlier version of chapter 8 appeared as "What's 'Justice and Dignity' Got to Do with It? Migrant Vulnerability, Corporate Complicity, and the State," *Human Organization* 69, no. 1 (2010): 19–30.

Portions of the postscript appeared as "Anthropology for Whom? Challenges and Prospects of Activist Scholarship," in *Public Anthropology in a Borderless World*, edited by Sam Beck and Carl Maida, 221–46 (New York: Berghahn Books, 2015).

Library of Congress Cataloging-in-Publication Data

Stuesse, Angela, 1975–.
    Scratching out a living : Latinos, race, and work in the Deep South / Angela Stuesse.
        p.   cm.—(California series in public anthropology ; 38)
    Includes bibliographical references and index.
    ISBN 978-0-520-28720-4 (cloth : alk. paper)
    ISBN 978-0-520-28721-1 (pbk. : alk. paper)
    ISBN 978-0-520-96239-2 (ebook)
    1. Chicken industry—Mississippi—Social conditions.   2. Foreign workers, Latin American—Mississippi—Social conditions.   3. African Americans—Mississippi—Social conditions.
    4. Mississippi—Race relations.   5. Industrial relations—Mississippi.   I. Title.   II. Series:
California series in public anthropology ; 38.
    HD9437.U63M778   2016
    331.6'2809762—dc23

                                                                                        2015028387

24   23   22   21   20   19   18   17   16
10   9   8   7   6   5   4   3   2   1

Contents

Illustrations

Acknowledgments

Acknowledgments are always a hearty reminder of the deeply collective nature of intellectual labor. A decade has passed since I began the work that produced this book; today my debts to those who have supported it are copious, and my memory far too feeble to do them all justice. Nonetheless, I am profoundly grateful to all who have nurtured this project since its inception in 2002.

In Mississippi I was fortunate to benefit from the kindness of hundreds of poultry workers and other research participants to whom I pledged anonymity. This book lifts up their stories and struggles, and I hope they will recognize themselves in its pages.

For making space for me at the table and believing in the potential of activist research to contribute something useful to their efforts, I am indebted to the many collaborators with whom I worked to establish and fulfill the vision of the Mississippi Poultry Workers' Center, including Tutu Alicante, Bill Beardall, Rev. Sally Bevill, Sibyl Bird, Israel Lucas Carbajal, Charles Carney, Bill Chandler, Rev. Jim Evans, Darrell Ezell, Sr. Pat Godri, Anita Grabowski, Slobodan Guerra, Laura Helton, Br. David Henley, Patricia Ice, John Jones, David Mandel-Anthony, Lia Ochoa, Sr. Terri

Rodela, Rick Slayton, Doug Stevick, Kathy Sykes, Milton Thompson, Danny Townsend, John Whittaker, and Nikita Williams.

Without the friends who made Mississippi a place I love, I could have neither conducted the research for this book nor survived my stay there. Thank you, José Aguilón, Oscar Aguilón, Realea Allen, Rodrigo Barabata, Luz Campos, Ann Clements, Amy Cohen, Mirta D'Angelo, Goyo de la Cruz, Guillermina Eugenio, Efrén Feliciano, Elias Feliciano, Coleman Harris, Moisés Hernández, Catherine Herring Weems, Addie Ruth Jones, Gaudencio Lopez, Elmer Matias, Celso Mendoza, Aracely Miranda, Osmar Miranda, Lillian Moore, Silvia Murature, Ramon Orozco, Edmundo Paz, Ana Ramirez, Fredy Salvador, Natanael Salvador, Magaly Taco, Danny Townsend, Mary Townsend, Daniel Vargas, and Faye Veasley. Anita Grabowski has been a cherished friend and colleague since we began working in Mississippi, and our years of collaboration at the workers' center were vital to shaping my analysis and writing during their early stages. I am equally beholden to Laura Helton, who not only taught me how to navigate historical archives and guided me as I struggled with citations of archival documents, but also was instrumental in shaping my understanding of central Mississippi's past and its relevance for today.

My mentors during my time at the University of Texas profoundly shaped my intellectual and political commitments, and words feel inadequate to express my deep gratitude. Richard Flores and Laurie B. Green provided crucial guidance and encouragement, as did Pierette Hondagneu-Sotelo from afar. Charlie Hale, Shannon Speed, João Vargas, and Ted Gordon, this work is a product of your teachings. Thank you for forging a rare institutional space for activist research, for training your students in the rigors of engaged scholarship, and for nurturing our commitments and dreams. I may never be able to pay back what you've given me, but I endeavor each day to pay it forward.

The bulk of my early writing for this project took place in the foothills of the Sangre de Cristo mountains, at the School for Advanced Research. Amid this natural beauty, coupled with the brilliant and supportive community of scholars of which I formed part, I encountered an idyllic setting for trying out new ideas, reflecting, and writing. I will be forever grateful for the care, mentorship, and friendship of Rebecca Allahyari, James Brooks, Catherine Cocks, Omri Elisha, Joe Gone, Laura Holt, John

Kantner, Nancy Owen Lewis, Tiya Miles, Malena Morling, Peter Redfield, Monica Smith, James Snead, and Silvia Tomášková. It was a magical, momentous, unforgettable year.

In various stages of writing and rewriting, my narrative and argument profited immensely from the individuals who offered inspiration and helpful critique to sharpen my ideas and brighten my prose. These included Robert Alvarez, Joe Berra, Jennifer Bickham Mendez, Ronda Brulotte, Heide Castañeda, Mat Coleman, Kathy Dill, Ruth Gomberg-Muñoz, Pablo Gonzalez, Andrew Grant-Thomas, David Griffith, Rubén Hernández-León, Sarah Horton, Don Lamm, Jamie Lee, Daniel Lende, Helen Marrow, Courtney Morris, Gilberto Rosas, Janna Shadduck-Hernández, Cheryl Staats, Chris Tilly, Roger Waldinger, Julie Weise, Jamie Winders, Kevin Yelvington, Becky Zarger, and many others.

I was able to refine my arguments thanks to the generous feedback I received when presenting this work at conferences and seminars, in particular the Social Science Research Council's "Translocal Flows: Migrations, Borders, Diasporas in the Americas" (2003), UNC–Chapel Hill's Andrew W. Mellon Foundation Sawyer Seminar (2007), the UCLA Migration Studies Group's "Labor Markets and Workplace Dynamics in New Destinations of Latino Immigration" (2009), and the Association of American Geographers' panel, "Latino/a Geographies of/in the American South" (2014). I also appreciated the feedback of students in my 2013 graduate seminar Engaging Ethnography, whose meticulous candor and validating feedback came at just the right time.

This project has been supported by numerous institutions: Ford Foundation Fellowship Programs; School for Advanced Research; Social Science Research Council; Society for the Anthropology of North America; Equal Justice Center; University of Texas; UCLA's Institute for Research on Labor and Employment; Ohio State University's Kirwan Institute for the Study of Race and Ethnicity; and University of South Florida's College of Arts and Sciences, Humanities Institute, Office of the Provost, and Tampa Library.

I also thank my colleagues at the University of South Florida, whose shared dedication to collegiality and engaged research have made the anthropology department there a treasured home. Department chairs Elizabeth Bird, David Himmelgreen, and Brent Weisman supported this project by granting me the gift of time, and the support and encouragement I've felt from everyone as a junior member of the faculty has been remarkable.

Catherine Herring Weems and her infant son, Griff (my tiniest research assistant), made a 2014 verification and validation trip back to Mississippi infinitely more productive and enjoyable. As I refined the manuscript, I benefited from Nicholl Cruz's unfailing childcare, as well as the research assistance of graduate students Cassandra Decker, Meredith Main, and Rachel Tyree. I am particularly indebted to the latter for her unfaltering cheer and availability amid the minutia of tracking down copyright permissions, citations, page numbers, keywords, and the like. LeEtta Schmidt at the University of South Florida library graciously helped acquire copyright permissions and missing citation details. Austin Kocher skillfully prepared the maps and chart found herein, while photojournalist Earl Dotter, filmmaker John Fiege, and family archivist Jack Rogers generously provided poignant images to complement and enliven the text.

Martha Bergmark, Lt. Shelby Burnside, Luis Cartagena, Linda Cromer, Tito Echiburu, Chris Foster, Miguel Martínez, Arnulfo Mundo, Jack Rogers, Monzell Stowers, and Rev. Rayford Woodrick found time to not only give interviews but also review drafts of my writing and provide crucial feedback. This book is stronger thanks to their munificence, as well as for the skillful attention it received from University of California Press editor Naomi Schneider, copyeditor Susan Silver, indexer Carol Roberts, and the rest of the editorial team, including Jessica Moll, Ally Powers, Will Vincent, and others. I am particularly appreciative of George Lipsitz, Eric Schlosser, Steve Striffler, and an anonymous reviewer for the time they have invested in my work and for their insightful critiques and corrections. I am also lucky to be surrounded by friends much more clever than I who lent their creative capacities to the imagining of a suitable title for this work. While only one made it onto the cover, several found their way into chapter titles, much to my satisfaction. Thanks, all!

Finally, my biggest debts are to my family, who remind me where I'm from and never cease to support me on life's short journey. My mother, Sherry Stuesse, has always been my champion as well as my earliest model that women in academia can be loving, dedicated mothers and have successful careers despite the inevitable hurdles. Her emotional and financial support have sustained me in more ways than I will ever be able to articulate.

I couldn't have imagined that I would find my life partner based on a mutual dedication to poultry worker justice in the South. Tutu Alicante inspires me to never give up on a better world, however daunting the climb. His selflessness and commitment astound me, and every day I am grateful for him. During the time I incubated this endeavor, we brought two other "projects" into the world, and his extraordinary coparenting—and willingness to take on more than his fair share of the responsibilities—enabled this book to see the light of day. Thank you, Tutu.

Djina and Sanze, you are my light. My greatest hope is that the problems of racial and economic injustice I document in this book will feel part of the distant past by the time you read these lines. Should they persist, may the courageous struggles documented herein inspire you to pick up the torch and continue the fight.

Figure 1. Chicken truck entering plant gates. Photo by John Fiege. Courtesy of FiegeFilms.com.

1 Southern Fried

GLOBALIZATION AND IMMIGRANT
TRANSFORMATIONS

"Her husband used to run whisky as a bootlegger," my acquaintance divulged in a low voice. It was December 2003 and I was visiting Forest, Mississippi, to secure a place to live in advance of my move there the following month. Among the many dead-end leads I pursued, someone suggested I call a widowed white woman who had some land outside of town where she rented a handful of trailers. I wasn't sure I wanted to live even farther out in the country—Forest, with its population of six thousand and hour's drive from the nearest city, seemed rural enough—but I was quickly learning that my housing options in the area were few and, thanks to the poultry industry's booming business in immigrant labor, mostly overpriced and poorly maintained. I spoke to the owner briefly by phone and then drove out along a narrow country road until I met her at the old trailer for rent. She opened the door, and I quickly looked around the dimly lit space. My eyes fixated on the threadbare, olive-colored carpeting in the cramped living area. The trailer did cover the absolute basics, but I hoped it wouldn't come to this.

As we stepped back out into the light of day, I looked around me and asked who else was renting on her property. "What can you tell me about who my neighbors would be?" Her response was surprisingly, painfully candid:

1

"Well, I don't rent to Mexicans. But I do have a Mexican family that is *very good* and helps me keep up my properties." A lump began to form in the pit of my stomach. She proceeded.

"Now, the one who lives down there," gesturing toward the end of the road about three trailers beyond where we stood, "He's a Black man. But he won't hurt you." The lump grew. While I had doubted this place's suitability when I was inside, I now found myself silently plotting my escape. Ultimately, the condition and hue of the wearied rug were insignificant; what made me queasy were my potential landlord's disgraceful views and the ease with which she had interpreted the shade of my white skin as an indication that I would share them.

As I drove away in dismay, wondering if I could ever feel at home here, the ethnographer in me found consolation—admittedly conflicted, but consolation nonetheless—in the realization that I had found fertile ground for my research on how new Latin American immigration was transforming the U.S. South. But I wasn't merely studying this phenomenon; my encounter had made clear that I was also living the very changes I was seeking to understand. I hoped that my work would speak to— indeed, have a transformative impact on—the experiences of everyday people.

·   ·   ·   ·   ·

Two years later I'm reminded of this moment as I sit at dusk on the make-shift porch of a different trailer with Pablo Armenta, a father of four from Veracruz, Mexico.[1] An occasional car passes quietly down the winding country road as darkness falls—headlights approach first, engine rumbling, and soon the red glow of taillights trails behind. Several hundred-foot pine trees stretch up, stoic, from the patch of lawn before us. Three pairs of yellow rubber work boots stand neatly at attention on the ground below the porch, accompanied by three purple plastic aprons that drape over the stairs' crude wooden railing, drying out after a long day's work at the chicken plant. Tonight the warm air is still, but we can't escape the familiar, pervasive odor of Forest—that stout, mealy, putrid aroma of chickens heading to and from slaughter. Around here they say it "smells like money," or so goes the timeworn joke.

I faintly hear the sound of the TV through the closed door behind us. I've asked Pablo to recount his story of how he came to Mississippi. "Mississippi . . . " He pauses for several breaths in a moment of reflection before continuing:

> I think God put it in my path. I was in Florida picking oranges. One afternoon I went to a Cuban store, and when I was walking home a van pulled over, and this guy says to me, "Hey, do you want to work in Mississippi?" And I told him, "Well, that depends." So he explained what it was about, a chicken plant, a factory where they process chicken, the work is like this, they pay this much. They were offering housing and everything, so yeah, it sounded good to me.[2]

I am incredulous. "So they just stopped you on the side of the road, and you said yes?" Pablo chuckles at my astonishment. Perhaps even he's a little surprised at the events that unfolded in its wake:

> Yes! So then they said, "Tomorrow we'll come get you around this time." So I told them where I lived, and I talked with my two brothers, and we decided to do it. They said, "You go ahead, and if it all checks out, we'll follow." The next day I left. We went in a van, all piled up on top of one another; you know, in one of those vans that you can rent to move furniture. It was so full! I arrived, worked one week, received my first paycheck, it seemed good to me, and I brought them all here to join me.

Despite considerable challenges, ten years later Pablo and his brothers have made Mississippi home. The migration he describes, which began in the mid-1990s, has changed the landscape of both the chicken-processing industry and rural southern communities. Such changes have taken place amid social landscapes with previously established categories, as my ill-fated interaction with a prospective landlord made abundantly clear. How these transformations came about, and their impacts on poultry workers, their communities, and their possibilities for workplace justice, are the focus of this book.

SOUTHERN TRANSFORMATIONS

For hundreds of years, the political, economic, and social fabric of the U.S. South has been spun from profound structural inequalities between Black and white.[3] A Latin American migration of unprecedented scope has begun to bring this foundational feature of the region into question. The Hispanic population is growing faster here than in any other part of the country.[4] With the exception of Louisiana, during the 1990s every southern state boasted a greater-than 100 percent increase, with several registering growth rates of more than 300 percent.[5] Over half a million Hispanics moved to the region in this period, and the trend has continued in the new millennium. It is home to seven out of ten states with the largest increase in undocumented migrants between 1990 and 2010.[6] The majority are young, single Mexican men, though the incidence of women as well as migrants from other places in Latin America is on the rise. They have scattered across the region in a patchwork of rural, suburban, and metropolitan areas, following the job opportunities of a global economy. So while immigration is not new to the South, the intensity and breadth of this growing trend is novel.[7] The phenomenon has become so incisive and widespread that some scholars have dubbed the region the "*Nuevo* New South," and white, Black, and new Latino communities find themselves grappling to make sense of the cultural changes and shifting social hierarchies sparked by these dramatic transformations.[8]

Mississippi is the most recent southern state to experience these changes. It has long been considered the "deepest" part of the South, holding a place of "symbolic importance . . . in the national imagination."[9] For many Americans the state conjures up images of the Mississippi Delta, the land along the floodplains of the Mississippi River that has, since the mid-1800s, been home to some of the largest cotton plantations and the most concentrated population of African Americans in the country.[10] Mississippi reminds others of pivotal periods in our nation's history, such as the Civil War or the Civil Rights Movement. For younger people the state may have entered their consciousness following 2005's Hurricane Katrina, which devastated the Mississippi Gulf Coast before decimating New Orleans.

When they hear the word "Mississippi," few people think of the poultry region at the center of the state. Yet this is precisely the area to which Latinos began arriving in the mid-1990s. Because the phenomenon is so recent—at least ten years behind other states in the region with more established immigrant populations—Mississippi's communities have limited infrastructure to support the integration of newcomers, and most residents know little about their backgrounds or reasons for coming. Similarly, new immigrants are generally unaware of the social and political histories of the United States or the South. Moreover, Mississippi's Latino population is extraordinarily diverse, with people from over a dozen countries across Latin America. These realities add to the complexity of social relations in communities and workplaces.

Mississippi is an important place to examine new Latino immigration to the South precisely because of these characteristics. Whereas in other parts of the country immigrants often replace a majority-white workforce, in Mississippi's poultry region they work alongside African Americans in some of the lowest-paid and most dangerous jobs in the country. While the state's high percentage of working-class Black residents and entrenched racial hierarchies have long contributed to the public perception of Mississippi as "the most southern place on Earth," these extremes also enable us to more acutely observe the effects that these new arrivals are having on the deeply engrained social order.[11] I am not suggesting that Mississippi or the Deep South are qualitatively different from other parts of the country. While their legacies of slavery and segregation produced particular social processes and relationships that continue to hold meaning today, the transformations taking place are emblematic of a larger shift throughout the United States, in which new Latino immigrants bring into question long-standing racial hierarchies and ways Americans relate to one another. Rather than seeing the Deep South as exceptional, then, let us consider what it can teach us about broader changes taking place across the country in the realms of social relations, racial identification, and the global economy.[12]

SLAUGHTERING AMERICA'S CHICKENS

America loves chicken. So much, in fact, that we eat almost ninety pounds of it per person, per year. That's nearly double what we ate when I was young (forty-eight pounds annually in 1980) and over ten times what our parents and grandparents consumed in 1950 (eight pounds per capita).[13] Our voracious appetite for this bird has fueled the transformation of poultry production from a backyard endeavor that supplemented families' dinner plates and incomes into one of the most highly specialized and labor-intensive forms of industrial agriculture in the world.[14]

But chicken processing is one of the worst jobs in America. Work on the processing lines is loud and fast. Communication is brusque and kept to a minimum. Pervasive fats and fluids ensure everything stays damp and slippery. Temperatures are extreme, knives often dull, and protective equipment in short supply. Supervisors regularly push bodies and patience past their limits and compensate it all with poverty-level pay. U.S.-born and immigrant workers alike complain of a litany of unjust practices, including wage theft, denial of bathroom breaks, unnecessarily hazardous working conditions resulting in high rates of injury, deceptive use of labor contractors, and abuse by supervisors and higher-level management, including discrimination and sexual harassment.

While corporate earnings continue to rise, poultry workers' real wages have declined steadily since 1970.[15] A national study found violations of minimum wage laws in 100 percent of poultry plants surveyed.[16] Jobs have been "deskilled" and production sped up through remarkable technological advances, and workers now repeat the same monotonous—and often hazardous—movement throughout their entire shift. As a result, repetitive motion injuries plague the workforce.[17] Plants are often out of compliance with federal safety and health regulations, and the government agency charged with oversight of these laws, the Occupational Safety and Health Administration (OSHA), is appallingly underresourced and, consequently, largely ineffective.[18] All workers are expendable; injured or disabled ones are typically disposed of. The annual turnover of workers is as high as 100 percent in some locations.[19]

Workers who try to organize to change these conditions are often met with stiff resistance. "There is no industry harder to organize than the poultry industry," said an international leader of the Retail, Wholesale, and Department Store Union at a gathering of poultry worker leaders from across the South in 2005. "I had heard stories and rumors about what went on in the plants, but I didn't really know till I got to visit a couple plants last year in Mississippi. There is no other place in this country where organizing is harder than in the South. There is no place else in the country where workers are facing such horrific working conditions. Poultry workers represent some of the most exploited workers in this world."

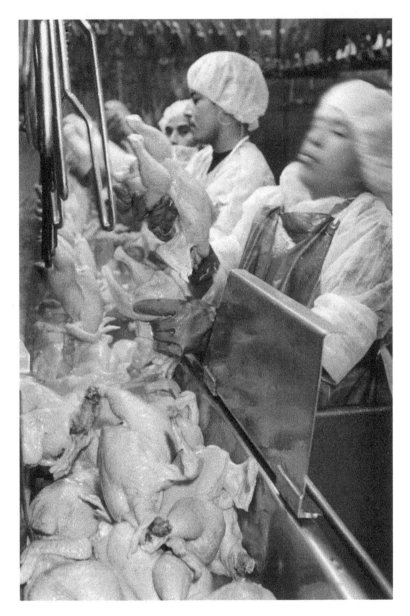

Figure 2. Poultry workers processing America's chickens. Photo by Earl Dotter. Courtesy of EarlDotter.com.

Aside from their claim to being the only major employer in many rural towns, poultry processors are giving their workers virtually no incentive to stay. As this ethnography shows, however, such incentives are unnecessary at the dawn of the twenty-first century, when workers, effortlessly recruited from across the world, are literally expendable and infinitely replaceable.

IMMIGRANT WORKERS IN THE GLOBAL ECONOMY

The dismal working conditions, poverty-level wages, and corporate resistance to collective bargaining that poultry workers endure are not new. Many of these problems were brought to the public's attention more than a century ago, when Upton Sinclair famously detailed the dangerous and unjust practices of Chicago's meatpacking industry in his acclaimed book, *The Jungle*.[20] Even the employment of immigrant laborers and other marginalized groups to weaken worker power is a legacy that extends back to (and before) Sinclair's lifetime.[21] Indeed, industrial capitalism has existed as the principal mode of production in the global economy since at least the nineteenth century, and this system has always reached beyond national boundaries.[22] Given these continuities, what has changed?

Anthropologists and others argue that we are in a unique historical moment in which the local and the global intersect in ways qualitatively distinct from the past.[23] Whether it is conceptualized as a "speeding up" or a "stretching out," globalization theory understands time and space as having been reconfigured through the development of new communication and transportation technologies—what some scholars have termed the "conditions of postmodernity."[24] Developments such as high-speed air travel, global telephone infrastructure, and the Internet have intensified human interaction on a global scale, fundamentally disembedding social and cultural relations from traditional spatially bounded contexts and linking distant places so that "local happenings are shaped by events occurring many miles away."[25]

Theories of globalization have been used to explain fluxes and flows ranging from money, commodities, and industries to people, ideologies, and ideas. Yet while these discussions recognize that transnational capital plays an important role in the globalizations they analyze, they fail to explain the economic, political, and cultural logic that fuels processes of globalization. In other words, while globalization theories help us understand *how*, they generally leave unanswered the question of *why* people, money, and goods are moving across international boundaries at such unprecedented rates. The answer lies in understanding what drives today's global economy.

Beginning in the 1970s neoliberal economic theory suggested that governments, or "the state," should interfere as little as possible with the market, instead allowing its "invisible hand" to guide economic, political, and social relationships.[26] But in practice, governments *do* regulate the market in all sorts of ways. In recent decades they have implemented policies to deregulate industry, divest the state of social responsibility for the poor, criminalize immigrants, weaken worker protections, invest public funds into private endeavors, and liberalize finance, among other interventions. Rather than shrinking away, states have become the principal enforcers of neoliberalism, wielding regulatory powers in ways that ensure that capitalist logic can govern society.[27] As a result, over the past thirty years global inequalities have grown significantly as wealth has consolidated around the globe.

Such inequalities are exacerbated by international trade agreements, structural adjustment policies, and U.S. foreign policy, which have disproportionately benefited capitalists and increased the vulnerability of the poor.[28] As a result, working people in the global South face increasingly bleak conditions in their sending communities and home countries, leading them to take advantage of globalization's new technologies to migrate in search of better opportunities.

In the meantime, corporate strategies such as outsourcing, contracting, part-time employment, and union busting allow for greater capital accumulation. Workers are on average being paid comparatively less, finding less job security, and laboring in increasingly dismal conditions. While companies have promoted these labor control tactics for achieving greater "workforce flexibility," from the standpoint of workers they are more accurately ensuring "job insecurity."[29] Corporations have come to count on the limited and underenforced nature of U.S. labor laws to shift the risks of capitalism onto individual laborers and thus secure greater profit.

While some companies have moved their manufacturing to other countries with advantageous trade policies and exceedingly low wages, some industries—like poultry—have figured out how to bring the global labor force to them.[30] One of the leading labor control strategies that has emerged in the global economy is the active recruitment of undocumented immigrant workers. These workers' social, legal, and economic precarity renders them hyperexploitable. Their heightened vulnerability makes them a "docile" labor force, weakening workers' potential for collective bargaining, putting downward pressure on wages, and showing local (often Black) workers the meaning of a "work ethic." The state's selective enactment and enforcement of immigration laws and labor protections facilitates this exploitation. This all enables corporations and their shareholders to maximize profits, which, under neoliberalism's economic and cultural logic, is the ultimate objective.

MISSISSIPPI'S POULTRY COMMUNITIES

As our consumption of America's favorite white meat escalated, the poultry industry harnessed globalization's technologies and neoliberalism's labor control strategies and began recruiting immigrant labor at unprecedented rates.[31] Whereas, traditionally, local whites and, later, African Americans supplied the industry's labor power, today in many U.S. poultry plants Latin Americans constitute the majority of workers. By 2000 over half of the country's quarter-million poultry workers were immigrants, the vast majority of these foreign-born Hispanics.[32] Since eight of the top ten poultry-producing states are located in the South, it's fair to say that shifting national food-consumption patterns and the poultry industry's heavy reliance on immigrant labor have contributed to the recent demographic transformation of the region. A mapping of the Hispanic population in the rural South confirms that poultry has been a major driving force; in Mississippi it has been *the* driving force (see map 1).[33]

Mississippi ranks as the country's fourth largest producer, and poultry has been the state's top agricultural product since 1994, the year after local processors began recruiting workers from Latin America. In 2010 the state's nearly twenty chicken plants processed 757 million chickens for an average of nearly 1,500 per minute, employing approximately twenty-eight thousand people and generating over $2.8 billion in revenue.[34]

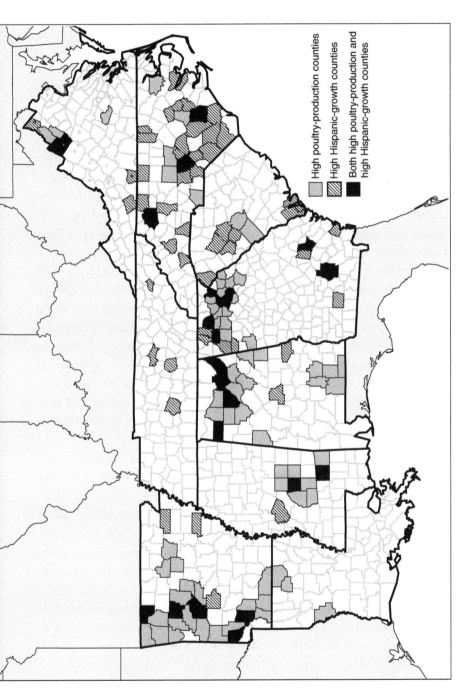

Map 1. Poultry production and Hispanic growth in the Deep South. Map by Austin Kocher, based on Kandel (2006), using data from the 1987, 1992, and 1997 Census of Agriculture and the 1990 and 2000 Census of Population.

High poultry-production counties

High Hispanic-growth counties

Both high poultry-production and high Hispanic-growth counties

Nevertheless, the average worker makes just over $23,000 per year, significantly below the federal poverty guidelines for a family of four.[35]

The core of Mississippi's poultry industry is Scott County. The county seat, Forest, is located approximately fifty miles east of the state capital of Jackson along U.S. Interstate 20. In 2005 Forest was home to five processing plants, with two others in nearby Morton and Sebastopol. Thirty miles north of Forest sits Carthage, in Leake County. Carthage boasts the largest poultry-processing facility in the country, owned by Tyson Foods, with a capacity to process 2.5 million chickens per week.[36] To the west, forming a triangle with Forest and Carthage, rests the city of Canton, in Madison County, with two more chicken plants. It is this area, formed by Scott, Leake, and Madison Counties, that I call central Mississippi's poultry region and sometimes just central Mississippi (see map 2).[37]

The country roads and two-lane highways connecting these towns wind over rolling red clay hills, around reservoirs, and through pine forests. Chicken farms dot the landscape, evidenced by groupings of large metal warehouses, set far back from the road, that glimmer in the evening sun. Older chicken houses made of wood beams and plastic sheeting decay on smaller plots nearby. Rickety trucks haul live chickens to slaughter, birds peering out from their cramped cages, tufts of white feathers littering the air in their wake. Amid the farms sit modest homes, decrepit trailers, and family-run corner stores in varying degrees of disrepair. The poverty here is palpable, even from behind the wheel of a car.

Forest, Carthage, and Canton, the main towns in their respective counties, serve as commercial centers that sustain more rural populations for miles around. Each is home to a variety of fast food options and gas stations and a more limited supply of small, family-owned businesses. Following Walmart's arrival to each of these towns, however, local retailers have been forced to close in growing numbers. Meanwhile, in many communities Walmart represents the most racially integrated space in town, with people flocking there to shop as well as socialize. Social outlets such as community centers, restaurants, and other entertainment options are limited; going to a mall or movie theater, for example, requires traveling a considerable distance into Jackson's suburbs.

Central Mississippi's poultry towns remain rigidly segregated by race. The literal and figurative railroad tracks often demarcate the line between tradi-

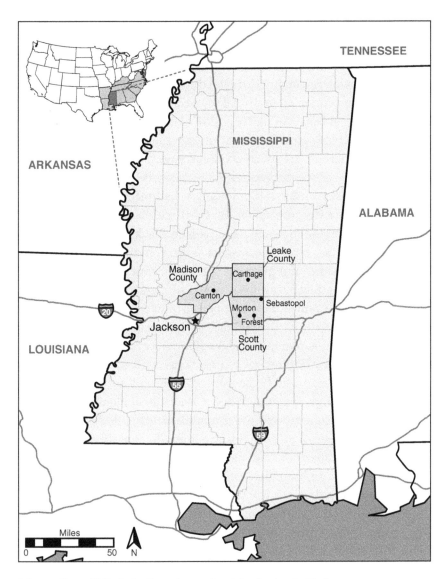

Map 2. Central Mississippi's poultry region. Map by Austin Kocher.

tionally white and African American neighborhoods. There's a church seemingly on every corner, and most of these, too, remain segregated. Some high schools elect separate Black and white student leaders or crown two homecoming queens. Many country clubs still deny entrance to nonwhite visitors. People tolerate and are often cordial to one another in public spaces, and some consider coworkers of the "opposite" race to be friends, but Black and white residents rarely socialize in more private realms. While perhaps, as one white pastor asserted, "at least a part of that overt racial tension [of the past has been] resolved," such quiescence at times feels no more than skin deep.

During my time in Mississippi, Canton had recently elected its first Black mayor since Reconstruction, but Carthage, Forest, and Morton have not followed in these footsteps. A successful Black attorney in the area told me a judge had recently called her "nigger" from the bench. She ran in a local election but lost after her opponent reminded people that she had represented a Black man who killed a white man and was acquitted. If elected, it was implied, no white person would be safe. The Ku Klux Klan remains active in parts of the state, appearing occasionally for marches, rallies, or autograph signings at the state fair.[38]

Neighborhoods are largely working class, with small single-family homes. Land is cheap, and home sales typically cost little more than the value of a lot's improvements. When I lived there, older two-bedroom homes in Scott County were often appraised for as little as $25,000. Beyond limited federal public housing options, few apartment complexes exist. Decrepit trailers abound, particularly just beyond city limits. The wealthy, too, tend to live outside of town (in Jackson's suburbs), though every poultry town boasts a few stately homes of its own.

Forest typifies distributions of wealth and poverty in Mississippi's poultry region. When I lived there, half of the city's households earned less than $25,000 each year, and barely 10 percent had an annual income of $75,000 or more. A mere 2 percent earned $200,000 or more per year, most of these hundred households making their fortunes in poultry and ancillary industries. Nearly half of adult individuals living without families were subsisting below the poverty level. Less than two-thirds of adults over age twenty-five had graduated from high school. By 2010 the median salary for full-time employed men was $36,023, while that for women was nearly half of men's earnings at $19,245. These statistics are illustrative of

rural Mississippi poultry towns dominated by low-wage work opportunities that have brought both enduring poverty and a more recent explosion
of migration from Latin America.[39]

Indeed, over the past twenty years central Mississippi has become
home to the state's greatest concentration of Latinos. The U.S. Census,
which regularly undercounts new immigrants, reported 3,024 people of
Hispanic origin living in Scott County in 2010, as compared to 1,660 ten
years before and only 141 in 1990. While the population nearly doubled
during the most recent decade on record, more astonishingly, it increased
by over 1,000 percent in the 1990s, when the poultry industry first began
recruiting Latin American workers. Hispanics now represent over 10 percent of the county's total population, and the vast majority of these are
foreign-born. This figure stands in contrast to the rest of the state, where
Hispanics make up just over 2 percent of the population.[40]

In central Mississippi's poultry towns Latinos join a population in
which Black residents generally outnumber white residents by a considerable margin.[41] The region also neighbors the reservation of the Mississippi
Band of Choctaw Indians and is home to a small but significant Native
American population. In Forest, Hispanics represent one quarter of the
town's residents, and a majority is from Mexico's newer sending region of
the southeast, particularly the states of Veracruz and Chiapas. Nearby
Morton (pop. 3,500) is home to more Cubans, Argentines, and other
Caribbean and South American immigrants, and Hispanics there make
up over 15 percent of the population. Carthage (pop. 5,075) has become a
principal receiving community for indigenous Mam migrants from
Comitancillo, a small town in the highlands of Guatemala. While Mam
leaders and local church representatives estimated the number at as high
as 1,000 individuals in 2005, the Census Bureau measured the city's
Hispanic population at half that, or just 12 percent.[42] Of the communities
included in this rendering of central Mississippi's poultry region, Canton
(pop. 13,000) has the lowest official count of Hispanics, at just 5 percent.
But because the city's geography is gerrymandered so as to locate the
chicken plants and a large neighboring trailer park—where many immigrants live—just outside the city limits, this figure does not provide an
accurate representation of the Latin American population in the Canton
area. A largely southeastern Mexican community at first, Canton became

Figure 3. Modern chicken houses on a central Mississippi poultry farm. Photo by author.

home to a growing number of Guatemalans moving from Carthage in search of work beginning in 2005 (see chapter 8).

The area's rural nature makes distances between poultry towns significant. I drove nearly fifty thousand miles in the two years I lived there and spent so much time in the car that I often took advantage of the ride by speaking my field notes into a handheld digital audio recorder. Such rurality can isolate people from one another as well as from bigger metropolitan areas. This limits education and employment options, keeps economies and wages depressed, and presents a real challenge for organizing workers dispersed throughout different plants and towns, not to mention regionally or across the industry. It is not a coincidence that poultry corporations have chosen to locate their processing facilities in some of the most remote areas of the South; indeed, the region provides them with just what they need.

ACTIVIST RESEARCH

I first went to Mississippi in the summer of 2002 in hopes of figuring out how research could support a budding coalition of immigrant and civil rights advocates, communities of faith, union leaders, employment justice attorneys, other politically engaged academics, and poultry workers grappling with questions of worker justice within the context of new Latino immigration into the area's chicken plants. My arrival there was a product of many months of conversation with my mentor at the University of Texas, Charlie Hale, and the Equal Justice Center, a nonprofit organization in Austin that was supporting poultry justice advocates across the South. In what ways could a politically engaged approach to research advance the work of this loose-knit Mississippi group struggling to help immigrant and U.S.-born poultry workers alike improve their wages, working conditions, and quality of life? And how might such activist scholarship breathe new life into a discipline that had long struggled with its colonialist roots?

My graduate training in activist research suggested a way forward in response to the dual concerns before me. Driven by a politics of liberation, the education I had received at the "Austin School" answered the question, "Anthropology for whom?" with an explicit political alignment with "people organizing to change the conditions of their lives."[43] This radical reconception of anthropological research, used as a tool that marginalized people could wield to effect social transformation toward greater equality and justice, held promise—I hoped—for decolonizing both the discipline and the world more broadly.[44]

My time in Mississippi that first summer helped me establish key relationships and identify some of the biggest problems poultry workers and their supporters encounter. It revealed local people's commitment and perseverance, as well as an abysmal lack of resources and information with which they were working to improve conditions in their chicken plants and communities. It also suggested that a better understanding of these challenges could help my interlocutors develop organizing strategies to begin to overcome them. Enthusiastic about the prospects for conducting activist research in this context, I committed to returning for long-term fieldwork, which I would carry out in dialogue and close collaboration with my new colleagues. In partnership with the Equal Justice Center and other supporters, I began helping to organize and facilitate Know Your Rights workshops in the area. Workers and advocates expressed interest in the idea of starting a workers' center to help them address ongoing obstacles to poultry worker justice.[45]

By the time I moved to Mississippi full-time in January 2004, the creation of the Mississippi Poultry Workers' Center, with a local advisory committee and the Equal Justice Center at the helm, was in the works. I took
on the title of community outreach and education associate, which, in
practice, meant I was the principal liaison between the workers' center's
leadership in Austin and the poultry workers and advocates it was being
created to support in Mississippi. "Research" became inextricable from my
everyday life supporting struggling poultry workers and helping them find
the resources—individual, institutional, and informational—to address
their problems. I interpreted for union representatives in plant break
rooms, accompanied injured workers to doctor's and lawyer's offices,
helped immigrants plan for and communicate at court proceedings, continued to lead popular education workshops, organized events, built relationships with community allies, attended coalition meetings, and participated in the organizational development of the fledgling workers' center.

In the first year, as the Equal Justice Center sought funding to sustain the
project, my work was unpaid and conceptualized as part of my role as an
activist researcher. Our partnership was mutually beneficial: my on-the-
ground efforts were vital to the establishment of the workers' center, serving
as an anchor between the Austin-based collaborators and those in
Mississippi, and this affiliation provided me with organizational support,
credibility, and access to spaces to which I may otherwise have struggled to
gain entry. To make ends meet, I also began teaching ESOL classes at a local
mission and community center.[46] This work advanced both my research
and the workers' center's efforts because it enabled me to build trusting
relationships with immigrant poultry workers of different backgrounds,
learn about their daily lives and struggles, meet others in their social networks, and connect them to workers' center efforts when appropriate.

By the start of 2005, the Mississippi Poultry Workers' Center had a
small office in Morton and had hired its first full-time Mississippi-based
community organizer, an African American woman who had been deeply
involved as an advocate for social justice in Jackson. The workers' center
had been successful enough in fundraising that it was also able to employ
me as part-time staff throughout that year. While I still felt I was always
scrambling to help the workers' center address the most recent violation
of people's human dignity and basic rights at the chicken plants—which

provided a wealth of research opportunities as well as loads of frustration and disappointment, alongside some key victories—this formalization of our relationship and the addition of other local staff enabled me to focus some of my time on developing more proactive programming. During this year I helped to establish the Workplace Injury Project and piloted Solidarity/Solidaridad: Building Cross-Cultural Understanding for Worker Justice, a popular education curriculum that brought African American and Latino immigrant poultry worker leaders into dialogue, which I continued to coordinate over the subsequent three years.

My activist fieldwork method might best be characterized by the term "observant participation," in which ethnography's cornerstone, participant observation, is inverted to emphasize one's role as a participant in the processes under study.[47] As the previous narrative suggests, my observant participation took place in a variety of settings, such as workers' center campaigns, workshops, and other gatherings; advisory committee planning sessions; English and Spanish classes; courtrooms; doctors' and lawyers' offices; kitchen tables; living rooms; soccer fields; police stations; church services; funerals; health fairs; union meetings; advocate conferences; community forums; chicken plant break rooms; industry recruitment events; and poultry farms, feed mills, and hatcheries. These activities included hundreds of informal one-on-one and group meetings and dozens of more organized small-group discussions among poultry workers. The latter were akin to focus groups, though they typically prioritized organizing or educational goals first, research objectives second.

Amid the intensity of fieldwork in this setting, I also conducted approximately sixty formal unstructured and semistructured interviews with people of diverse backgrounds. These included poultry workers from Mississippi, Mexico, Guatemala, Nicaragua, Honduras, Cuba, Venezuela, Peru, Uruguay, and Argentina; former and current poultry plant executives; union organizers and business agents; faith leaders; teachers; small business owners; local civil rights veterans and historians; immigrant rights advocates; law enforcement officers; injured workers; Black and Latino victims of racial profiling; and workers' center staff and advisory committee members. In addition, I carried out approximately two months of concentrated archival research in the Mississippi Department of Archives and History, the Forest Public Library, and local, privately held archival collections.

In early 2006, as I prepared to wrap up my fieldwork and leave Mississippi, the workers' center hired a second community organizer, a Salvadoran woman who had previously worked in the chicken plants. While she took over some of my responsibilities, I continued to support the workers' center, first from Austin and later from Santa Fe, until 2008, when completion of my doctoral program coincided with a cross-country move, a postdoctoral research appointment, and the birth of my daughter. A period of six years of engagement, punctuated by two intense years of round-the-clock immersion and political participation in the issues at the core of this book, had come to a bittersweet close.

Many aspects of my identity shaped my fieldwork experience, including my positioning as a young, white, non-Mississippian woman fluent in English and Spanish. I wore multiple hats, including those of graduate student, advocate, organizer, interpreter, and part-time teacher of English. Coming from a middle-class, educated, U.S. citizen background also influenced the process of research. When I failed to secure funding to support my fieldwork, I didn't have to turn to the chicken plants to make a living. I considered seeking a job there only as a research strategy, to build relationships and heighten my own understanding of and empathy for the struggles of poultry workers. When I decided the risks of crippling injury were too great and the returns on my "investment" too low, I had the luxury of revising my research design and dropping the idea altogether.

Permitted to obtain a driver's license, I didn't worry that in a traffic stop I might lose an entire month's earnings to fines or be detained or deported. I might be pulled over because of my out-of-state license plate, but not likely because of my fair skin and hair. With a social security number, I had a bank account and thus didn't have to worry that my savings could be stolen from underneath my mattress. Despite my concerns that I would have a hard time finding affordable rental housing in Forest, I was ultimately able to find a two-bedroom house on an acre of land for far less than most poultry workers pay to share a dilapidated trailer. These privileges of race, class, and citizenship were palpable as I went about my daily life in Mississippi, fighting alongside others as they fought to access such basic human rights as dignity on the job, a living wage, minimal health and safety protections, affordable housing, and the ability to help their families thrive. In the book's postscript I consider this experiment in activist research in greater detail, outlining the genealogies of politically engaged scholarship, analyzing the promises and pitfalls of this approach, and further considering how my positionality molded my experiences, conclusions, and contributions.

ORGANIZATION

This book addresses the transformation of rural Mississippi, its relationship to capital and labor, and its human implications for established southern communities as well as new immigrant groups. It explores the ways in which people of different backgrounds understand and experience immigration, shaped to a large degree by the historical and contemporary political economies of race in this region. It examines the changes in the poultry industry over time that led to its strategic recruitment and exploitation of immigrant laborers. It illustrates the ways in which difference is constructed and maintained among people of diverse backgrounds in both communities and workplaces, and it discusses the implications this has for possibilities of workers' political mobilization in the twenty-first century. Finally, it points to new strategies of organizing across difference emerging from the efforts of people and organizations working to build more just workplaces and communities in Mississippi's poultry region today.

I begin in chapter 2 by locating the development of central Mississippi's poultry industry within the area's deep tradition of racial apartheid. From the region's "founding" amid Choctaw removal and the institution of slavery through repeated claims of the birth of a "New" South to a budding industry in the 1950s, the chapter illustrates early poultry processors' reliance on these relations of inequality—as well as on the melding of state and industry power—from its very inception. Playing on the industry's buzzword of "integration," I expose the very dependence of such early integration on rigid structures of racial segregation.

Chapter 3 examines the relationship between central Mississippi's Black communities, the state, and the poultry industry during the Mississippi Freedom Struggle. Presenting previously untold histories of Black struggles for civil and labor rights between 1950 and 1980, I trace the path of local African Americans into the chicken plants and their attempts at unionization as the industry gained power and the seeds of neoliberal globalization began to take root.

Then, as the industry's growth accelerated, local plants began recruiting immigrant workers from Miami. Reconstructing the story of B.C. Rogers Poultry, chapter 4 reveals the logics and elaborate mechanics through which an extraordinarily diverse cross section of Latinos came to call central Mississippi home. It suggests that they entered the plants not in response to a simple "labor shortage," as management suggested, but amid a climate of neoliberal restructuring that responded to growing efforts to organize the area's poultry workers. It also shows how calculated recruitment led to chain migration with increasing reliance on immigrants' social networks.

Chapter 5 examines the reality that when people of any background in central Mississippi talk about immigration, they tend to talk in terms of race and work. Beginning with the area's first encounters with immigrants, then focusing on concerns over housing and residential segregation, and finally considering the various discourses in circulation among white, Black, and Latino Mississippians that attempt to explain the area's demographic transformation, I analyze the roles of whiteness and Blackness in shaping and constraining immigrants' social positions, carving out a contested third space between white and Black.[48] Communities' relationships to these categories, as well as to the poultry industry, play a key role in molding their beliefs about the immigrant work ethic and its impact on African American workers.

In chapter 6 the reader enters the chicken plants to witness the labor regimes management strategically wields to govern workers and ensure maximum profits. Revealing a remarkably hostile, hazardous, and hurtful work environment, I interrogate the industry's exploitation of identity categories of race, gender, and other forms of difference to suppress worker organizing. While some strategies reflect old "plantation mentality" approaches to labor control, neoliberalism heightens their effects and provides new opportunities for worker division and exploitation.

Chapter 7 introduces the recent efforts of unions to confront the new realities of chicken plant labor and improve wages and working conditions. A discussion of language barriers, immigrant diversity, divergent ideologies surrounding organizing and resistance, and anti-Black racism lays bare the major obstacles to bringing Black and Latino workers—as well as immigrant workers of different backgrounds—together across difference. An assessment of recent union organizing strategies that highlights their prospects and limitations in light of social movement theories and considers the potential of increased collaboration with the Mississippi Poultry Workers' Center suggests that unions' efforts to partner with community organizations offer a possible, if conflicted, path forward.

Chapters 8 and 9 focus on the issue of migrant worker illegality as a particularly acute challenge for organizing poultry workers in the early twenty-first century. I present two different cases analyzing the role of the state in constructing heightened vulnerability among undocumented workers while increasing protections for corporations. Chapter 8 chronicles a Tyson Foods campaign to rid its Carthage plant of its largely unionized Guatemalan immigrant workforce through the reverification of workers' "papers." Chapter 9 narrates the struggle of undocumented workers who sought to unionize a Koch Foods chicken plant in Forest, revealing the impossibilities of organizing in the context of third-party labor contract work. Together, these cases demonstrate how the present immigration and employment policies of the United States, contrary to their stated purpose, effectively incentivize employers to hire and abuse undocumented workers, further complicating worker organizing efforts today.

Chapter 10 returns to the question undergirding my activist research engagement in central Mississippi: what does all this mean for poultry workers' possibilities for organizing in the rural South for better pay, working conditions, and basic human dignity? It considers the Mississippi Poultry Workers' Center's efforts to create spaces for poultry workers to come together across difference and begin to build a shared political consciousness about the ways their lives are affected by neoliberal globalization, structural racism, and the criminalization of migration. While not fully realized, these attempts suggest an approach to organizing that values differences in identity and experience as well as a political and ethical bottom line.

Finally, in the postscript, I consider in greater depth the collaborative nature of the research that gave life to *Scratching Out a Living*. The discussion offers a concrete case through which to consider issues of power, accountability, and reciprocity in anthropological work concerned with social justice. It rejects the notion that one can be an unperceived observer and recognizes that all research is political and all encounters have consequences. By making my positioning—both personal and methodological—explicit, I seek to illuminate the ethical and practical challenges I faced as an activist anthropologist "in the field," rejecting the artificial divide between theory and practice and contributing to a growing conversation on the promises and pitfalls of engaged scholarship.

This book's narrative moves intentionally from a heavier reliance on archival and oral historical sources (chapters 2, 3, and 4), to the words and lived experiences of Mississippians of diverse backgrounds (chapters 5, 6, and 7), to my own activist ethnographic activities and experiences (chapters 8, 9, and 10), and, finally, to the more self-reflexive postscript on the potentialities of engaged scholarship. I chose this structure to privilege the voices and lives of Mississippians new and old, using the book primarily to share their stories of change, while also creating space for the reader to position me, the author, vis-à-vis the narrative.

Readers primarily interested in the story I have to tell about southern transformations and the poultry industry should proceed in the order the chapters are presented. Those who find a deeper discussion of the research process necessary for interpreting my analysis may want to read the postscript first. Whichever the proclivity, it is my hope that the postscript will provide readers an opportunity for sustained consideration of the methodological and epistemological potential of activist research.

2 Dixie Chicken

RACIAL SEGREGATION, POULTRY INTEGRATION, AND THE
MAKING OF THE "NEW" SOUTH IN CENTRAL MISSISSIPPI

"The Wing Dang Dash 5K run/walk will start the day off with a bang. After the run the wing cooking contest begins. Cooking teams begin preparing a year in advance to take home the top prize for the best chicken wing. Bring your lawn chair and relax under the shade trees as you enjoy a great lineup of bands who come from all around."[1] Nearing its sixtieth anniversary, this festival—known today as the Wing Dang Doodle—brings residents of Scott County together each year to celebrate the chicken. Under the pines families group together in folding chairs and on blankets. There's excitement in the air, as this year a favorite Mississippi blues artist, Super Chikan, has come all the way from Clarksdale to headline the festival. We gather in Gaddis Park, named for a man who dedicated his life to making Forest the heart of one of the leading poultry regions in the country, and prepare to enjoy the show.

But chicken hasn't always been the area's principal economic driver. Throughout much of its history, central Mississippi has scrabbled to attract investment. "There's a Future for You in Forest," boasted the town's chamber of commerce around 1950. While the affirmation prefigured similar promises poultry processors would make to migrants from across Latin America half a century later, this one appeared in an official brochure seeking to entice businesses to the burgeoning seat of Scott County. Mules were still pulling cotton wagons down mostly dirt roads in these parts as Forest began its push for industrialization. Among the offerings of the "IT town of central Mississippi," the promotional material claimed confidently, were cooperative community leadership, ample intelligent labor, adequate shipping facilities, modern utility services, a moderate year-round climate, and an unlimited water supply. This last point, in particular, would prove key for the poultry industry.

At the time of the brochure's writing, Forest was home to two lumber mills; three manufacturers turning wood into ski billets and pick handles, straight chairs and rockers, and railroad ties, respectively; a cotton compress; a bentonite transporter; an ice company; a frozen food locker; and a National Forest ranger station. For each, the brochure noted in detail the number of white and "colored" employees on payroll. The brochure did not include any poultry or cotton operations in its list, but it did note that cotton was still the leading farm product of the county, though it had "ceased to dominate the economy many years ago, as farsighted farmers turned to cattle, hogs, and chickens."[2] These words would foretell the decades to come, during which poultry would scratch its way to the top of the area's economic, social, and political power structures and come to be feted at the annual Wing Dang Doodle Festival.

.   .   .   .   .

The chamber of commerce's mid-twentieth-century efforts to portray the rural Deep South as a new, untapped budding industrial market awaiting eager investment represented a pivotal moment in the development of the area's poultry industry. Yet while the period predates more recent claims of a Nuevo South by over half a century, it also came eighty-five years after the first proclamations of southern newness. Certainly, many things have changed since slavery was abolished in 1865, but key elements of social control, including structures of white supremacy and labor exploitation, endure. This chapter provides an overview of central Mississippi's local history through the 1950s, with a focus on the often highly racialized features that primed it to become the heart of the state's poultry region.

"NEW" TERRITORY

Historian Ronald Takaki argues that the American Revolution, which ushered in the independence of the United States from Britain in 1776, fostered an ideology of rationality, self-governance, and civilization. Its doctrine called for Christianity and control over the emotional and sexual sides of one's being, and it was believed that only white men could possess these traits. Women and people of color, who the "founding fathers" believed lacked self-control and the ability to live up to the new country's formative ideals, were constructed as marginal to civilization, and thus the nation's hegemony of white supremacist patriarchy was born.[3] This system of racial, ethnic, and gendered hierarchy remained central to economic and social life in the United States in the centuries that followed.

When, in the late eighteenth century, early white Americans brought the transatlantic slave trade with them into the area that is now Mississippi, they confronted established Native American communities. Leaders of the new nation debated strategies for white domination of groups of color, coming to the conclusion that people of African ancestry should be incorporated into the nation, while "Indians" must be removed. The colonists' ideologies and actions were largely motivated by economics—Black labor was central to the success of the U.S. market, and Native Americans occupied lands into which colonists wanted to expand.[4] Hence, throughout the early nineteenth century, as white settlers moved west, the system of slavery of Afro-descendants was expanded and Native Americans were slaughtered, exterminated, or otherwise removed by forcing them beyond the Mississippi River.

Under U.S. president Andrew Jackson, Indian tribal units were abolished throughout the South, and federal jurisdiction was extended to "reduce" them to citizenship. In addition, white settlers were legally permitted to appropriate native lands, and Native Americans could agree to receive an allotment from the U.S. government and be forced into a market economy or move west. Mississippi became a state in 1817 and the area's Choctaw Indians became the country's first experiment in Indian removal when, in 1830, the Treaty of Dancing Rabbit Creek forced the Choctaw Nation to assimilate or leave "as early as practicable."[5] Organized groups of Choctaws left Mississippi in 1831 and 1832, forced to travel west over five hundred miles on foot through the winter. Many died of cholera, exposure, and other ailments.

Ultimately, approximately 12,500 Choctaws were relocated to Indian Territory (present-day Oklahoma), and few were permitted to remain in Mississippi. Socially and economically disenfranchised, the descendants of those who stayed now comprise the Mississippi Band of Choctaw Indians, located throughout central Mississippi and headquartered in Pearl River, just twenty miles east of Carthage.[6] As a result of the Treaty of Dancing Rabbit Creek, a young Mississippi was greatly expanded through the formation of sixteen new counties, including those that today form central Mississippi.

In the cases of both Native American and Afro-descendant peoples, the forms of racial subjugation enacted by whites were congruous with these two groups' positioning within economic relations of production of the white marketplace. Native lands (but not individuals) were needed for agriculture, and Black slavery became crucial to southern agricultural production. As an economic system, slavery in the United States can be credited with the white accumulation of wealth and power that ultimately made possible both national independence in the eighteenth century and the country's position as a world superpower in the twentieth century.[7]

It was under these conditions in the 1830s that most of central Mississippi was founded and settled. The area was largely agricultural, with cotton as the chief crop. The early settlement population was small, and plantations were not as large as in the Mississippi Delta region to the north, but wealthy landowners nonetheless relied on slave labor. In Scott County, for example, the first official census in 1840 counted only 1,653 people, but twenty years later the population had risen to 8,139, including "850 voters and 3,051 taxable slaves."[8] Similarly, in 1860 the enslaved population in neighboring Leake County was 3,056.[9] Because nearby Madison County was closer to the Delta, it had larger cotton plantations and therefore a slightly higher percentage Black population, a demographic particularity that holds true into the present.

Slavery and agriculture grew dramatically in the South in the early nineteenth century. In the 1830s in Mississippi, cotton production increased by four times and the enslaved population doubled.[10] This growth happened slightly later in the central part of the state, however, as the area developed following the appropriation of indigenous lands. The increase in the Black population precipitated greater social tensions throughout the South, and white folks of all classes shared a growing fear of slave insurrection and rebellion. By the mid-nineteenth century in Mississippi there were four Black persons to every white citizen, and white anxiety ran so high that "in some counties women and children were gathered into guarded places at night."[11]

Public displays of white-on-Black violence were key to maintaining racial divisions and white dominance, setting a precedent for centuries to follow. One such event took place in Madison County in 1835, when "at least six white men and a dozen Negroes were strung up until dead, in the courtyard . . . by the Committee of Safety. The Committee said it was putting down a slave insurrection."[12] Working in concert with these acts of violence, the racial hegemony of the South was strengthened through white fear of Black rebellion and takeover, thus solidifying slavery as a "common sense" ideology and widely accepted institution among the majority of white southerners regardless of class.

While the local and state economies depended largely on agriculture, and more specifically cotton, in central Mississippi as early as the mid-nineteenth century signs of early manufacturing were present. The area was covered in natural pine forests, and a handful of sawmills had begun processing pine trees into lumber.[13] Other industries included a tannery that turned raw hides into highly valued skins, a blacksmith who produced plows, and numerous cotton gins and compresses.[14] By 1858 the Alabama and Vicksburg Railroad was built on the former stage road, enabling the rapid shipment of goods along its route, including in and out of Scott County.[15] Accompanying this growth on a local level, southern "boosters" across the South began pushing for industrialization, making plans for the expansion of slavery out of agriculture and into factories.[16]

These dreams were cut short and economic development came to a standstill when the U.S. Civil War broke out over the disputed rights of the white southern slaveholding class. Controlled by dedicated southern loyalists, central Mississippi's white communities "supported secession and furnished [their] full quota of men to the Confederate army." Most of the war action happened away from home, with the exception of a few months in 1863, when Gen. William T. Sherman's army came through, destroying the railroad, its equipment, and the towns in its path.[17] These central Mississippi communities suffered during the war, as land lay fallow, schools were closed, and families were separated, but the loyalties of many white Mississippians to Gen. Robert E. Lee and his army never wavered.

THE BIRTH OF THE "NEW" SOUTH

The end of the Civil War cemented the Emancipation Proclamation, and in 1865 the Thirteenth Amendment to the U.S. Constitution abolished the system of slavery, freeing Black men, women, and children across the South. The Union's victory changed the structural relationship between Black and white in the United States forever, though arguably less than many would have hoped, as its promise remains only partially fulfilled. In the period known as Reconstruction that followed the war, the federal government sought to establish basic civil and political rights for all, and Black men across Mississippi began to occupy elected positions of political authority after the Fifteenth Amendment granted them the vote in 1870. In Scott County, where three thousand enslaved people were freed, Sam West, a Black preacher, was elected to the position of county supervisor. African American political power following the war was significant but short-lived, in part because the Reconstruction acts were not accompanied by the federal funding and oversight necessary to bring them to fruition in the long run. In hindsight, some consider the process a failure. The 1914 opinion of a northern "carpetbagger" who lived in Mississippi during and after Reconstruction offers a glimpse into this analysis: "The Negro had the ballot and enjoyed his rights as an American citizen during the years the National Government was disposed to stand behind the reconstruction policy it had itself inaugurated, but today the Negro residing in the Southern States once in rebellion has about as much voice in the politics of those states as has the mule with which he cultivates his crop of cotton."[18] The withdrawal of federal troops from the South in 1877 effectively marked the end of the Reconstruction era, dramatically shaping social, economic, and political relations between white and Black southerners into the present.[19]

Mississippi struggled as its economy went through a deep economic depression following the war.[20] The regional boom that was enjoyed in some parts of the South in the 1880s seems to have missed much of the state. Thus, while the *economic* ideology of the New South—which publicized the region as a newly modern place with economic opportunity in agriculture and industry like that never seen previously in the North or the South—did not come to Mississippi until many decades later, the *social* ideology of the New South, which promised a static racial and political order, served to reassure whites in Mississippi and across the region of their superiority over Black folks.[21] In sum, as the postbellum South shifted from plantation agriculture to small farming and, in some places including central Mississippi's poultry region, eventually to industry, African Americans remained socially and economically subjugated to whites. The South was a "new" place—the days of slavery were over—but in its stead were scarcely improved race relations predicated on continued social, economic, and political subjugation of Black Americans.

Sharecropping

Newly freed Black families faced limited work and housing opportunities off the plantation. This reality gave rise to sharecropping, in which poor families would live on and cultivate (mostly white) land in exchange for a portion of the crop at the end of the season. This economic system of domination persisted in central Mississippi for over one hundred years, and most older Black (and some white) residents I had the privilege of knowing in Mississippi shared their childhood memories as sharecroppers. When I asked one why she left Mississippi in the 1950s, she recalled,

> We was living on this farm, and every year we would like pick fifty, sixty bales of cotton. And if school had gotten started, we could not leave and go to school until we got finished with all the cotton. So if school started the latter part of August, it would be sometimes the latter part of September before we could go to school.
>
> Well, that wasn't really the reason. The reason that really got me the most was how we were treated. We were treated like dogs. And, like, we would pick all that cotton every year. And we would go and sell a little bit. [The landowner] would always say we'd come out in the hole. I mean, every year. And, like, Mama'd promise us, "When we settle up . . . we going shopping, and I'm gonna buy y'all this," and everything. We never could go buy nothing. And we'd always come out in the hole.

Many told me about starting to pick cotton as very small children, and when the conversation involved more than one person with such memories, talk nearly always turned to who had begun work at a younger age and who had been paid a more miserable piece rate. I heard stories of clothing made of flour sacks and of the sacks with floral patterns used to decorate the hems of girls' (and dolls') dresses.[22] Tales were told of learning how to ride the mules, Will and Bill, and of the mail carrier being the only man in town with an automobile. Memories arose of children going hungry because the landowner took a family's only hog and crib of corn, which they had been saving for Christmas dinner, as settlement for part of their debt. "I remember I got so mad," recounted a poultry worker leader fifty years later. "You know, I was just a boy, but I just almost went crazy. And so I got me two of those long cotton sacks—nine foot—that we picked cotton in. The largest cotton sacks back in those days." He laughed as he continued: "And I went to that corn crib that night around midnight, when I knowed everybody was gone to bed, and I filled 'em full and brought 'em in the house that we was staying in and hid them under the bed. I said, 'We gonna have some corn.' And I peeled that corn off and put it in that little black pot on the fireplace, boiled it, and we ate hominy for Christmas that year." His family moved shortly thereafter to sharecrop on someone else's land. "It was better because these new people made sure that you got food. . . . But it was still just like slavery, you know."

Sharecropping forced Black southerners into a permanent debt economy, in which sharecroppers often had to borrow money from the landowner to purchase their farming supplies, tools, seeds, and so on. This obligation was to be paid off at the end of the season when the crop came in, but the loan was often higher than the worth of the crop, forcing families further into debt with each passing year. So while this "new" economic system tendered free Black men and women some degree of independence and allowed them to maintain control over their labor, it also served white southerners as a particularly effective means of social control.[23]

Jim Crow

Modernization, industrialization, and urbanization had begun throughout the South, but these were spotty and incomplete and had not yet made their way into central Mississippi.[24] Some southern cities grew rapidly, as with Birmingham, Alabama, where the population increased from three thousand to forty thousand between 1880 and 1900. Mississippi, however, continued to be largely rural. The South retained qualities that set it apart from the rest of the United States, particularly in terms of demographics, and overall the region was home to equal numbers of white and Black residents. Despite gradual industrialization and a successful history of economic subjugation of racial minorities, white southerners continued to innovate new ways to delineate the color line.

By the late nineteenth century, intensified practices of social segregation had become another key component to maintaining white control. De facto Jim Crow social norms were already in place, but the 1896 *Plessy v. Ferguson* U.S. Supreme Court decision ratified these racially "separate but equal" facilities. Grossly unequal facilities and opportunities were sanctioned under law over the next sixty years and have endured, extralegally, for much longer. Southern states further disenfranchised Black residents through the implementation of a poll tax and "literacy requirements" for voting, and Mississippi's practices at the polling place were notoriously transparent in their racist underpinnings.[25]

Accompanying these political changes, the practice of white-on-Black lynching had become increasingly popular by the 1890s.[26] In his bold description of the dehumanizing practices of lynching in Mississippi, Charles Payne writes that these experiences

> were as much a part of the ritual of lynching as the actual act of killing. They sent a more powerful message than straightforward killing would have sent, graphically reinforcing the idea that Negroes were so far outside the human family that the most inhuman actions could be visited upon them. . . . The point was that there did not have to be a point: Black life could be snuffed out on whim, you could be killed because some ignorant white man didn't like the color of your shirt or the way you drove a wagon. Mississippi Blacks had to understand that viscerally. Those who wanted to work for change had to understand that they were challenging a system that could and would take their lives casually.[27]

Many people throughout the South endured these acts of terrorism and disenfranchisement for generations. Others left home in search of better opportunities "up North." The biggest exodus of Black southerners, known as the "Great Migration," took place between 1916 and 1929, during which hundreds of thousands of people sought economic, social, and political security in northern cities such as Chicago and Detroit. In rural Mississippi, those who stayed behind continued struggling to make ends meet as sharecroppers and tenant farmers.[28]

A CHICKEN IN EVERY POT

Beginning in the 1930s the U.S. government acknowledged its responsibility to look out for the welfare of its citizens and began promoting more progressive social policies through the New Deal federal programs and protections, such as the Social Security Administration, the Works Progress Administration, the National Labor Relations Act, and the Fair Labor Standards Act, among many others. In part, these policies stemmed from the country's shifting racial ideologies that questioned biological notions of superiority and inferiority, suggesting that raising the economic status of Black Americans would in turn decrease white racism and help meet increasing demands by communities of color and poor whites.[29] Of equal or greater importance, however, James C. Cobb explains that the programs were enacted with the needs of American capitalists in mind, aimed primarily at "stabilizing an industrializing society and vaulting it over some of the earlier stages of economic development by providing it with the modernized system of transportation and public services and the reliable, competent labor force thought necessary for more advanced industrial economies."[30]

The New Deal programs were implemented unevenly. Thanks to heavy lobbying by capitalists, many of them white landowners in the South, they were often designed and implemented in ways that disenfranchised African Americans, women, and other minorities. For example, some industries, including agriculture, were (and continue to be) exempt from Fair Labor Standards Act regulations of minimum wage and overtime pay. Similarly, Laurie B. Green documents that in the early 1940s African Americans in Memphis were kicked off the federal Works Progress Administration relief rolls when their labor was needed to harvest cotton in the Mississippi Delta.[31] Moreover, state and local governments were permitted to administer certain grants, and in the South white politicians often disproportionately allocated opportunities away from African American residents. As such, few of the social welfare policies of the New Deal era significantly disrupted the poverty or positively impacted the lives of Black Mississippians.

Mississippi's Poultry Entrepreneurs in World War II

While the Mississippi Delta remained dependent on large-scale cotton production, central Mississippi inched slowly toward industrialization. The area continued to rely on small cotton farms and increasingly on pulpwood and hardwood production, even after the Bienville Lumber Company closed its operations in the 1930s and donated its land to the federal government, but a new industry was beginning to develop.[32] The nation took President Herbert Hoover's promise of "a chicken in every pot" to heart, and Scott County did its part to make it a reality. Up until this time, chickens had been grown mostly by women in backyards and on small farms for family consumption and to extend meager incomes.[33] By the time the industry began to develop in central Mississippi, it was entrepreneurial businessmen, not necessarily farmers, who gave it wings.

Bennie Clyde (B.C.) Rogers from Morton, who at the time was the largest Purina dealer in the world, started the poultry business there in 1932.[34] Because of the demand for powdered eggs for American troops during World War II, what began as a live hen-and-egg operation quickly grew. Rogers ran a successful egg-drying business during the war, and when this niche disappeared, he opened his first chicken slaughtering plant in 1949.[35] B.C. Rogers Poultry processed between ten thousand and eighteen thousand chickens weekly and sold them whole.[36]

As Rogers was beginning to build his business in Morton, just twelve miles down the road W.J. Sharp likely became the first commercial chicken dealer in Forest in 1936.[37] He is credited with mounting the first chicken display at the Sebastopol Fair and convincing the president of a Forest bank to invest in the poultry business, lending money to farmers so they could grow chickens. The local financial industry boomed in central Mississippi throughout the second half of the twentieth century, thanks to the growth of poultry.

Figure 4. The "Chicken King of the South," B. C. Rogers' refrigerated truck, circa 1959. Photo from *Rogers Report,* 1990, 4 (1): 7. Courtesy of Jack Rogers.

At the time these entrepreneurs were beginning their poultry operations, they likely looked for inspiration from innovations occurring in other parts of the country. The Delmarva Peninsula was already a thriving poultry region, selling seven million chickens annually up the East Coast.[38] Anthropologist Steve Striffler's historical research on the industry suggests that by the mid-1930s the first innovation in chicken production had taken place there:

> Birds were "New York–dressed": slaughtered and defeathered but left with the entrails and feet intact. Although it was a long way from nuggets and patties, this basic processing would eventually transform the industry. Birds no longer had to be transported alive; they could be processed near growing areas, then packed on ice and trucked to market. This allowed growers in Delmarva to ship their chickens to more distant markets, but it also reduced their competitive advantage. Indeed, the advent of processing opened up the possibility of chicken farming to rural folk throughout much of the United States.

Shortly thereafter, another innovation further opened the doors to the development of poultry production in the South. In 1942 the War Food Administration appropriated Delmarva's ninety million birds per year— more than half of the country's chickens—for federal food programs. With

Delmarva no longer competing in the market, the nation's chicken supply waned, creating opportunities for producers in other regions. These wartime policies forever changed the geography of the industry, and, as a result, "by 1950, the South was the most dynamic broiler-producing area in the United States."[39]

Why the South?

In addition to the technological and political conditions previously outlined, poultry has thrived in the South due to the region's fulfillment of a range of conditions. Terrain in other parts of the country was perhaps more valuable when used for other purposes, but in places like central Mississippi, where land is typically valued at far less than the improvements built on it and the clay-and-sand-filled hills roll on into eternity, there were fewer alternative uses, enticing local businessmen and farmers to invest in poultry. Poverty was another key component. This was caused not only by the South's largely infertile land and limited resources, and restricted access to credit, but also by an abundance of struggling family farmers and ample supply of available workers.[40] Further enticements for poultry capitalists included the region's mild climate, local boosterism that encouraged manufacturers to locate there, state and local policies offering subsidies to industry, antilabor legislation and citizen sentiment, and weak or nonexistent labor unions.

Even with these incentives to locate in the rural South, investing money in poultry was risky for family farmers as well as for entrepreneurial small businessmen. Striffler identifies three key obstacles to its success in the rural South: First, southern markets were relatively small and distant from the large population centers of the country. Would southern poultry find a market that would enable its growth? Second, growing chicken wasn't cheap, and family farmers rarely had extra money to invest in their budding businesses. Could they make a living on poultry? Third, at the time Americans got most of their protein by eating meats other than chicken. Could chicken overcome its sketchy backyard image, and could it be purchased cheaply enough for Americans to increase their consumption? These questions could only be answered with time.[41]

Figure 5. White women on the line at B. C. Rogers' new Morton plant, circa 1959. Courtesy of Jack Rogers.

Wartime Legacies and the Erosion of White Male Supremacy

During World War II a shortage of white male workers led to increased employment opportunities for some women, communities of color, and foreign workers across the United States. As we will see in later moments related to Mississippi poultry, however, some scholars argue that this "shortage" was, even then, due to employers' unwillingness to pay living wages and desire to flood the market with low-wage workers.[42]

It is likely that white women first began working in Mississippi's chicken-processing plants during the wartime period. Workers of color would still have to wait decades before having the opportunity to join the processing lines. Black residents of central Mississippi for the most part continued to sharecrop and work in the homes of wealthier white families during and after the war. They were excluded from many forms of industrial employment, and those who did find jobs in manufacturing nearly always occupied the lowest-paying, most difficult and dangerous positions. Work, like society, was rigidly segregated by race and gender.

Outside the workplace, leisure activities were governed by the same rules. In 1948 the city of Carthage planned a multiracial event for which residents were carefully instructed, "Negro people will occupy the eastern side of the field, white people the western side and Indians will be at the north end of the field."[43] The following year the event was repeated, and the (white-controlled) newspaper touted, "Negro and Indian leaders of Leake County—boasting that the three races have been living working and playing together for over a century—will hold the second annual 'Tri-racial Good Will Festival' in Carthage."[44] Following the event one paper asserted that "although participants in the festival automatically grouped themselves by races, there were no reserved sections. Movement about the Carthage high school football field was free, easy, unrestricted. Men and women of different races approached and met without guile, and with no condescending gestures. A spirit of friendship and goodwill fellowship permeated the air."[45] Despite the reporter's celebratory tone, the shift from rigidly enforced segregation in year one to purportedly unpoliced but equally obvious racial divisions at the festival the following year suggests that, whether externally enforced or internally governed, Black and Choctaw residents of central Mississippi were well aware of white society's expectations regarding spatial segregation of the "races" in public facilities at the time.

Meanwhile, progressive Black leaders were fighting for society to live up to the "equal" in "separate but equal" facilities and were beginning to contest this system in the courts. The Mississippi State Conference of the NAACP was formed in 1945, and the Regional Council of Negro Leadership was founded in 1951 and active in the Mississippi Delta by the following year. Participation in the labor market and in the military during World War II had helped people of color across the country find a voice, and following the war they asserted their needs and desires in ways that white society had not anticipated. Thus, courageous southern leaders and communities of color during the 1930s and 1940s, while they didn't know it at the time, were laying the groundwork for the more concerted political and social contestations of racial inequality to come.[46]

RESURRECTING THE "NEW" SOUTH

Following World War II Mississippi increased its efforts to entice manufacturers to locate in the state, and its economy, in part due to the growth
of poultry, finally began an upward climb.[47] In 1944 the state legislature
passed the Balance Agriculture with Industry plan, which allowed cities
and counties to issue voter-approved bonds that would finance the growth
of industry using taxpayer dollars. Under BAWI, the city or county would
own the buildings in which the manufacturer operated, and the newly
established manufacturer was eligible for ad valorem and property tax
exemptions for a period of ten years.[48] In exchange, the manufacturer
would provide jobs and pay minimal rents to the city. This period of state-
funded economic growth represented a second coming of the New South
for central Mississippi, and industrialization was heavily encouraged by
local governments and chambers of commerce, illustrated, for example,
by the "IT town" brochure discussed in this chapter's opening.[49] While
many corporations took advantage of the incentives offered through
BAWI, poultry processors may have benefited the most.[50]

Early Poultry Integrators

Fred Gaddis, whose life began and ended in Scott County, played a key
role in making the area one of the top poultry-producing regions in the
country. In 1947 he started his poultry business with just $1,665, and over
the years he built an empire that included dozens of chicken farms, hatcheries, a feed mill, multiple processing plants, and an equity company.[51] By
1949 Scott County produced over a million birds annually. Around the
same time, three hatcheries were operating at full capacity but could not
keep up with demand, so baby chicks were shipped in from Georgia.[52]
Soon after, farmers began importing up to ten thousand bushels of corn
from the Midwest each week to feed and grow the chicks.[53]

In 1954 a group of local businessmen, including Gaddis and his friend
Erle Johnston, who will emerge as a central figure in chapter 3, financed
the building of a grain elevator in Scott County to store, shell, and dry the
corn to be used by local feed mills. Furthermore, the businessmen pledged
to purchase "all of the No. 2 yellow corn which can be grown in this area."[54]

Thanks to poultry's growth, five banks now operated in Scott County.[55] And by the mid-1950s the industry had grown so much that Forest was producing between five and six million birds annually.[56]

At the same time, just to the north of Forest, in Leake County, businessmen Curtis T. Ramzy and M. D. Reagan formed a partnership and began their poultry operations. In many ways their success paralleled that of their colleagues B. C. Rogers and Fred Gaddis. In 1948 they began by providing feed for poultry growers. As grower capacities increased, in the early 1950s they incorporated as R&R Industries and opened a processing plant that slaughtered five thousand chickens daily. But they encountered a local shortage of birds. In an effort to hatch enough chicks locally, they founded R&R Farms and built laying houses. By 1961 R&R was producing four hundred tons of feed, feeding forty thousand laying hens and nine hundred thousand broilers, and processing twenty-five thousand chickens each week. A few years later eight local companies, including R&R, established Central Laboratories, which conducted feed analysis, furnished the industry with medications and supplies, and disposed of chicken carcasses and waste. The massive expansion of R&R in the 1950s illustrates the awesome growth of the industry in central Mississippi during this decade, in the form of family-owned companies run by a few resourceful men like Rogers, Gaddis, Ramzy, and Reagan.[57]

Each of these cases resonates with Striffler's research on poultry tycoon John Tyson's development of his family company in its early years, in that "the process of vertical integration, whereby previously independent facets of the emerging industry were brought under the control of a single entity, initially occurred as a response to problems encountered along the chain of production."[58] Yet the trajectories of Mississippi's poultry entrepreneurs illustrate that vertical integration was due to other factors as well. As with previous moments, in the late 1960s government regulations also played a role. Reflecting on her family's poultry business, one white Scott Countian recalled,

> All we did was process chickens, and that's the worst thing you can do as far as the tax bracket, because it makes you a manufacturer, which is taxed higher than a farm operation. [The owner] was paying 80 percent of his income in taxes. So he became partners with [another local poultry entrepreneur,] who owned a lot of growing operations and hatcheries and that

kind of thing. Then they were able to call themselves a farm and get a better break on the tax. So that's one of the things that drove the changes in the industry.

Propelled by both the market and tax policy, the process of vertical integration led to poultry companies being referred to in industry lingo as "integrators."

Poultry Power Grows

In small-town Mississippi, poultry company owners quickly became powerful leaders in their communities, as economic power translated with ease into cultural and political influence. With local chicken fervor growing, in 1954 Fred Gaddis organized the first Chicken Festival Dinner to celebrate the budding industry. The newspaper advertised, "Beauty events, listed as Queen and Rooster contests, will be held in six different classifications," which included Baby Chick, Junior Broiler Queen, Senior Broiler Queen, Hen Queen, Bathing Beauty Queen, and Rooster King. The article went on to remind would-be participants that "no evening dresses are allowed. Ladies and children must be in cotton or wash dresses (except the bathing beauty contest which will be in bathing suits)."[59] As with all other officially sanctioned social events during that time in central Mississippi and throughout the South, the event was strictly segregated by race; only white residents were invited. In an area where visits from out-of-town friends and extended family still merit publication in the local newspaper, the 1954 Chicken Festival Dinner is emblematic of the poultry industry's growing cultural and economic significance.

Fred Gaddis was elected mayor of Forest in the early 1960s and held this position on and off until just before his death in 2001. When an important out-of-town guest visited in 1963, Mayor Gaddis took him on a "tour of the various poultry operations and other interesting sites in Forest."[60] Gaddis was elected eight times, serving as mayor for a total of thirty-two years, and upon his death he was honored for his contributions to the poultry industry and his public service.[61]

Similarly, in addition to operating B.C. Rogers Poultry, over time the Rogers family has owned many of Morton's businesses, including a farm-supply store, a livestock operation, a butane company, an oil well, a construction company, the grocery store, the phone company, and even the Bank of Morton. While the man who would become known as the "Chicken King of the South" never held office, his economic and political clout were palpable.

And the legacy continues. Today the city of Morton is led by Mayor Greg Butler, who worked in management for B.C. Rogers Poultry for twenty-five years before being elected. Moreover, Gaddis's 1954 Chicken Festival Dinner caught on. By 1957 the celebration became a statewide Broiler Festival, and it lives on today in Forest's ever-popular Wing Dang Doodle Festival—"We hope to see you at the Doodle!"[62]

INTEGRATION AMID SEGREGATION

The problems of racism and white supremacy have been central to constructing and maintaining social, political, and economic relations in the South over time, shaping their contours into the present. The poultry industry is no exception; to the contrary, a critical history of its development in central Mississippi underscores its reliance on racialized structures of power in the region since its inception. It also benefited immensely from a myriad of federal, state, and local interventions, which ensured the area's growth from a budding "new frontier" in the mid-nineteenth century into the birthplace of the state's poultry region a century later. Through it all, despite two renditions of a New South, a static racial order flourished.

Ironically, at the same time poultry industry pioneers became known as "integrators"—in reference to their vertical integration of the myriad phases involved in chicken production, from the fertilization of eggs to the shipment of a packaged product—the social structures in which they operated and from which they drew the labor needed for such integration remained strictly segregated. Power remained in the hands of white men, while Black Mississippians clung to the lowest rungs of the area's social and labor hierarchies. Thanks to World War II, by the 1950s white women were likely the principal workforce in most of central Mississippi's chicken plants, but African Americans would have to fight for nearly two more decades to earn the right to labor in the burgeoning industry.

3 The Caged Bird Sings for Freedom

BLACK STRUGGLES FOR CIVIL AND
LABOR RIGHTS, 1950–1980

"This office will be closed next Monday in observation of Robert E. Lee's and Martin Luther King's Birthday," announces a notice taped to the door of the hulking gray Scott County Courthouse. On my way into court to interpret for an acquaintance, I breathe in the crisp January air, glance up at the cloudless blue sky, and, sighing, read it again. The racial justice activist in me is disgusted by the implications of this joint commemoration; the ethnographer, pleased that I happened to stumble upon this cultural tidbit. It turns out, I later learn, that the remembrance of Lee's birthday was adopted by the Mississippi legislature in 1987, though it appears it was unofficially celebrated in conjunction with MLK Day long before either were officially sanctioned holidays.[1] I dig through my bag but find no camera (in the days before smartphones). I hurriedly scribble the quote in my notebook before swinging open the heavy door and slipping inside.

The following year I glimpse a sign with the same message as I enter the Mississippi Department of Archives and History (MDAH) in Jackson. My shock dulled this time, I still cringe at the tribute to these two individuals side by side. The irony that I have come in search of some trace of a civil rights archive for central Mississippi's poultry region is not lost on this visitor. After several years here, I am still trying to uncover the untold histories of civil and labor rights organizing in this part of the state.

I enjoy my trips to the MDAH, both because I always uncover a new fragment on this topic and because I can sometimes find my colleague, Laura Helton, in her office and convince her to join me for a break. Today we head to Hal & Mal's honky-tonk down the street. Over fried pickles and iced tea, I share my latest discoveries, and we consider their interpretation within the context of Mississippi's poultry communities.

Helton, who is working as a field archivist for the Mississippi Digital Library and will later go on to earn a PhD in African American political history, first came to Mississippi as a student in 2003 to collaborate on our activist research project in Mississippi poultry (see postscript). Since then, we have read accounts of the Mississippi Freedom Struggle; conducted oral history interviews with the area's civil rights leaders, elected officials, and industry forefathers; spent days poring over old newspapers; poked around local libraries' holdings; and scoured all the MDAH's subject files with a hint of potential relevance to central Mississippi's past as it relates to poultry, race, and labor. But the histories of Black Scott Countians' activism during the Civil Rights Movement, the desegregation of the poultry industry that followed, and union organizing in the chicken plants since then remain elusive.

·   ·   ·   ·   ·

This chapter presents a patchwork of tenuous histories, using the fragments that we managed to assemble through the methods described above. Beginning in the 1950s this story is largely one of continued subjugation of Black Mississippians, the strengthening of poultry industry power, and the collusion of the state and the media with regard to both. It is also a story of profound change, in which African Americans in parts of central Mississippi finally gain the power necessary to contest the conditions that have constrained their status as full citizens, demand new economic opportunities, and start to organize for improved wages and working conditions. Partially in response to these developments, by the 1980s the neoliberal restructuring of the poultry industry takes root, speeding up the processing lines, increasing total production hours, and cutting costs by any means necessary. By that time, African Americans constitute the majority of workers in the chicken plants and have fought some hard-won (but mostly hard-lost) battles to establish unions in their workplaces, paving the way for poultry producers to expand their horizons in search of cheap, unorganized labor.

ERLE JOHNSTON AND THE MISSISSIPPI STATE SOVEREIGNTY COMMISSION

One of the most influential men ever to live in Scott County was Erle Johnston Jr. In addition to investing in the area's budding poultry industry, he also owned the *Scott County Times* for over forty years and eventually became the mayor of Forest. With regard to the state's dual King/Lee birthday commemoration, he noted in his memoir, "It could be said that . . . Mississippians share a common holiday but not necessarily a common hero."[2] Indeed, Johnston was a key architect of white Mississippi's fight to maintain racial segregation during the 1960s. Not only did he serve as a speechwriter and strategist for a number of Mississippi's prominent politicians during this decade, including Gov. Ross Barnett and Senator James Eastland, but he also served as public relations chair and later director of the Mississippi State Sovereignty Commission, the state's official weapon against the Civil Rights Movement. I argue that the dearth of archival evidence of civil and labor rights organizing in central Mississippi is due in large part to the fact that Erle Johnston called Scott County home.

In 1956, in panicked response to the U.S. Supreme Court's *Brown v. Board of Education* ruling, the Mississippi legislature created the Sovereignty Commission. Facing the prospect that schools throughout the country would be forced to desegregate and Black and white children required to study side by side, southern lawmakers scrambled to pass legislation ensuring the steadfastness of their states' long-standing structures of racial hierarchy. As a state agency, the Sovereignty Commission was to carry out "any and all acts deemed necessary and proper to protect the sovereignty of the state of Mississippi" from encroachment by the federal government.[3] During its nearly twenty years in operation, it remained the state's main avenue to spy on those who would challenge the racial status quo and advise local officials on how to thwart federal civil rights legislation.[4]

While the Sovereignty Commission was small, with only a director, public relations chair, and a handful of secretaries and investigators, its reach was expansive. With functions similar to the FBI, it was responsible for surveillance of "race agitators" across the state, suppressing efforts focused on the political, economic, and social empowerment of African Americans. The commission colluded with local officials and employers to ensure that they intimidated and controlled would-be activists, compiling detailed information about their physical appearance, their activities, their home addresses, and their places of work.[5] The commission even secretly collaborated with private detectives and provided funds to pay undercover informants to undermine organizing efforts.[6] Over the years it produced thousands of reports, correspondence, copies, photos, and other documentation on the activities of civil rights activists and state-sponsored strategies for stopping them:

> Investigator Scarborough and myself proceeded to Canton on the early morning of January 22, where we met with Sheriff Cauthen, City Attorney Bob Goza, Billy Ray Noble, County Patrolman and Deputy Sheriff. . . . [We] informed these officials that in the past, we had found it most effective with local Negroes to photograph them individually while they were participating in demonstrations, etc. Usually when local Negroes find that they are being photographed, they are hesitant to participate in demonstrations. . . . We also learned that on Monday night [there was] a [mass] meeting. . . . These officials recorded the tag numbers of all vehicles at this meeting, checked the ownership of these vehicles, and furnished this investigator with a list of the local Negroes whose automobiles, that were registered to them, were observed at this meeting.[7]

THE FIGHT AGAINST SCHOOL DESEGREGATION

By the 1950s racial segregation had been the backbone of Mississippi's society and economy for well over a century. White Mississippians, particularly those in positions of power, were increasingly aware of a movement toward racial equality building in their state and elsewhere in the nation, yet they were determined to maintain their "way of life." Over the

next two decades, this struggle to uphold institutionalized white supremacy in Mississippi would become bloodier and more bitter than ever in the
state's history. It crystallized in the battle over school desegregation, and
the events that followed played a large role in shaping the contours of
unequal opportunity and ongoing racial inequality in Mississippi today.

Perhaps we might gauge the average white Mississippian's sentiments
on segregation by their politicians' emphatic stances on the issue during
electoral campaigns following the *Brown v. Board of Education* ruling.
While every campaign for Mississippi governor between 1956 and 1968
addressed whites' concerns for maintaining segregation, no politician was
more emblematic of that fight than Senator James Eastland. Serving as a
powerful member of the U.S. Senate for more than thirty years, Eastland
was raised in Scott County and periodically returned to his roots. In 1954
he visited Forest to announce his race for reelection. One month prior
Eastland had defied the U.S. Supreme Court during a speech in the
Mississippi Senate, booming, "Let me make this very clear. The South will
retain segregation! ... Southern people will not surrender their dual
school system and their racial heritage at the command of this crowd of
radical politicians in judicial robes." In Forest, with Erle Johnston as his
publicity manager, Eastland's speech was distributed to reporters while a
crowd of five thousand assembled to hear the senator's proposal for maintaining segregation. As attendees enjoyed a meal of barbecued chicken in
Mississippi's budding poultry capital, Eastland and Johnston's combined
power was palpable.[8]

Over the next decade, Johnston and colleagues resisted federal orders
to desegregate the schools with every defense they could muster. The
Sovereignty Commission scrutinized actions of Black teachers, principals,
parents, and other activists in central Mississippi and across the state,
punishing organizing activity with intimidation and economic strangula-
tion.[9] It organized a Speakers Bureau in which Johnston traveled the
country to convince white people of Mississippi's racial harmony under
segregation.[10]

Oral histories suggest that when African American families tried to
send their children to white schools, they encountered treacherous and
powerful resistance. On one occasion white residents shot a Black leader
in the head and his wife in the shoulder. Monzell Stowers, the first African

American elected to the Scott County Board of Supervisors since Reconstruction, recounts, "They said he shouldn't 'a messed with white folks' business. That was white folks' business, and he should've stayed out of it." Johnston secretly requested the school superintendent submit names of Black Scott County residents in touch with federal authorities so Sovereignty Commission investigators could track them down for interrogation.[11]

In Morton the Rogers family found themselves between a rock and a hard place when, in 1963, their nanny's children became part of the first group of Black students to matriculate at the Morton Attendance Center. Some of the most vocal opposition to this integration attempt came from local Klan leadership, who also worked in management at B.C. Rogers Poultry and threatened to harm the Rogers family should they fail to control "their" help. While B.C. Rogers, now a grandfather, pressed his son, John, to take action to protect the family, John Rogers, who now ran the family business, was conflicted. He relied heavily on the nanny and her family, and his children adored her. Moreover, giving in to the Klan would mean ceding to the demands of an organized group of his own chicken plant employees, a precedent he wasn't ready to set. Instead, after his children witnessed a cross burning in their yard, he hired sharpshooters, who took turns keeping watch from his roof at night. In this moment John Rogers's personal and business interests won out over white supremacists' demands, but despite his refusal to bend, the social pressure became too great. The families leading Morton's earliest school integration effort eventually yielded and withdrew their children from the enrollment lists.[12]

The area's Black residents would participate in other failed school integration attempts in subsequent years. It wasn't until 1971, after every last legal and legislative option had been exhausted, that the white schools in "holdout counties" like Scott County finally opened to Black children, over fifteen years after segregation had been deemed unconstitutional. Both the archival record and the historical memory of area residents offer confirmation that local desegregation efforts were quickly silenced through acts of physical and economic terror at the hands of a white supremacist populace and state. Few possessed the resources to successfully resist.[13]

THE SUPPRESSION OF VOTER REGISTRATION EFFORTS

Leading up to and throughout the struggle for school desegregation, racial violence escalated across Mississippi.[14] Perhaps the most well-known racial injustice of these decades is the murder of fourteen-year-old Emmett Till in 1955. Visiting his uncle in the Mississippi Delta during a vacation from school in Chicago, Till was badly beaten and killed after speaking to the wife of a white shop owner where he had gone to buy candy. His murderers were acquitted by an all-white jury after only an hour of deliberations. Indeed, "criminal justice" was nearly always decided by white residents, as juries were chosen from the available pool of registered voters, and African American residents were systematically excluded from voter registration.

In Scott County that year, only 15 "negroes," or 1 percent of the total number of qualified electors, were registered to vote.[15] The following year a newspaper reported that the first Black man "since Reconstruction days" had been selected for jury duty in Madison County.[16] In Leake County not a single Black resident was permitted to register to vote between 1955 and 1961.[17] Blocking African Americans' access to voter registration would not only exclude them from having a voice in the electoral process but also ensure minimal participation in the justice system.[18] For the white power structure, keeping control of both was key.

Thus, as African Americans across the South pushed for conditions that would allow them to exercise their right to vote, a new terrain of struggle emerged in the battle for civil rights. Nowhere was this fight more significant than in Mississippi, where Black Mississippians had been blocked from meaningful participation in the political process since the end of Reconstruction. Monzell Stowers remembers from his childhood, "In 1953 my mom and dad were [among the first] African Americans registered to vote in Scott County. At the time that they registered, the sheriff said some people might want to do something to my dad, and me, and the family. Matter of fact, we were used to people hanging people, and shooting 'em, and bombing 'em, and killing 'em when they attempted to register to vote."

A decade later nearly 90 percent of eligible white voters were registered in nearby Madison County, while this was true for fewer than 2 percent of Black citizens, and the Madison County Movement brought national attention to the fight for the right to vote in Mississippi.[19] In the spring of 1964 the Congress of Racial Equality (CORE) organized a day of action in which three thousand people were expected to line up at the courthouse to register. In the eight months prior, of a thousand attempts, only thirty had been successful, and over three hundred complaints had been registered with the U.S. Department of Justice.[20] The Madison County Movement distributed a leaflet, the *Canton Liberator*, calling folks to action:

> THE BATTLE FOR FREEDOM IN CANTON has begun. Our goal is a decent chance for every Negro in Miss. A chance at a decent education, a chance at a decent job, a chance for a decent home. We have waited too long for the white man to give us these things—he will never *give* us a thing. We must fight for our Freedom, not with violence but lawfully, through the ballot. We in Canton can get these things if we are all willing to step forward and become registered voters. The world is watching you, and your black brothers and sisters all across the South. . . . Well, What are YOU going to do? ? ? GO DOWN TO THE COURTHOUSE NOW! ! ! ! ! REGISTER TO VOTE! **FREEDOM NOW!**[21]

Some white Mississippians employed heavy intimidation tactics leading up to Freedom Day, as documented by the Sovereignty Commission: "It has been reported (not established) that there is a group of white citizens who . . . will probably arm themselves and serve somewhat in the capacity of vigilantes. . . . Informant in Jackson (Not X) states his associate in Canton advises local lawmen will set up two machine guns on square at [sic] riflemen in top of courthouse."[22] Despite these actions, the line of would-be registrants ended up being three miles long.[23] That day only three people were given the exam to pass the state's "literacy requirement," a policy in which applicants' interpretations of a section of the constitution were judged by the local county registrar, and, as was customary, none passed.[24] True to practice, the Sovereignty Commission investigator's report logged the names of each applicant for its files.

Thanks to the Madison County Movement's careful documentation, the county registrar was charged in federal court for intimidation and discrimination against Black applicants, and the FBI went to Madison County to investigate.[25] The Madison County Movement organized additional Freedom Days throughout the spring of 1964 as violence escalated across the state.[26] But it wasn't until the passage of the 1965 Voting Rights

Act that federal registrars went to Canton to take over the voter registration process from local authorities. According to a local newspaper, they "set up shop in a vacant store in Canton's business district and . . . within minutes . . . more than 100 Negroes were filling out the application forms."[27] The Sovereignty Commission took careful note of the activities.[28] Johnston and his cohort were alarmed by what was happening, as they began to see the writing on the wall:

> Large numbers of Negroes are registering to vote in Madison County and especially in the city of Canton, and since the population of the county is predominantly Negro, if they continue to register at the rate they are registering at the present time, they would definitely be able to control future elections in the city of Canton as well as the county, as a whole. If they nominate Negro candidates in the next election, it is possible that the majority of the city, county and state officials will be Negroes in this county.[29]

The tide had finally begun to turn in Madison County.

Unlike this high-profile effort, in Leake and Scott Counties, no significant voter registration efforts were organized by any of the state's civil rights organizations, and despite requests by several groups, federal registrars did not intercede as they did in Canton.[30] Still, on a much smaller scale, courageous individuals took the lead, organizing vehicles to carry people to register. But without organizational backing or the larger population found in Madison County, fear of reprisals kept many people from taking the risk. Leake County activist Winson Hudson recalls, "one thing for sure—who plain didn't register or vote, was people working for white people. The easiest folks to get to help us and to register were the farmers. At that time, farming was going out of business, and people didn't have nothing to lose and were glad to get that little money to help carry people around."[31]

The Sovereignty Commission records contain virtually no information about voter registration attempts in Scott County. My oral history interviews, however, suggest that the effort there took place largely after the Voting Rights Act passed and was mostly organized by progressive white residents. One of these was Eva Noblin in Morton, daughter of state representative Dick Livingston. She was in her twenties when she and her family began helping Black Scott County residents register to vote. "You had to go to Forest," she remembered shortly before her death. "I would pick people up and drive them to register. They would watch the car I was coming in, so we went out the other side of the courthouse and came back down another road or in a different car to throw 'em off. I knew the work was dangerous, but it was so exciting."

I asked her to tell me more about the dangers she and other organizers faced. Though her speech was belabored toward the end of her life, she drew breath and memories from deep within and continued. "Getting Blacks registered was a *hard* thing. Sometimes [Ku Klux Klan Imperial Wizard] Sam Bowers would call, and he would say, 'Listen, you do know we're gonna kill you?' But Daddy said to me, 'Now, Eva, they're not going to hurt you. They'll threaten, but you're too high profile.'" At the time she was leading the singing at the local Methodist Church, which had taken an early stand on the issue of racial equality. "'The church will come down on them,' Daddy said. 'Erle Johnston knows that. Sam Bowers knows that. They're not gonna hurt you. But *they will kill* Black people, and racist white people do not *know* one Black person from another.' Now *that* was a real shock to me."

Another elderly white couple in Scott County recalled that for nearly ten years they had attended Black church services, and in this way they built relationships and drove people to register. African American movement supporters would guard their home with shotguns whenever they took people to the courthouse, a signal to would-be terrorists that they were being watched. They say they were never retaliated against, but many they registered received threats, and they saw several homes and crosses burned over the years. An African American activist I met praised their commitment, saying, "Don't many white like 'em because they helped Blacks and came up to the polls and all of that. And white folk don't like Eva Noblin, neither. She was great!"

As many white Mississippians feared, registering Black voters did dramatically alter state politics. Today Mississippi has the highest percentage of Black elected officials, and one of the lowest Black-to-white ratios of incarceration in the country.[32] By 1966 the number of Black voters in Mississippi had increased from 30,000 to 170,000.[33] A year later the first African American was elected to the Mississippi legislature since Reconstruction.[34] Within five years, over 300,000 Black Mississippians were registered, representing over a quarter of the state's electorate.[35] Again, Scott County moved at a slower pace. The first Black alderman in Forest wasn't elected until 1977.

THE MADISON COUNTY MOVEMENT'S ECONOMIC BOYCOTT

In places where the Black community was larger and more organized, economic boycotts became a key terrain of civil rights struggle. Erle Johnston reflected in his memoirs that "Negroes found that even with their minimal purchasing power because of limited employment, they were numerous enough to force concessions from whites by boycotting merchants."[36] In Canton, where 80 percent of residents were African American, the Madison County Movement began a "selective buying campaign" in 1964 that continued on and off for more than five years and resulted in the closure of many white businesses unsympathetic to the ideals of racial equality.[37]

The campaign encouraged Black residents and white allies to avoid buying from businesses until they agreed to hire Black sales clerks, treat Black customers with respect, and desegregate their facilities.[38] Until these principles were met, the campaign called on supporters to avoid allowing "the white man [to continue] growing fat on our money." A leaflet circulated in the first year of the boycott offered further rationale:

> The Madison County Movement has tried hard and has waited long for consent to talk and negotiate with the white power structure and business community of Madison County. . . . Discriminatory practices in hiring and firing Negroes in our stores and other business places is damaging not only to the Negroes' dignity as human beings, but also to the economic progress of our town and county. . . . We have chosen a selective buying campaign because we believe it the most effective means of showing our unwillingness to let these evils persist. The stores chosen were chosen, not because they alone have been guilty of discrimination, but because they have proved themselves the worst offenders. We all know the long histories of incidents connected with each. . . . DON'T SHOP AT ANY PLACE THAT IS LISTED ON THIS SHEET.[39]

The leaflet then named about twenty stores and a handful of manufacturers targeted by the campaign.

The boycott coincided with the Madison County Movement's voter registration campaign, and within weeks white politicians and businessmen were fighting back. Canton created a "Visitor's Registration Form," requiring nonresidents to declare their presence and indicate the purpose and length of their stay.[40] The city's aldermen also made it illegal to distribute "handbills" or leaflets without a permit and threatened those not in compliance with a fine and jail time.[41] Senator Ed Henry, owner of a Canton grocery store that the boycott eventually put out of business, soon introduced a similar "anti-boycott" initiative at the state level.[42]

Violence escalated as well, as organizers reported in the boycott's second month: "The Freedom House in Canton (the building in which the staff lives) has been raided twice by police. . . . George Raymond, CORE Task Force worker, was told by Constable Herbie Evans that every time the Justice Department comes to Canton it will cost the Negro community $5,000. In January, Raymond was pistol-whipped by Evans. After the beating, Raymond was charged with intimidating an officer and resisting arrest. He was never tried and is out on $70 bail."[43] In anticipation, the Sovereignty Commission warned local officials that such "false" claims were to be expected from this "gang of agitators," cautioning, "All kinds of false charges of police brutality will be made by them, and in all probability some of the local agitators' home will be fired into. This of course will be blamed on white people and in all likelihood some fires will be set to some of these local agitators' home. Of course, whites will be accused of this and furthermore, all of this will be reported immediately to the Justice Department and the various national news media throughout the country." The commission's warnings proved eerily prescient. A few months later shots were fired into the Freedom House, and in June it was firebombed. By September grocery stores owned by supporters of the boycott were also bombed. In October the Sovereignty Commission reported that "Canton in Madison County seems to be, with the possible exception of McComb, the area where civil rights workers are most active in Mississippi at the present time."[44]

Erle Johnston and his investigators were hard at work. They used informants to try to establish who was leading the boycott and determined based on scant evidence that "two grocery stores owned by Negroes" were at the helm "because it has benefited their business."[45] Johnston and Senator Henry determined which wholesale companies supplied these

stores and contacted the wholesalers to brazenly ask them to stop supplying stores owned by African Americans. They also threatened that Canton's
white store owners would boycott their products should they fail to comply. When Pet Milk Company responded that it could not refuse sales to
any buyer, mastermind Johnston was ready with a counterargument:

> We proposed that he discontinue sending a truck to Canton, and thus cut off
> all grocery outlets using as a reason that because of the tense situation now
> existing, he could not run the risk of his truck being damaged or his driver
> being intimidated. I told him this would accomplish the purpose of depriv-
> ing the Negro owned stores of Pet products and at the same time would
> regain the good will of the white merchants, and when and if the boycott
> was lifted, he could resume trading with all stores.[46]

Industry had been growing in Canton, and Black workers were finding
jobs in enough new manufacturing plants to provide them with sufficient
buying power to make the boycott effective. So when these intimidation
measures failed to end the boycott, Johnston met with local business owners to discuss other options: "I said they could end the boycott by firing
every Negro employee at their stores and manufacturing plants. 'But,' I
quickly added, 'you can't do that because you depend too much on Negro
labor for your own income.'"[47] Instead, he suggested that local officials

> ask the manufacturing plants with these payrolls to pay their employees,
> both white and colored, in order that there [be] no discrimination, in 50%
> cash or check and 50% in specially printed specie. On the face of each specie
> would be printed words like this "This note is worth $ when properly
> indorsed [sic] and presented for cashing at any of the following stores:
> (then the list of stores would be printed). . . . At the same time, the mer-
> chants could adopt a promotion known as "cash your payroll check and win
> a prize." . . . This plan, if carried out successfully, could induce the Negroes
> to go back into the stores. . . . I believe the best approach is to try to out-
> think and out-maneuver those who have caused the boycott.[48]

Johnston's plan was strategic in targeting the Black community's growing
class of manufacturing workers. But despite their collective purchasing
power, the median annual income of African Americans in Madison County
was still low—only $1,862—and over 33 percent earned under $1,000 per
year.[49]

Despite Johnston's plan to break the campaign, momentum continued to build against industries that refused to hire African Americans, particularly poultry processing. On one boycott handbill these letters were typed, in capital letters, at the very bottom of the page: "DO NOT BUY PRODUCTS OF MOSBY MILK, HARTS BREAD, OR CANTON POULTRY." Another campaign flyer stated the problem even more clearly: "Don't buy Canton Poultry—they don't hire Negroes."[50] The inclusion of Canton Poultry in the boycott is important because it is one of the only instances in central Mississippi's archival record that illustrates Black workers' attempts to organize for racial integration of the white-only chicken plants. This marked the beginning of a change in the local poultry industry's labor force.

INDUSTRIAL GROWTH AND RACIAL INTEGRATION

As the Mississippi Freedom Struggle wore on, officials worried about the movement's effects on their efforts to bring industry to central Mississippi: "Pointing out that the local economy has been greatly expanded in recent years through new industries and development in business and agriculture, Mr. Henry, of the [Canton] Chamber of Commerce, . . . said, 'there are now outside agitators among us who would destroy that which has been developed over the years.'"[51] While statements such as this may have discouraged organizing, they also reflected what had become an obsession of central Mississippi's elected officials—"smokestack chasing," or the never-ending quest for manufacturers willing to locate in the area.[52] Throughout the 1950s and 1960s, the Balance Agriculture with Industry (BAWI) plan was these officials' biggest strength, luring industries on the taxpayers' dime. The new industries in the area included furniture plants, garment and textile factories, electric parts manufacturers, chemical companies, defense contractors, paper processors, frozen-pastry producers, and others.[53] Often these employers opened and closed their doors within a matter of years, leaving poultry as the steadiest employer in central Mississippi despite what was perceived as ongoing economic growth.

Local newspapers were quick to report on industrial growth and the passage of new BAWI bonds, which were typically valued between

$100,000 and $200,000 and passed at the polls by wide margins. In Forest, however, a subsidiary of Sunbeam Corporation, which produced clocks and electric knives and ice crushers, was lured to the area in 1962 with a BAWI bond in the amount of nearly $1 million dollars.[54] The funds were used to build a state-of-the-art air conditioned factory, which provided jobs to mostly white Scott County residents for over twenty years.

The area's chicken processors also benefited from BAWI, supporting their growth. A 1963 industrial survey of Forest reported that two poultry companies were helping pay off the city's bonded indebtedness of over half a million dollars.[55] In Carthage, R&R Processors' expansion was representative of developments across Mississippi's poultry industry. With the support of BAWI bonds worth nearly $500,000, in 1968 R&R opened in a new location north of Carthage: "The plant was built complete for processing 3000 broilers per hour. Space was allocated . . . to double production when growth of the company indicated it. [The plant] included a water system pumping 1000 gallons of water per minute, a rendering plant . . . to make poultry product meal, and its own lagoon system for waste water disposal. It was one of the most modern and efficient plants in the United States."[56] Production and profit continued to rise, though plants still typically ran just one shift through the mid-1970s.[57] Workers from that period recall that R&R had just three departments—live hang, evisceration, and cut-up.

Despite this growth, as late as the early 1960s most chicken plants would not hire African Americans. Those that did typically placed Black workers in outdoor or nonprocessing positions such as truck drivers, loaders, or cleaning crew. Production lines were staffed almost entirely by white women. One white woman who spent time in the plants during those early years explained just how bad it was: "Blacks couldn't work *anywhere*. Not *even* the chicken plants."[58]

Beginning in the 1960s, bending to the intense pressure of the Civil Rights Movement, some industries previously closed to African Americans began allowing Black employees to fill manufacturing positions. African Americans were still often relegated to the heaviest, most difficult, most dangerous work, but increasingly they were able to secure work on the line instead of just outdoors.[59] For example, a Sovereignty Commission investigator who visited Canton in 1964 stated, "I observed Negroes and

Figure 6. Cross burning at Sunbeam Corporation, 1965. Mississippi State Sovereignty Commission. Courtesy of the Archives and Records Services Division, Mississippi Department of Archives and History.

whites working together at the Madison Wood Works (furniture plant). This is customary at several manufacturing plants in Madison County and has been for years. I found no one that objected." Still, many new manufacturers continued to hire only white workers. When Sunbeam hired "two colored males for positions formerly held by white personnel" in 1965, protesters burned crosses in front of the factory and in the general manager's yard.[60] The company reverted to an all-white workforce for many years to follow. One elderly Black resident recalls, "A *long* time they didn't have nothing up there but white folk. And they used to tell you had to have a high school education. But I found out that a bunch of white didn't have no high school working there."

AFRICAN AMERICANS ENTER THE CHICKEN PLANTS

Despite acts of violence like the cross burning at Sunbeam, by the mid-1960s workplace segregation had begun to break down. Even though Black workers were not welcome everywhere, the increasing availability of new manufacturing jobs to white workers meant that jobs in less desirable industries, particularly poultry, finally began to open to African Americans. At the same time, federal agricultural policy, seeking to create a tighter market for cotton, created an incentive to keep cotton fields fallow in central Mississippi. This program disproportionately hurt small Black farmers, making it increasingly difficult for them to make a living. This, combined with the rising prominence of the mechanical cotton picker, gave many local African Americans no choice but to trade the fields for the factories. "The chicken plant replaced the cotton field," said movement veteran Monzell Stowers. "You have to have work and earn a living, so you have to go wherever the job's at."[61]

Others saw the opening of the chicken plants to Black workers as an opportunity to escape low-paying jobs as cooks, housekeepers, and nannies in the homes of wealthy whites. Such was the case of Fannie Bradford, who, two decades later, would become the first Black woman to serve as Scott County voter commissioner: "When Southeastern opened up, I went down there and put in an application. A lot of the Black peoples was going there trying to get on, and the white folks was calling the plant, telling them don't hire their cooks, their this and that. But I went there, and they called the house where I was working and said, 'Fannie, we want you to come in the morning for work.' So I told the lady I worked for, 'Miss, I'm going to the chicken plant in the morning!' And you know what she said? She was a sweet lady. She said, 'Well, they oughta have something for the Blacks to do. I hope you have success.'"

She said that Southeastern Poultry in Forest began hiring Black workers after folks up north refused to buy the company's product because it came from segregated plants: "And them chicken ruined, so as of then they went to hiring Black folk 'cause they couldn't take the consumer pressure." This, in combination with the poultry industry's expansion, the deskilling and intensification of its labor, the increasing availability of new manufacturing jobs to white workers, the waning of opportunities for small Black farmers, and mounting political pressure, likely contributed to the widespread integration of Black workers into Mississippi poultry.

Helton suggests that labor disputes may have also played a role. One of the first African Americans to integrate Southeastern Poultry recalls that "the Whites had a walk-out, so they called the Blacks in."[62] The way she remembers it, African American workers received slightly less pay than whites and had to stand while other workers sat. Companies thus relied on the introduction of African Americans as a wedge against potential grievances from white workers.[63]

Women made up the majority of Black workers desegregating Scott County's chicken plants in the 1960s. They recall having more difficult jobs than their white counterparts. Frequently this entailed "cutting buttonholes," which required carefully inserting a knife just under the bird's tail in order to pull out the entrails: "It was white and Black folk working along together, but you know, we [Black folk] had it rough. You know, some of the peoples quit. I used to stand there and cut oil bags, and the ladies next to me had they hands in there pulling chicken guts out. But nowadays, they tell me they got those machine to do all of that. I would like to go inside of a plant now to see. The line was going fast back then, but they tell me now it go faster. I said, 'I don't see how it could!'"

Another former plant employee remembered how hard she worked for her weekly seventy-five-dollar paycheck: "Your fingers was sore and your arms and shoulders. And I come home, and lotta nights, I would be so tired. But I held in there. I stayed there and worked." In addition to doing

Figure 7. Black workers packaging chickens in Forest, circa
1980. Photo of unknown origin, in Forest Vertical File. Courtesy
of Forest Public Library.

the dirtier work, many Black women who integrated the chicken plants
believe they were paid a lower wage than their white counterparts. But
because they received their paychecks in sealed envelopes, they were unable to prove their suspicions.

Before long, there were fewer and fewer white women in the plants
with whom to compare salaries or workloads. At Southeastern Poultry,
within the first week of opening to African Americans, so many white
women abandoned their jobs that the plant was forced to temporarily shut
down. "They quit because they didn't wanna work with Blacks," a woman
hired the following week says. "So many whites left, they couldn't even run
the line. But the more walked out, the more Blacks they was hiring."
Slowly, she and others corroborate, some white workers came back to the
plants, but the workforce became, and stayed, majority African American
and largely female—the result of a combination of white flight, continued
occupational mobility for white families, and increasing African American
migration from farms to towns in Scott County. Thus, by the end of the
1960s central Mississippi's chicken plants were typically run by white
management, overseen by white supervisors, and staffed by line workers
who were almost entirely Black women and men. "White, too," one former
executive recalls, "but mostly Black."

THE MISSISSIPPI POULTRY WORKERS' UNION

By the 1970s socially progressive individuals throughout the United States were eager to harvest the fruits of the Civil Rights Movement. Their political struggles increasingly yielded to economic priorities, driven by the understanding that "newly-won access to the electoral process would be truly meaningful only in the context of adequate job opportunities, wages, and education."[64] And in Scott County, poultry workers began to organize. Out of the Civil Rights Movement, the Southern Conference Educational Fund (SCEF) had established its Grass Roots Organizing Work (GROW) project, an antiracist organizing initiative that sought to help Black and white workers improve their economic conditions.[65] Led by Bob Zellner, a leader in the Mississippi Freedom Struggle, GROW had been organizing pulpwood haulers and woodcutters since the late 1960s. It had a chapter in Forest, and family members of some GROW participants worked in poultry. Encouraged by the organizing efforts of their husbands and brothers and fed up with management's refusal to give breaks after one woman urinated on herself on the line, in 1972 Black women at Southeastern Poultry walked off the job. GROW sent two organizers to Forest to support the budding poultry worker mobilization, and that year the independent Mississippi Poultry Workers' Union (MPWU) was formed.

Tonny Algood, a white Mississippian and recent college graduate, was one of the MPWU organizers in Forest. The first year his position was grant funded, but by year two Algood was dismembering chickens at Gaddis Packing Company to make ends meet while helping the area's poultry workers organize. By year three Gaddis's management laid Algood off "after they tried to work me to death." The MPWU won National Labor Relations Board (NLRB) elections at Southeastern Poultry and at Poultry Packers and was in the process of organizing Gaddis Packing Company when the plant's ownership changed hands.[66]

Organizing poultry workers was difficult for many reasons: the state's Right to Work laws weakened unions; local politics were dominated by poultry tycoons and white segregationists who weren't afraid to use violence and intimidation to maintain their power; the rural landscape meant people lived and worked over a relatively large and isolated geographic area; no core group of workers had union experience; and companies were in the midst of constant transition and mergers.[67] Where workers did successfully organize, plant management resisted contract negotiations.

Soon, employees at Poultry Packers' went on strike in hopes of bringing their employer to the bargaining table. They sought support for the strike by reaching out to activists: "The Mississippi Poultry Processing Industry saw its first strike this month in Forest, where 72 of 200 $1.60 an hour workers demanded a 15 cent raise, collective bargaining, pay during breakdowns and two week paid vacations. The plant is 80% Black. Poultry Packers, Inc., the second largest employer in the county, promptly fired all the strikers. Food and checks may be sent to Ms. Merle Barber, c/o Mississippi Poultry Workers' Union, Rt. 2, Box 11, Forest, Miss."[68]

The plant's white workers did not strike. In fact, new white workers were hired as strikebreakers to cross the picket line, and Mississippi's engrained divisions between white and Black made it impossible for the union to organize across race. "I think a lot of 'em were just afraid to speak out at all," recalls Algood. "You know, it was still a very hostile environment at that time, and I think a lot of it was fear. For years and years you had the whites who were in leadership, telling the poor whites that they were better off than the Blacks. And there were certain privileges allowed to them that were not allowed to Blacks in Mississippi. [So they just] weren't willing or were unable to see how they would benefit or what they had in common with Black workers."

Algood recalls an incident on the picket line in which a driver hauling chickens tried to run over a striking worker while pulling out of the plant's gate, and the worker was forced to dive into a ditch to avoid getting hit. Later that day the same driver mumbled something at Algood and then "slung gravel all on me" on his way into the plant. The next thing he knew, the 250-pound driver had knocked Algood's slight frame to the ground and was towering over him. At least two police officers witnessed the incident. "I looked up and the police officers had their shotguns out," Algood says, "and they had 'em trained not on the guy, but on the strikers, just threatening 'em to go ahead and take one move and they would empty their shotguns off."

Algood and other strikers went to the police station to file a report, and an officer threatened to beat him up right there in the police station. The police chief told him, "We're getting some calls saying they gonna get that white boy. I don't know who they are, but I know they're real rough people." He told Algood that no one would be able to recognize him by the time they got through with him.

Like so many civil rights organizers in Mississippi before him, Algood began sleeping on the floor of his home and got a gun permit.[69] But it was his Black neighbors who kept him safe: "I got home and one of my neighbors, a little Black man, he was boxed up in the middle of the afternoon with a shotgun. He said he had talked to all the neighbors, and if I had any problems to call him, and they figured they could all be there in just a matter of minutes. So I told the Police Chief, 'They may see me out alone, but I'm not by myself.'" Some white folks in the community also showed public support, making it clear that "they didn't wanna see this turn into another Philadelphia," in reference to the murder of three civil rights workers in neighboring Neshoba County that had focused the nation's attention on the Mississippi Freedom Struggle nearly a decade before.

With state-sanctioned violence and strike-breaking tactics, by 1974 Poultry Packers successfully forced workers back into the plant without a contract. The company hired a New Orleans law firm with a reputation for dragging out contract negotiations and beating its opponents by attrition. Martha Bergmark, a lawyer and founding director of the Mississippi Center for Justice, took the Mississippi Poultry Workers' Union as her very first client upon moving to Mississippi in the early 1970s. She represented the MPWU and participated in the contract negotiations with Poultry Packers.

The contract negotiations were "very painful," she remembers. "This guy would come up from New Orleans, we'd sit in a room, and the workers would present proposals. They would describe circumstances that justified why they needed better break policies or why they needed better pay and safety conditions. And it was just a total stonewall. Their strategy was just to sit there and wait us out. It was such a depressing experience, 'cause it was so clear that they weren't gonna agree to anything." Adding insult to injury, after hearing hours of worker testimony about the hazardous work of processing chickens, Bergmark remembers breaking for lunch to find that the meal of the day was Kentucky Fried Chicken. "They'd bring in whole buckets of chicken, and we'd all sit around eating chicken for lunch! And it was just sickening, the whole thing."

The employer and its law firm never budged. They offered only the status quo, and the workers refused to agree to those terms. "It just basically broke the backs of the people," says Algood. "They couldn't afford to continue just staying out. There was no real strike fund." The MPWU continued to negotiate after the workers went back to work, but the workers never got a union contract. After the incident on the picket line, Algood couldn't get hired anywhere in Forest. Like the workers, he couldn't afford to continue without an income, and by late 1974 he moved away. The first successful union organizing effort in Mississippi poultry, and quite possibly the most radical to date, was over by 1975.[70]

In hindsight, Algood and Bergmark wonder if affiliating with an international union might have provided the organizing workers with more support and power. A parallel effort a few years later at Sanderson Farms in Laurel, a poultry-processing stronghold one hundred miles to the south of Scott County, in which the largely Black female workforce self-organized and carried out a prolonged strike, garnered the support of the AFL-CIO and led to an affiliation with the International Chemical Workers Union (ICWU).[71] Their efforts did result in a contract, albeit a weak one that received little sustained support from the international union leadership. These events, which seem to justify the MPWU's reluctance to affiliate with the broader (and in their eyes, co-opted) union movement, received considerable national attention, and plant managers in Scott County likely followed their unfolding closely.[72] Companies around the state spent large amounts of time and energy to undercut growing labor unrest, aiming to keep the unions out at all costs.

In the decade that followed, numerous union organizing attempts failed at plants in Morton, Hazlehurst, Laurel, Jackson, and other poultry towns. Pitting Black and white workers against one another, as happened at Poultry Packers in Forest, became a central tactic to industrial restructuring in the post–civil rights South.[73] Moreover, central Mississippi's poultry management became expert at employing intimidation, threats, bribes, and lies to instill fear in workers and defeat most NLRB elections during the next twenty years.

CONCLUSIONS

Organizing by African American poultry workers in the 1970s took place in the context of centuries of institutionalized white supremacy. Despite these obstacles, such efforts grew from the seeds planted by the Mississippi Freedom Struggle of the 1950s and 1960s, in which local people built the power necessary to begin to challenge structures of racial inequality. Companies defeated union organizing attempts though a careful blend of the kind of racialized social control perfected over the course of Mississippi's history and the newly emerging sensibilities of neoliberalism.

Corporate violations of federal labor laws became increasingly wide-spread across the country during the seventies and eighties, such that in places and industries where unions had been strong, their abilities to effectively organize were weakened.[74] In meatpacking, for example, unions and the wages and benefits they had fought so hard to obtain went into decline around 1980, never to recover.[75] In poultry, however, where the industry had always relied on marginalized, low-wage workers (first white women, followed by Black women and men), a plunging of wages and benefits was hardly possible.[76] Still, management tactics ensured that few workers succeeded at organizing for better pay and working conditions and led the growing national turn toward "low road" labor strategies. This rising economic, political, and cultural logic—what some have termed the "race to the bottom"—soon led to Mississippi poultry's recruitment of immigrant workers as a form of labor control.

4 To Get to the Other Side

THE HISPANIC PROJECT AND THE RISE OF THE
NUEVO SOUTH

"It's amazing," booms the director of production into his microphone. "You've just got to see it to believe it! Very soon, our birds will have never been touched by human hands. The chicken business is high-tech, folks. It's not the mom-and-pop operation it used to be. And it needs you!" An expansive hotel dining room in Laurel, Mississippi, brims with eager young people considering professional careers with Sanderson Farms, the only remaining major poultry processor headquartered in Mississippi. He's right to emphasize that poultry is no longer a "mom-and-pop operation." When I first came to Mississippi, 55 percent of the state's twenty-two plants were locally owned; a decade later this figure had fallen to just 37 percent—and in central Mississippi to zero percent—thanks to buyouts that have reorganized the industry into the hands of a few major producers. "Well, I *am* a student," I reasoned when I came across an e-mail inviting college students to the Super Chicken Road Show, a two-day event through which Sanderson Farms sought to recruit graduating seniors into its ranks. Fortunately for this ethnographer, the registration process required minimal information. Tonight we dine on chicken (of course) atop linen tablecloths as the corporation's highest executives talk up the exciting world of poultry production. The promise of a prototypical automated chicken-catching machine to crate birds for transport to slaughter, which would eliminate the need for human chicken-catching crews altogether, is hyped as the latest and greatest advancement.

But here at the Super Chicken Road Show, it is just one of several technological innovations Sanderson Farms has touted as proof that it is on the cutting edge of profit and growth. We also learn that the company's chicks are vaccinated in-egg and that once they hatch (averaging three hundred thousand a day per hatchery), an automated "chick separator" removes their shells and neatly packs the hatchlings one hundred to a box for shipment to the farm. Its broilers take only seven weeks to grow to full capacity, and in the 1990s Sanderson Farms began producing a bigger bird, resulting in more valuable pounds of flesh per animal.[1] "'Growth' became the word for the 1990s," the speaker proudly announces, "and our company tripled in size in the decade between 1994 and 2004." Indeed, with 5.5 million birds a week literally untouched by humans until their untimely demise, processing facilities that never close, and management with fewer and fewer connections to the communities and workforces it exploits, Sanderson Farms—and the industry as a whole—barely resembles its earlier years. Today it is one of the most highly specialized and integrated agricultural sectors in the world.

.   .   .   .   .

But what caused these remarkable changes? Scholars point to Americans' skyrocketing consumption of chicken in the 1980s as it became more affordable, cholesterol became a national health issue, and the industry funneled top dollar into marketing. During this decade consumer preference shifted from mostly whole birds to boneless, skinless, "further processed" chicken products. For example, Striffler notes that in the early 1970s industry giant Tyson Foods sold seven different cuts of chicken. By 1980 it produced two dozen, and by the 1990s it marketed thousands of different products. Accelerated by the literal and proverbial chicken McNugget, today only 20 percent of chicken consumed by Americans resembles its original form.[2]

Another factor fueling the industry's transformation is that profit margins on chicken sold in its most basic form are slim.[3] There are many financial variables in chicken production, most notably feed and labor, and even minute fluctuations in the market can cause small producers to go under. I heard this repeatedly from people involved in the industry's early development. One explained,

> You'd do good if you could make one cent a pound. One! Well, not all companies are created equal. Some of them are holding a lot of one cents. It all relates to ingredient prices and labor cost. When I was in the business, ingredients were 65 percent of the total cost and at the mercy of the market conditions. Successful companies tried to minimize labor costs by buying equipment to replace workers. Many of the small, family-owned companies, like ours, never had the economic strength to buy this equipment due, in part, to lack of profitability. We just couldn't compete.

Another Scott Countian whose family spent many years in the business concurred:

> This is a volatile industry; the profit margin is very small. You only make a couple three cents a pound off a bird. If you have a bad year and you don't have resources to carry you through, you can't make it. So a lot of small plants spring up and just fade away. Tyson bought our company out. They're big and fairly diversified, which has lowered their risk and increased their profit margin. But a lot of companies in Scott County were family-owned businesses, and when the competition got really hard they just couldn't keep up.

As a result, the number of producers has shrunk, allowing larger operations to monopolize a disproportionate share of production. Those that have survived turned to a neoliberal business model to minimize variables in the cost of production to the greatest extent possible and have worked continually to acquire new plants and increase their market share. Champions of this reorganization tout that its efficiency made the industry what it is today, but critics argue that it effectively "placed a ninety million dollar industry in the hands of only five companies."[4] A former plant administrator confirmed the local reaches of this shift, saying that in the 1970s there were at least fifteen poultry companies "just in this area." Today central Mississippi is home to only four. Charting changes in the ownership of Mississippi's poultry plants over time illustrates this dramatic shift away from local ownership.

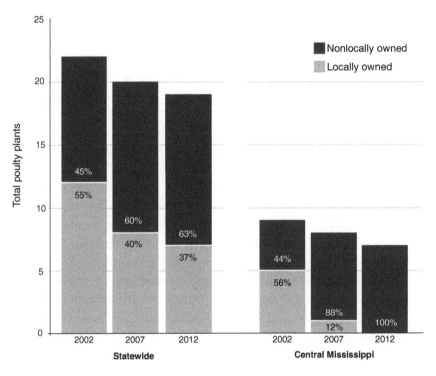

Figure 8. Changes in poultry plant ownership over time. Chart by Austin Kocher.

Consumer demand and the drive for profit have led agricultural scientists and industry leaders to innovate previously unfathomable technological advances, "domesticat[ing] the chicken into a completely industrial animal, bearing little genetic similarity to the chickens of only a century ago."[5] A commercial bird in the 1990s, for example, "grew to almost twice the weight in less than half the time and on less than half the feed" than did a broiler in the 1930s.[6]

But with escalating demand for greater quantities and more specialized processing, profit as the ultimate goal, and many production expenses out of their hands, in addition to genetic modification and developments in animal husbandry, poultry producers have focused on cutting costs in the area over which they have most control—labor. They have done this through developments such as the automated chicken-catching machine, along with thousands of other implementations that have decreased the industry's reliance on humans and increased workers' efficiency and speed.[7] They have also reduced costs by aggressively suppressing worker organizing and identifying untapped pools of cheaper and more exploitable workers, as illustrated in chapter 3. Thus, by the 1970s, right when many of Mississippi's poultry workers began to organize for higher pay and better working conditions, the industry's massive transformation was afoot. It was the confluence of these factors that led central Mississippi's poultry producers to seek out the Latin American immigrant workers that would forever change the landscape of the rural South.[8]

Using the case of B.C. Rogers Poultry in Scott County as a primary example, this chapter illustrates how these changes taking shape in the seventies, eighties, and nineties gave rise to the industry's recruitment of migrant laborers. In turn, through their evolving strategies to control labor to maximize profit, Mississippi's poultry processors became agents of the neoliberal globalization that would transform the state's poultry region. Here I trace the local history of migrant recruitment, exploring the mechanics, logics, and shifts in approaches over time, to illustrate how and why Mississippi's poultry region became home to immigrants from across the Americas and to highlight the poultry industry's role in catalyzing this shift.

CENTRAL MISSISSIPPI'S FIRST LATIN AMERICAN?

The story of Latin American migration into Mississippi poultry takes us back to the early 1960s, when Tito Echiburu, Chile's top junior tennis player, arrived in South Florida to compete in a tournament. Foreshadowing the path he would later lay for many others, Echiburu was recruited to Mississippi, where he would study and compete at the all-white Mississippi State University. He graduated in 1966 with a degree in accounting, and after returning to Chile for a couple of years, he found himself again in Mississippi working as a tennis pro at a country club in Jackson.

It was during these years that he met John Rogers, the son of local poultry tycoon B.C. Rogers, whose company of the same name, founded in Morton in 1932, was the second-oldest poultry business in the country. John Rogers was a tennis fanatic. By the time the family business started producing an employee newsletter in the 1980s, it reported industry news, recognized employees of the month, documented the county's annual chicken festival, and periodically celebrated the Rogers family's tennis achievements.[9] Sharing a bond over their favorite sport, as young men John Rogers and Tito Echiburu became fast friends.

Echiburu went back to Chile and worked for some years in international business, but as political unrest grew there in the early seventies, he began to consider the possibility of returning to the United States. Soon after, in 1973, John Rogers called. His father had passed away, and he was now leading the family poultry business. Rogers asked Echiburu to come work for him, taking responsibility for the company's finances. Echiburu and his family moved to Scott County, where he became chief financial officer of B. C. Rogers Poultry, and probably the first Latin American in the area.

MIGRANT LABOR RECRUITMENT IN THE 1970S

As with the industry as a whole, throughout the 1970s B. C. Rogers Poultry grew, and with the death of its founder, Black workers quickly became a majority on the processing lines. One would expect this growing employment opportunity in Morton to attract Black workers from across the county, as had occurred in neighboring towns. After all, with the decline of sharecropping and the mechanization of cotton, chicken plant work was *the* job opportunity for African Americans, to whom other factory work was still largely unavailable.

So it is surprising that, in 1977, B. C. Rogers Poultry began to recruit Mexican migrants from El Paso amid claims that "there was no labor available to us" in Mississippi.[10] An interview with a former manager offered further explanation: "People didn't want to work," he reasoned. There was a lot of "absenteeism and welfare," and there "just wasn't enough people."[11] This response, which reflects emergent rhetoric of the 1970s and 1980s about the Black "underclass," surfaces as an industry justification for migrant recruitment in later periods as well.[12]

B. C. Rogers had trouble retaining the migrant workers it recruited in the 1970s and stopped after a few years. Echiburu, who did not play a role in recruitment at that time, suggests management "didn't understand the changes for workers they brought to Mississippi. They were left on their own when they came and weren't accustomed to this culture and society, so most left. It was very hard for them." He estimates that only four or five families stayed in the area over time.

Furthermore, the defeat of a union organizing attempt at B. C. Rogers in 1980 meant that the company managed to maintain enough power over its local workforce to continue reaping profits without the added expense of immigrant recruitment, at least for the time being. Helton found a former manager credited welfare reform, however, not tighter labor control, with the industry's success. He claimed the company stopped recruiting migrant workers because "the labor got better; the government done a lot of things to make people work." Though B. C. Rogers' experiment with migrant labor in the 1970s was short-lived, this episode, now forty years in the past, represents an early attempt at leveraging the new opportunities for labor control just as neoliberal globalization began to take hold. It helps contextualize the contemporary moment by showing that today's talk of work ethic, workplace divisions, labor shortages, and welfare is embedded in local history.[13]

GROWTH AND A LABOR SHORTAGE AS NEOLIBERALISM TAKES HOLD

By the late 1970s the pace of expansion among the area's poultry integrators picked up speed. For example, R&R owners Curtis T. Ramzy and M. D. Reagan in Leake County had started a second company, Choctaw Maid Farms, and acquired the feed mill, hatchery, and processing plant facilities of smaller companies in the area. By 1984 Choctaw Maid employed over 1,200 local people, had more than five hundred contract growers, and slaughtered close to a million birds each week.[14]

With John Rogers at the helm, during the eighties B. C. Rogers Poultry acquired three new processing plants. Each slaughtered chickens for a minimum of sixteen hours a day, and by the early nineties they employed between 3,000 and 4,000 workers. The company's participation in American Poultry International, formed in 1978 to increase producers' capacities for cultivating an international market, was producing extraordinary results, and B. C. Rogers was exporting fifty-four million pounds of chicken annually to Russia, the Middle East, and the Caribbean.[15] But amid this intense growth, the plant struggled to fill vacancies on the line. It was bussing in around 450 workers a day from surrounding counties and even as far away as Alabama.

At the same time, throughout the 1980s the conservative Right led a rising tide calling for the rollback of state supports for the working class. In earlier moments the state had seen as its responsibility the maintenance of citizens during times of unemployment, sickness, and old age, even if these provisions were unequal and often failed to protect more marginalized groups, including many Black southerners. Such policies had supplemented the growth of industry, as state initiatives to help people make ends meet had effectively sustained the practice of paying unlivable wages. But as neoliberal logic began to take hold, the state assumed less and less responsibility for social welfare, and citizens were increasingly expected to fend for themselves.[16]

By the early 1990s the local newspaper ran a series of stories about Scott County's low unemployment rate and reported that "it has become difficult for local poultry producers to staff late shifts because of labor shortages."[17] When remembering that time, company executives cite 90 percent turnover rates, 50 percent absences on the night shift, and three hundred employment vacancies. One former manager assessed the difficulties simply: "The night shift started at three in the afternoon and ended at midnight. Nobody likes working at night, including me."

The objective cause of any perceived labor shortage is debatable. In other industries, the neoliberal "race to the bottom" of many employers led workers to look elsewhere for better opportunities, creating a void that needed to be filled.[18] But in central Mississippi, poor Black workers had few alternatives to chicken plant work. Rather, it appears that as America's appetite for chicken expanded, the industry's remarkably low pay for backbreaking work was not sufficient incentive to ensure labor demands were met. As Helton and I have argued, the term "labor shortage" merits careful examination because it is often employed to justify racialized strategies of labor control.[19] For example, I asked Echiburu why B. C. Rogers had so many problems filling the night shift. He explained, "Well, I can tell you theories, but I really don't know. You hear that Blacks don't want to work. I don't know if it's true or not. Poultry work is difficult. I'm not minimizing that, but Hispanics do it."

Rationalizations of a labor shortage, then, offered palatable ways to talk about racist perceptions of Black laziness, a discourse promoted heavily by the neoliberal Right in the early 1990s.[20] Public discourse of the time suggested that the country's economic problems were caused by "big government" and that poverty was worsened by individuals' dependency on the welfare state. The media demonized individual welfare recipients, particularly African Americans. Black men were depicted as shiftless and irresponsible, and the term "welfare queen," referring to single Black mothers who relied on the welfare system, circulated widely.[21] These racialized discourses of poverty and deservingness were finally cemented in the federal Personal Responsibility and Work Opportunity Reconciliation Act of 1996. The legislation denied aid to children born to women on welfare, instituted a five-year lifetime limit on welfare eligibility, and instituted the "workfare" program, which requires welfare recipients to work off their benefit in public- or private-sector jobs.[22] It also denied welfare benefits to immigrants and banned state and local governments from providing all but emergency services to undocumented individuals. In these ways, welfare "reform" served to further shift the burdens and risks of capitalism from states and corporations to individuals, a majority of them minorities and women, virtually forcing them into low-paying and unsafe industries such as poultry processing.

In this context, explanations of a labor shortage fail to recognize that most people receiving welfare in the early nineties carefully weighed the option of public benefits against their other life and work opportunities.[23] And while the southern economy was growing, wages and opportunities on poultry-processing lines remained stagnant. At $6.00 per hour, workers were earning less than $250 a week, not even reaching the federal poverty threshold for a family of four. Plant work no longer promised African Americans the opportunity for upward mobility it had represented twenty years prior. The notion that African Americans opted for state support out of blind laziness fails to consider both the valid reasons Black Mississippians had for contemplating options other than poultry and the myriad concerns that rational individuals take into account when making choices for their families.

In Mississippi today the labor shortage discourse is still widely used, and it revolves around questions of "hard work," the "immigrant work ethic," and the perceived "laziness" of local Black residents. As one woman told Helton, "If they were paying ten or twelve [dollars] an hour, people would be coming from all over the county for those jobs." A Black elected official echoed this sentiment: "[Immigrants] were brought in for cheap labor, not a shortage. . . . The labor's here but the jobs don't want to pay."[24] For many residents, then, "labor shortage" is not merely a race-neutral term for a period of low unemployment, but is instead a pejorative way to talk about the available (and mostly Black) labor pool. It delegitimizes individuals' reasons for avoiding dangerous conditions and below-poverty wages in the plants while disregarding the industry's violations of federal labor law, health and safety regulations, and human rights. Despite these critiques, Scott County's labor shortage led B.C. Rogers Poultry to South Texas in search of workers.[25]

SOUTH TEXAS, 1993

Echiburu's career at B.C. Rogers was successful, and in time he helped family members secure management positions. One was his brother-in-law, Luis Cartagena, who, in 1993, was charged with recruiting workers from South Texas. He recounts, "I would go by plane to Brownsville. I would arrive on a Tuesday. I would go to the Employment Commission and on Wednesday I would interview a lot of people. And right then and there, I decided who to hire. I would tell them, 'Tomorrow the bus leaves for Mississippi, Thursday.' Then I would fly back, and on Friday I was here waiting for them with money, housing, everything." Cartagena says he brought between seven hundred and eight hundred workers— mostly men without their families—from South Texas over a period of six months, but few stayed. He reasons that the deal was too sweet, as the company initially offered two weeks of rent-free housing plus a ten-dollar daily allowance for meals. People came but would leave after two weeks, or they would stay a few months and find a better job. Turnover remained high, and management couldn't figure out how to get it down.

THE HISPANIC PROJECT, 1994–1998

After B. C. Rogers' six months of intense recruitment, the Texas Employment Commission continued to send workers from the Rio Grande Valley, though on their own and at a slower pace. Cartagena reimbursed people for their transportation costs upon hire. Meanwhile, B. C. Rogers refocused its recruitment efforts in South Florida. Echiburu remembers that a television program gave John Rogers the idea that would forever change the landscape of Mississippi poultry: "John saw a program about immigrants in Miami who didn't have enough work, so he asked me what I could do to bring them. That's what started it! We had a Cuban friend there, so I set up an office in his company and advertised in the local paper. It worked great—after only one week there, we brought a Greyhound bus full of Hispanics. And we'd bring them every week, fifty-something a week. This was the beginning of what we called our Hispanic Project." Fidel Briceño, a Venezuelan who today drives trucks for the chicken plant, remembers seeing that advertisement in the paper in Miami. His cousin encouraged him to go to Mississippi, but he had doubts, so he went to the recruitment office to inquire:

> I talked to this Cuban guy and he told me that the next group was leaving that weekend, on a bus, and they would pay my way. In that office they put on a video that showed the plant, the workers with their white smocks, and the chickens going by on the line. It showed the city, the bank, the police station, the grocery store. And it said this was a good place to live and work, a tranquil place that didn't sell beer, with a school for children and all the comforts one could hope for.

So, like so many others, Briceño's family came to Mississippi on the next bus. They were taken straight to the chicken plant, where they started work that very night. Most who made this journey say they began work the same day, or within just a few days, of their arrival.

Basic Needs and Cost of Living

Providing jobs was not a problem, but providing for workers' basic needs was, starting with housing. Cartagena was in charge of ensuring a place to stay for all new recruits. With rental properties in short supply, in the early nineties most landlords did not want to house B. C. Rogers' Latino employees. Sometimes Cartagena was able to change their minds by offering higher rent. More often, he was not. He began working closely with a couple of local businessmen: "I told them, 'Hey, do you want to make money? I need houses. Buy as many as you can get your hands on near the chicken plant, and I will rent them all. Okay?' They agreed, and that's how we did it."

Workers who remember this time recall regularly sharing a one-bathroom home or trailer with up to a dozen people. These memories are cause for resentment to this day, and their vivid recollections best speak for themselves:

> When we arrived we were in a house with ten people, and everyone worked nights and wanted to sleep during the day. But my kids were on summer vacation, and they made noise. And one woman who lived with us kicked them out of the house one day and locked the door so they couldn't get back in. Imagine that! What were they supposed to do?

Immigrants recall never knowing when they would come home from work to find a stranger in the kitchen—their newest housemate:

> One day we arrived home and there was a man there in our house. We were like, "Who is this guy?" But we couldn't do anything because the house wasn't ours.

> You would leave for work and come home and find people in your house. You just never knew. There was a time where there were three people sleeping in the living room and seven of us in a little house meant for four.

Advocates, too, were dealing with immigrants' housing problems. "They were just cramming as many people as they could into a trailer and charging 'em by the head," recalls Mary Townsend, an ESOL teacher and Catholic outreach volunteer. "And it would take *ages* for repairs to be made. Holes in the floor, heaters that didn't work, I mean, really big things." Stories abound about the barely livable condition of many of B. C. Rogers' residences: "The houses were in deplorable conditions when we moved in, and filthy. There were people who came and as soon as they saw where they would be living, they turned around and never went to work, not even for a day."

But others say they were grateful despite the conditions. "We were lucky. We arrived to a house that was deteriorated and dirty, and we had to sleep on the floor the first night. But it had a refrigerator and stove, and one fine day we decided to clean and paint it, and it turned out beautifully."

In Echiburu's opinion, organizing the Hispanic Project was a thankless job, and not enough workers were appreciative of B. C. Rogers' efforts. "We did a really good job of taking care of them, but there is certain Hispanics that take things for granted. I hate to say it. I'm not trying to be prejudiced, but, my goodness, 'Why this?' 'What that?' And we were the only company that I knew of that was doing all this outside work."

By the mid-1990s B. C. Rogers rented or owned 166 houses in the areas around its plants in Morton and Forest. Cartagena managed a team of nineteen people working on the Hispanic Project. They gave orientations, assigned and maintained housing, collected rent, and arranged social activities. They coordinated a soccer team, provided transportation to and from work, and even offered an optional weekend transportation service that taxied people to the supermarket, Laundromat, and church. Cartagena recalls, "I would take them to Mass in Jackson, to the Saint Peter's Cathedral by bus, and after Mass we would take them to the mall." When I joked that there were probably a lot of non-Catholics attending Mass so they could go shopping in the city on Sunday afternoons, Cartagena playfully conceded that it was most certainly the case.

The services were not free of charge. Most accounts suggest B. C. Rogers charged $25 a week for housing, $20 for transportation to and from work, and $12 for the weekend services. Earning wages of approximately $6.50 an hour, workers' take-home pay after these deductions was typically under $200 a week.[26] A union organizer remembers, "The workers would make they money, but when they'd get they check sometime they didn't have nothing left." Meanwhile, the Hispanic Project was grossing up to $1,000 per month from each rental property.

The Hispanic Project Closes Its Doors

Though business appeared to be booming, in 1998 John Rogers sold the family business and the doors of the Hispanic Project were closed.[27] In its roughly five years of operation, the Hispanic Project recruited nearly five thousand workers to Morton and Forest, towns with a combined population of under ten thousand. The program made B. C. Rogers a leader in immigrant recruitment, as well as a model for other employers nationwide. "One time I went to make a presentation somewhere close to Miami," Echiburu reminisced. "It was a huge meeting of people from all over the U.S. working in the area of migrant worker employment, and I spoke to about sixty or seventy people there. None of them had the program that we had. At the time there was nobody bringing them, giving them houses, taking them shopping. . . . We were front-runners, far ahead of anybody else."

Roughly 80 percent of workers brought under the project were Cuban. The other 20 percent were mostly Central American (Nicaraguan, Honduran) and Caribbean (Dominican, Puerto Rican). As with B. C. Rogers' recruitment efforts in the 1970s, most did not stay over the long term. "I've noticed a trend that a lot of people are unhappy with the situation here," reflected ESOL teacher Townsend. "They haven't gotten what they were promised, and the working conditions are much, much harder than they anticipated. After they've been here a while and meet some other folks and find their way around, a lot of them leave the area. It just takes one or two to get there and say, 'It's better here,' and they all follow."

Poultry worker Briceño concurs but notes the role of immigration status in enabling people to leave. "Many people didn't stay precisely because of how they were treated, the poor supervision, the abuse. You know that when a Cuban lands on American soil, he immediately has rights, and he knows it. So Cubans came here from Florida and when they felt bad they asked, 'Why are we here? We can go somewhere else and find work where they treat us better.' And little by little, they left." In fact, many—though certainly not all—workers brought by the Hispanic Project were able to legalize their status. Due to the United States' policy toward Cuba, since 1966 its refugees have been eligible for legal residency. Similarly, migrants fleeing hurricane-devastated Nicaragua, El Salvador, and Honduras in the 1990s were often able to attain Temporary Protected Status, allowing them to live and work legally in the United States. With "papers," immigrants' work and life prospects broadened substantially, and few opted to continue enduring the conditions and poverty-level wages of chicken processing.

A RETURN TO SOUTH TEXAS

While there are few recruits from the mid-1990s still in the area, new migrants kept coming. At the end of the decade, a new human resources manager at B.C. Rogers from Mexico reinitiated a scaled-down recruitment program in South Texas. "The following year, more Mexicans started to come," remembers Townsend. "And they would let the people back home know that this was a good place to be and there was work, and then more would come. But I'm not sure what the pipeline was or what the network was because people were coming from *all over* Mexico."

Mexican migrants to Mississippi have been particularly mobile, coming from Texas, Florida, and elsewhere and spreading out throughout the state's poultry region, but some general demographic trends are discernable. The majority come from the newer sending states of Veracruz, Oaxaca, and Chiapas of southeastern Mexico. By 2005 Forest was home to a large population from Veracruz and a smaller group from Chiapas. These are mostly men, many with families back home. Many Chiapanecos come from indigenous communities near Guatemala and speak languages other than Spanish. The Jarochos tend to be monolingual Spanish speakers hailing from rural communities in central Veracruz. An indigenous Oaxacan community is budding to the south, in Laurel. Though smaller in number, there are also men and women throughout Mississippi's poultry region from more traditional migrant sending states like Guanajuato, Michoacán, and San Luis Potosí. This diversity makes it a challenge to trace the particular paths that have led Mexican migrants to Mississippi poultry.

SOUTH FLORIDA TRANSIT

B.C. Rogers set an example, and it didn't take long for other poultry operations and ancillary industries to catch on. After only a year of the Hispanic Project's activities, a handful of other processors in the area were also recruiting from Florida, Texas, and beyond. One paid its own Spanish-speaking line workers to drive vans to Miami and bring them back full of fresh laborers. Another sent recruiters to Texas and perhaps even Mexico to recruit migrant workers during a union organizing drive in the mid-1990s.

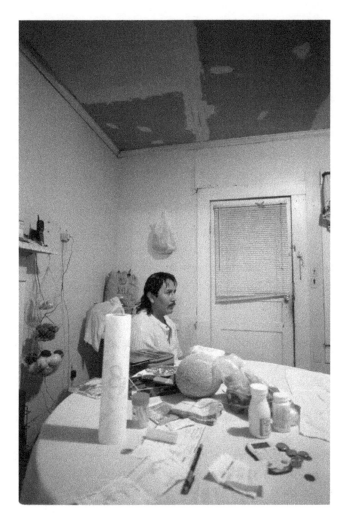

Figure 9. Immigrant from Veracruz, Mexico, in his Forest, Mississippi, kitchen, 2004. Photo by John Fiege. Courtesy of FiegeFilms.com.

By 2000 most chicken plants in the area were operating around the clock. A number of informal and more formalized recruitment and transportation ventures flourished, and migrant workers continued to arrive in record-breaking numbers. It was around this time that South Florida Transit—remembered by local immigrant rights advocates as the most notorious of recruitment agencies—began bringing immigrants to Scott County from South Florida. The vast majority were no longer Cubans; they were Argentines, Uruguayans, and other South Americans. Fleeing economic decline and political unrest, the lack of steady work in Miami led these visa-overstayers to piece-rate work in chicken processing.

The economic crisis of Argentina, beginning in 1999, put pressure on people of all social classes.[28] Those that eventually found their way to Mississippi were mostly working- and middle-class families. Back home they had earned a living as bus drivers, bank tellers, real estate brokers, and salespeople. They arrived in Miami as "tourists" but knew they would be seeking work and would likely stay beyond the six months their visas allotted. In many cases Argentine men came first and, upon securing jobs in Miami, sent for their families.

Generally, it didn't take long for them to realize they couldn't keep up with the cost of living in Miami. Those who found work struggled to make ends meet on their meager construction, restaurant, or gas station salaries. Many overstayed their welcome on the couches of friends while they looked unsuccessfully for employment. Some worked briefly in agriculture, grumbling that the growing presence of Guatemalans had driven wages even lower. One entrepreneurial couple put their business experience to work and began selling roses in stopped traffic. They maintain that together they earned $250 per day, but when the city cracked down on street vendors, the income stopped. Soon after, with only $40 in their pockets and desperation mounting, they learned about the possibility of work in Mississippi's chicken plants.

Like many other South Americans, they came across advertisements for South Florida Transit through Spanish-language newspapers, Hispanic stores, or by word of mouth. Vicente Suárez, from Córdoba, Argentina, remembers, "an acquaintance told me there was work in Mississippi. I had just recently arrived in the U.S., and I didn't know what he was talking about. I had always thought Mississippi was a river. 'What do you mean Mississippi?' 'It's a job in chicken production, cutting something like breasts, I'm not sure exactly,' he said. 'But it's a new department that they're opening, and nobody works there yet. They will pay you thirteen cents a pound, and the more you cut, the more you will make.'"

In exchange for $125 per person, South Florida Transit promised a secure job, respectable pay, and decent housing. Suárez came with thirty others packed into two vans on the outfit's pilot journey to Mississippi in 2001. At least half of the passengers were Argentine. Mariana Paz was far from pleased by the prospect of chicken plant work, but relieved to quit her job serving drinks to men in a seedy Miami nightclub, she was willing to give it a shot. She and her husband, Adrian Vera, along with their two elementary school-age children, made the journey to Mississippi a few weeks after Suárez. Four years later, in the home they had purchased with their wages in the plant's "debone" department, they recounted their harrowing trip with much animation. Vera began,

> It was July 22, 2001. We left Miami at 4:30 in the afternoon and had no idea where we were going. We only knew the name, Mississippi. We knew we were going to work in a chicken plant, but we had no idea what that really meant. We had our own car, but the company wanted to make money, so they still charged us the usual rate, and on top of that we had to pay for our gasoline. We traveled through the night—

Paz jumped in to continue the story:

> Adrian drove the car, and I rode in the van with our children. But the company didn't save seats for the kids, so we were packed in like canned sardines. You have no idea what it was like to travel that distance with my daughter in my arms. The other passengers were so good to us and let her lie across their laps while she slept. I will never forget that night. The driver was falling asleep. He ran off the road. He hit the cones. I was terrified. When we stopped for gas, I begged Adrian to take us with him in the car, but it was full of our belongings.

Luis Cartagena remembers fondly that during this era "families started to arrive." For him this meant not only that they might stay for longer periods but also that his life would get easier. Though his title had changed to out-of-state employment department supervisor, he was still overseeing newcomers' housing and serving as a community liaison for the company. During his tenure with the Hispanic Project, he had often received calls from the police to interpret for migrants who had been arrested for public intoxication, DUIs, and disturbing the peace. More families, he hoped, meant fewer single men, fewer calls, and more sleep at night.

Laborers brought by South Florida Transit went to work cutting "tenders" in a new production area of the plant, where they soon numbered sixty. New hires were drawn to this work because of the piece-rate pay, which rewarded them for dexterity and dedication. Suárez recalls getting so good at his job that he could cut a hundred pounds of tenders each hour. His weekly paycheck was typically over $450, and he proudly recalls his most productive week ever, when he cut 4,079 pounds of tenders and took home $530. Pay by the pound offered the opportunity for higher wages, and reward for hard work resonated with many immigrants entering Mississippi. The remuneration was short-lived, however.

With most positions full, the plant no longer needed new workers at such a rapid pace. This did not deter the recruiters of South Florida Transit. They continued to bring at least a van of workers per week, with the same promises as before, charging their recruits by the head. "They promised one thing and gave you something else," one worker recollected. "Even the plant management got mad at them. In our trip from Miami, they brought twice as many workers as the plant had positions for. The housing wasn't ready for us, either. We didn't even have beds!"

Within eighteen months South Florida Transit was run out of town. A local immigrant rights advocate remembered, "they were dropping people off and charging 'em and then not going back to get 'em because there was no work. We complained to the plants, the police department, and the mayor, and we managed to get them shut down. We called the Miami newspapers to tell 'em what they were doing up here and not to run their ads anymore. We were very aggressive with them."

By 2001 B.C. Rogers' new management couldn't make ends meet and declared bankruptcy.[29] With the industry still expanding and cheap labor in abundant supply, they had taken a gamble and bought new equipment (on credit), ultimately sinking the company deep into debt under a heavy load of loans and interest payments. And the city of Morton still had over ten years to pay on the substantial loans it had taken out to renovate the city's water treatment facilities expressly for the chicken plant. In analyzing the closing of a poultry processor elsewhere, Cedric Chatterley and Alicia Rouverol assert that bankruptcies are not always due to failed business, stating that "92% result from disinvestments, restructurings, 'runaway plants,' and the like."[30] This appears to have been the case with B.C. Rogers, as Chicago-based Koch Foods agreed to acquire the company on the condition that it first file for bankruptcy. The move would decrease the liability to creditors that Koch Foods would inherit in the acquisition.

Echiburu was hired to negotiate and administer the details of the bankruptcy in exchange for a percentage of the proceedings. The arrangement worked out especially well for him, he says, and he went on to serve as the chief financial officer of the Bank of Morton and chair of the Morton Chamber of Commerce: "I got twenty million dollars for them, and I got a percentage of that," he relates. "So financially, it was very rewarding to me, even though it was bad for the company. That was like my retirement."

By the end of 2001 Koch Foods had bought B.C. Rogers Poultry.[31] Within a few months Koch Foods had divested itself of the residential properties it had inherited from B.C. Rogers, selling its houses and trailers to one of Cartagena's old business collaborators for $1 million dollars, or just over $6,000, per property. Koch Foods also brought new management to Mississippi, getting rid of the old administrators. They soon eliminated the factory's "tender" operations altogether.

Workers formerly cutting tenders were transferred to other areas of the plant, and most new migrants learned to debone chicken thighs. Piecerate pay was reduced from thirteen to eleven cents a pound. With this disincentive, numerous Argentine workers moved to Jackson, where they found work in restaurants, housekeeping, and retail. Others relate that they had a comparative advantage over other Latin Americans and African Americans, enabling them to secure work as servers at the casinos on the nearby Choctaw reservation. Meanwhile, in early 2002 the U.S. State Department realized that a disproportionate percentage of Argentine tourists were not returning home, and it revoked Argentina's (and soon after, Uruguay's) participation in the Visa Waiver Program.[32] By the end of that year South American migration from Miami to Mississippi—and the operations of South Florida Transit—had come to a screeching halt.

RECRUITMENT INCENTIVES AND FAMILY NETWORKS

During roughly the same time as South Florida Transit's operations, Choctaw Maid in Carthage began paying its employees $600 for each new worker they recruited who stayed a minimum of three months. This enabled one entrepreneurial Peruvian to bank tens of thousands of dollars. He advertised in a newspaper in his hometown of Arequipa, Peru—for those who had a tourist visa to enter the United States, could afford a plane ticket, and desired to work in poultry processing, he would bring them to Miami, then to Mississippi, and guarantee a job. In Mississippi I met agronomists, engineers, doctors, librarians, and psychologists from Arequipa, now taking English classes, deboning chicken, and learning how to file workers' compensation claims.[33]

Similarly, Baldomero Félix, an indigenous Guatemalan worker at the same plant, claims he more than doubled his annual income through the plant's recruitment incentives:

> They put up announcements inside the plant that if you recruited someone they would pay you money. Well, I never did it in self-interest, but I thought, "They're going to have to give this money to someone, so as long as they're giving it out, I'm not just going to let it sit there." One time about twenty Mexicans arrived. I don't know how they got my name, but they called me. They wanted to know if anyone could help them get a job. So I took them to work, and the plant ended up paying me $12,000. They had that incentive for many years. And yes, I recruited a lot of people.

Such employee recruitment bonuses are not new, as similar schemes were documented among poultry producers in North Carolina and Georgia some years prior.[34]

Félix has been instrumental in further transforming the demographics of Mississippi's poultry towns. The majority of new immigration into the plants in the first decade of the new millennium came from the villages surrounding Comitancillo, which Félix calls home, in the indigenous Mam-speaking highlands of San Marcos, Guatemala. In 1995 Félix was among the first group from Comitancillo to arrive in Mississippi. A decade later he was considered by many to be the patriarch of a community of approximately one thousand Comitecos in Carthage. Even *coyotes* in Comitancillo have used his name to recruit migrants.[35] "They would say, 'If you come with me, we have contact with Baldomero Félix, and when you get there, he will get you work.'" Félix says new arrivals would visit him, saying that their *coyote* told them that he could get them a job. "I don't mind if I've gotten a little bit of fame for this over the years," he chuckles.

When they came to the United States, Félix and his brothers were escaping Guatemala's armed conflict that had lasted over thirty years—their entire lives. While San Marcos was not one of the areas worst affected by state violence, when Félix spoke at his labor union's regional conference in 2004, he vividly recounted his memories of childhood terror and his painful work as a young man in the Guatemalan army before making the journey to the United States.

Félix and his brothers arrived first in Arizona but didn't know where they were headed. Félix imagined going somewhere that sounded familiar—California, maybe New York. Instead, at their *coyote*'s insistence, they found themselves in North Carolina. "There was no particular place we had to go. Not like now that everyone knows they are coming to Mississippi. I simply wanted to be in the United States; it didn't matter where. They put us out on a little old ranch at the edge of a river. The house didn't even have a floor; it was made of dirt. We stayed for about a month picking cucumbers." They then picked tomatoes in Kentucky for five months before heading to Florida, where they harvested oranges for another six. In each location they were out of a job when the harvest season ended.

They eventually crossed paths with a Cuban woman who told them about the opportunities in Mississippi, so they left farmwork for the relative stability and indoor-nature of chicken processing. "What motivated me was that farmwork was very hard," Félix explains. I was in North Carolina, Kentucky, Florida, and the jobs were very difficult. Cutting oranges is tough. What I lived through in Guatemala was tough. So for me the work that we're doing here is okay. Many people who come now say that the work here is really hard. I think maybe that's because they haven't been through so many things in their lifetimes. They are much younger, and they don't really know what suffering is."

The Comitecos in Mississippi are indeed young, and were even more so when I lived among them a decade ago. Many do not remember Guatemala's armed conflict, instead identifying as refugees of the global economy. Most arrived before they were twenty years old, often as young as fifteen or sixteen. The majority are young men, though newcomers are increasingly women. Like other undocumented immigrants, they have to purchase papers to get hired, and their new identities typically place them in their early twenties, thus making them old enough to work in chicken plants. Though Mississippi law would permit these young people to attend public high school, most do not enroll; economic necessity typically requires that they work full-time.[36] Comitecos attend ESOL classes at higher rates than do immigrants from other places, and they tend to pick up English quickly, perhaps due to their bilingual upbringing as Mam and Spanish speakers. This has enabled a handful of Comitecos to move into "lead person" and even supervisory positions on the processing lines. Others, typically girls and women, are monolingual Mam speakers, which isolates them not only from broader Mississippian society, but also from most other (non-Mam) immigrants.

Efrain López, who was fifteen when he migrated from Comitancillo to Mississippi in 2000, says that migrating at such a young age had a profound impact on his life: "When I came I was very young. I didn't know much. I've learned so much here. Most of my life experiences have happened here." López barely survived his journey across Mexico, let alone his swim across the Rio Grande and his subsequent travels on foot in shoes two sizes too small. Though reluctant, he brought two brothers to Mississippi after him, but he hopes that together they can send enough money home to keep their five youngest siblings in school in Guatemala. López's brothers and sisters notwithstanding, when I visited their village in 2006, I noticed that young people—particularly young men between the ages of fifteen and thirty—are conspicuously absent. Their presence is felt in the DVDs and video games occupying their younger siblings in adobe and dirt-floor homes, in the numerous new cement block homes being built in the municipal capital of Comitancillo, and in the long line of patient family members waiting outside the local co-op to pick up remittances on market day.

Félix, López, and hundreds of others in their footsteps saved the money they earned slaughtering chickens and sent it home for family members to make the journey across Mexico, through the desert, and into the United States. Once receiving word that their loved one had arrived in Houston or Phoenix, they would send more money for the *coyote* to release him or her and arrange for transportation to Mississippi. As Félix recalls, "I brought my brothers and sisters, then my cousins. Then my cousins brought their brothers. Then they brought their families, like a chain." By 2004 up to fifty Comitecos would arrive in Carthage in any given month.

Anthropologists have long been interested in social networks and have noted the crucial role they play in shaping immigration patterns in the neoliberal era.[37] And many labor migration scholars note the roles that social networks have played in the creation of job opportunities and the concentration of new immigrants in the lowest rung of segmented labor markets.[38] Certainly, for both Choctaw Maid and the many people from Arequipa, Comitancillo, and parts of southeastern Mexico who have spent time in Mississippi, immigrants' abilities to leverage social ties in the creation of transnational work opportunities have been vital to their economic survival. As a result, by the first years of the twenty-first century, Mississippi's chicken plants no longer had to leave the state to recruit foreign workers. In the words of the Hispanic Project architect, Tito Echiburu, "They were right here."

HOW DID THESE PEOPLE GET HERE?

So it is in this way that today Mississippi's poultry workers are Americans from nearly every part of the continent. They are Black, Brown, and occasionally white; men and women; rural peasants and former blue- and even white-collar workers; speakers of English, Spanish, and a handful of indigenous languages. Their histories, cultures, and experiences have been vastly different, creating both tensions and alliances within and between groups that will be explored in greater detail in subsequent chapters.

Tracking the logics and mechanics that brought Latin Americans to Mississippi demonstrates that none of the various waves of migration into Mississippi poultry have happened accidentally, nor were they random. To the contrary, they were produced; they were patterned.[39] History teaches us that they were propelled by elaborate neoliberal corporate projects and calculated recruitment, with the goal of constructing an expendable and infinite pool of disempowered low-wage workers. "Indeed," writes David Griffith, who has extensively studied the use of immigrant labor in industrial agriculture, "one of the hallmarks of advanced capitalism has been its success at the continued reliance on 'marginal' workers." Moreover, he argues, low wage labor forces in the U.S. do not just emerge, naturally, as responses to market conditions. Instead, they are constructed, reorganized, and maintained by means of a few common practices. . . . Each of these practices also depends on the development and use of myths about specific kinds of workers as compared to others, particularly myths about "the work ethic." By looking at these processes of constructing labor forces, we can more fully understand how low-wage industries come to use new immigrants, minorities, and other workers considered "marginal."[40]

Understanding how immigrants have leveraged social networks to journey and find work in the area's chicken plants further demonstrates that it is insufficient to explain migration to new destinations by pointing to the "pulls" of economic expansion and industrial restructuring.[41] Looking further back in time demonstrates that poultry's immigrant-recruitment strategies do not exist merely to decrease costs and maximize profits. They also serve to weaken both immigrant and local workers' prospects for collective bargaining by cultivating divisions along lines of race, nationality, language, gender, and legal status, as we will explore further in subsequent chapters.

Finally, deeply examining the histories of immigration in Mississippi poultry reminds us that the circumstances that give way to the movement of people, into new spaces, by new actors, are unique to every locale. It teaches us that local knowledges and experiences do matter, in bigger ways than we might imagine. Toward the end of my time living in Mississippi I asked Tito Echiburu if he realized, when he and John Rogers first initiated recruitment of Latin Americans, the potential it had for changing the Mississippi landscape and the contours of the poultry industry. He says they never predicted the impact of their Hispanic Project, and he is amazed by how rural areas like Scott County have changed.

> It's funny you're asking this, because something strange happened about three months ago. John is getting older, and he's beginning to forget things. He came to the bank with his wife, and I was in the lobby talking to him. It was a Friday, and a lot of people come to the bank on Fridays. And, of course, I'm Hispanic, so, you know, I say, "*Hola, ¿Cómo estás?*" to about five or six people. John was beside me and he looked at me and said, "Tito, how did these people get here?" And I looked at his wife and she looked at me, and we both died laughing. And I said, "That was you, John. That was you!"

5 Pecking Order

LATINO NEWCOMERS, RECEPTIONS, AND
RACIAL HIERARCHIES

"I think some of our new Hispanic guests have unfortunately been victims of racism." Chris Thompson, a lean, thirty-something white man, leans toward me, his green eyes briefly scanning the stacks of papers scattered across the oversized desk that divides us. I shift in my seat too, eyeing my digital recorder to ensure it's capturing his words. In Mississippi and beyond, white people rarely speak openly about racism, despite the persistence of thinly veiled structures of white supremacy that permeate society. But Thompson appears relaxed and laughs often during our conversation in his wood-paneled office. The overcrowded space would be dim but for the large glass panes on the front wall that let in the early spring sunshine. Beyond where I sit, past a few artificial houseplants and the block lettering advertising his realty services to passersby, he can see the comings and goings at the Mexican store across the street in downtown Forest. Thompson was born and raised here but left for college and worked in another state for a few years before he returned in the mid-1990s to find his community transformed by immigration. Today he has been generously talking with me about these changes.

"I find it interesting that, well, the white people that seem to be racist against the Hispanics are the very same ones that are racist against the

Black people. But what I find *really* interesting is there's *Black* people that are racist against them as well—the people who have been victims of racism themselves!" A long, low train whistle interrupts us. When the air clears, Thompson cracks a joke about life in small-town America, where conversations still pause when a train comes through. We share a brief laugh, and he picks up where he left off, without missing a beat. "I will tell you strictly my opinion. I'm crazy about 'em. I think they're making a real effort to assimilate into our society, and I applaud that. I'm glad they're here. They're providing the work that otherwise would go undone here in our county. Anytime a group wants to come here and work, I'm all for 'em. I don't care what color they are or what they look like or what language they speak. I don't know what our poultry industry would do without our Hispanic guests."

Thompson's observations about the area's "new guests" and their reception by local people of different backgrounds captivate me. They echo concerns I have heard repeatedly throughout my time in the South, shared by community leaders, the media, and academics alike: Latin American immigrants stick out because they look and sound different, but will they—can they—assimilate? Are they putting a strain on local resources, or are they growing the area's economy? Do they do work that Americans "don't want," or are they "taking our jobs"? And what will become of America's "color line"? Such questions hold a magnifying glass up to the nuanced, layered—indeed, complicated—nature of cross-cultural and cross-racial relations blooming in the wake of immigrants' arrival. With population experts predicting that the United States will become a "majority-minority" country by 2042, the political and social stakes are high.

·   ·   ·   ·   ·

Thompson's comments that afternoon went to the heart of a fundamental problem scholars have been debating about the region's demographic transformation: in what ways is the growing presence of Latino communities transforming social hierarchies of race in the South? This chapter explores how people of different backgrounds in Mississippi's poultry region answer this question. And when folks in Mississippi—white, Black, and Latino—talk about immigration, they are often also talking about race. Indeed, I argue that race serves as the principal lens through which people are living out the demographic changes around them. Experiences with and attitudes toward immigration vary greatly depending on people's racial identities, which often determine the contexts of interactions they have had with people unlike themselves. Examining the ways and spaces through which Latinos enter into a society that continues to uphold rigid distinctions between white and Black highlights the racial diversity that exists within Mississippi's Latino immigrant communities. Ultimately, I conclude that despite astute analyses emerging from Black poultry worker leaders, rather than reconfiguring the area's rigid social hierarchies of race, immigrants' arrival is largely reinforcing a system in which whiteness maintains its privilege and Blackness persists at the very bottom.

WHITENESS, BLACKNESS, AND THE U.S. COLOR LINE

Popular conceptions of racism in the United States often cast it narrowly as individual prejudice based on racial characteristics that leads to discrimination. But not only is racism a question of structures and institutions, as introduced in previous chapters, it is also just as much about privilege as it is about disadvantage. Society encourages white Americans to invest in whiteness, "to remain true to an identity that provides them with resources, power, and opportunity."[1] The role of whiteness in governing relations of power is ubiquitous, yet it is rarely recognized as an organizing principle because its workings are unconscious and unnamed. Naming whiteness as constitutive of social relations refocuses our understandings of the ways in which race and racism operate, always shaping individual and group opportunities. One does not have to consciously be a "racist" or hold biases based on notions of race to be complicit with a system of racial oppression. In fact, regardless of their politics, people with lighter skin benefit from the workings of white supremacy.

But whiteness holds meaning only in opposition to the denigrated and degraded racial category of Blackness, and African Americans "remain the defining other despite how much they conform to 'White standards.'"[2]

Indeed, George Lipsitz teaches us, "the power of whiteness depend[s] not only on white hegemony over separate racialized groups, but also on manipulating racial outsiders to fight against one another, to compete with each other for white approval, and to seek the rewards and privileges of whiteness for themselves at the expense of other racialized populations."[3] In other words, this racialized system incentivizes people of diverse backgrounds to invest in the workings of white supremacy in hopes of reaping its benefits at the expense of those identified as Black.

Throughout U.S. history, groups deemed nonwhite have fought to be accepted as white to secure the advantages of this social category. For example, many European immigrants to the United States in the nineteenth and twentieth centuries were initially deemed nonwhite, such as Irish Catholics, Italians, Eastern Europeans, and Jews.[4] While at first they struggled to purchase homes in white neighborhoods, over time they achieved acceptance into the category of whiteness and gained equal access to quality housing.

Similarly, the term "Hispanic" has been traced back to an elite political project that sought to unify, through the creation of a common identity, those ethnic and linguistic groups with historical ties to Spain. Those who agreed to "become" Hispanic were promised a chance to "trade up," to join the "new paradoxical category [of] Hispanic Whiteness," a "whiteness of a different color."[5] Such was the case when Mexican American migrants who came to the South in the 1920s and 1930s enlisted the help of their consulate to ensure their children could attend white schools. Over time, their family members who stayed in the South came to be understood— and understand themselves—as white.[6]

These experiences have often been contrasted with those of more recent immigrants of color. How will new Latino immigrants identify and be identified racially, and where will they be positioned vis-à-vis our country's invisible "color line?"[7] Will the category of whiteness expand to include (certain) Latinos? Will it remain closed to these newcomers? Who will be considered Black? Will another racial category emerge to house those who don't fit into the social categories of either white or Black? By uncovering how the power-laden categories of whiteness and Blackness shape social relations, we can consider how they influence racial self- and community-identification.

IS THAT A CHOCTAW?

When Latinos began arriving to work in central Mississippi's poultry plants, local people didn't quite know what to make of them. One middle-aged white woman first saw the newcomers at the grocery store: "I went, 'Wow! Who are these people?' It seemed like overnight, and it was astounding! I had evidently missed the changes that were happening around me." A retired white man agreed that grocery stores, especially Walmarts, were where migrants became noticeable in the late 1990s. Standing in checkout lines, people marveled at the strange language being spoken around them.

Others noticed there were new people in town because there was more foot traffic than there had been in three decades. "All of a sudden they were everywhere, walking on the streets. Had they all had cars, I probably never would have noticed, but nobody used to walk in Forest! And I was like, 'Where are these folks coming from? What's happening here?'" High school students laughed with one another about the "Mexicans" waiting on benches in front of a Forest bank. In the rural South, where people get in their cars to go even two blocks to the corner store, migrants' use of road shoulders for walking and decorative benches for sitting constituted different uses of public space that contradicted longtime patterns.

With the headquarters of the Mississippi Band of Choctaw Indians nearby, people of many backgrounds remember confusing the newcomers with Choctaw people:

The first comment I remember hearing was an elderly [white] lady who had to stand in line behind "them foreigners" at the grocery store. She said, "I just don't know why they don't go back home." And I asked her who she was talking about. She said, "Well, Choctaws or, I guess . . . they said they was from Mexico, I think. They were speaking a language I couldn't understand." People don't know the difference, and sometimes I'm actually not sure myself, even after I listen to them talk for a little while.

My cousin said that when he first arrived from Mexico, people looked at him strangely. They thought we were weird because the Indians here normally don't have moustaches. They confused us with Choctaws. We look a lot alike—even the police get us mixed up. One time when my cousin was arrested, the cop who released him wanted to throw him back on the reservation!

See, Black people really didn't know what to think. When I heard them speaking Spanish I thought this was, you know, Indian. We all did. I didn't know that Indians and Spanish people have their own language. It was a long time before we realized that they were, you know, Spanish-speaking Mexicans. Finally somebody at the chicken plant said, "Hey those aren't Indians. Those are Mexicans!"

In the early days of Latinos' arrival, many locals placed people with brown skin speaking a language other than English in the only category they seemed to fit—as part of the small but long-standing local Native American community.

I asked immigrants to recall the biggest adjustments they went through when they first arrived. They shared stories of struggling to be understood, getting accustomed to new foods, learning to drive instead of walk, and realizing that one cannot bargain with salespeople to get lower prices at the store. Their racialization as darker-hued, strange-tongued foreigners has further impacted their adjustment to life in the small-town South. Some felt uncomfortable leaving their houses for years because of the stares they received. "There was a lot of discrimination! I endured all that; I lived through it. Especially the whites—the ones we call Americans—didn't want us here. I could tell by the ways they looked at us that they didn't like us."

Some immigrants have come to terms with the region's strict racial divisions through events with particular impact, as did one woman who painfully recalled, "When we first arrived there was this bar in town. They told me, 'Don't you even think about going in there, because it's a bar for white people. Blacks and Hispanics are not permitted inside, only whites.'" More commonly, however, Latinos have learned the local workings of white privilege and anti-Black racism of their new surroundings on a more intuitive level, through the daily acts of living in Mississippi.

HOUSING, RACIALIZED EXPLOITATION, AND THE POLICING OF WHITE PRIVILEGE

It's Thanksgiving and winter has arrived in Forest. I pull up to the dilapidated rental I fondly call the "Green House," for the color of its faded and peeling exterior paint, to visit poultry workers from Veracruz, Mexico. As

I step through the back door, I see plastic aprons and gloves from the plant neatly spread out on the bushes and kitchen chairs. I wonder how they will dry in this cold weather. Greeting a handful of acquaintances on my way through the kitchen, I join Artemio Murrieta seated on a sagging sofa. Bundled in coats, hats, and gloves, we half-watch a *telenovela* as he tells me about a conflict with a coworker on last night's shift. The coils are red hot on the tiny electric heater working overtime in the middle of the room. The floor slopes down considerably toward one wall, and there is a two-inch gap under the front door. Interrupting himself, Murrieta motions toward the breach, "No wonder it's impossible to heat this house." The pipes have been frozen for three days now, the central heat won't come on, and the plumbing is out of commission. This is no small problem for a household of thirteen men who work handling raw chicken for at least eight hours a day. They've reported the problem to their landlord, but no one has come. The house is literally falling apart.

The roommates sleep in shifts opposite their work schedules. They share two large bedrooms, and personal space is but a distant memory. Some have photos of wives or children tacked to the walls above their sheetless mattresses. Murrieta sometimes mentions wanting to find another place to live, somewhere with fewer roommates. But on his meager earnings of under $300 a week, this shared space is all he can afford if he is to continue sending money home for his children's school and wife's medical care. It's a matter of priorities, he explains. "Coming to Mississippi is, without a doubt, a sacrifice, but it's one I must bear for my family."

Ten years and as many different living arrangements from now, Murrieta's utilities will be cut off for failure to keep up with the bills. In desperation, on a cold winter night he and several roommates will move a generator indoors so they can run a couple of space heaters in hopes of keeping warm. They will never awaken, victims of carbon monoxide poisoning and casualties of an unearned and inescapable poverty.

. . . . .

Housing for the new Latino community has been a contentious social problem since B.C. Rogers first began importing workers. When the

Hispanic Project proposed building a large trailer park next door to its Forest plants, there was great uproar. Racial tensions present but unspoken, white residents claimed they didn't want "300 strangers living next door" and defeated the initiative.[8] Immigrants face housing discrimination from white residents and predatory practices of unscrupulous landlords of all backgrounds. At the same time, the housing market is one realm in which immigrants' presence seems to further marginalize and stigmatize Black residents, and the gradual dispersal of Latino families throughout traditionally white neighborhoods points to the nuanced race, class, and gender components of housing discrimination. This section considers the issue of housing as one site that illustrates Latinos' complicated insertion into the racialized social hierarchies of the South.

Housing has long been a terrain in which the privileges of whiteness have been closely guarded. From refusing people of color entrance into homeownership in traditionally white neighborhoods, to denying them credit to secure mortgages, to promoting the movement of the white middle class away from more urban centers into suburbia, white-dominated institutions have been largely successful at maintaining residential segregation into the present.[9] Yet by finding cracks in these strategies, some immigrant groups have gained a foothold into the privileges of whiteness.

Discrimination and Displacement

Following the defeat of the Hispanic Project's initiative to build a trailer park in the early 1990s, Forest and Morton passed ordinances forbidding the introduction of any new trailers inside city limits.[10] As a result, trailers in these towns are old, terribly dilapidated, and limited in number. The majority of Latino workers live in rental houses within walking distance of the plants. In contrast, expansive trailer parks flank the chicken plants in Carthage and Canton.

Carthage's was built in the mid-1990s, as the plant began to recruit migrant laborers. Sections were added gradually as the Latino population's demand for nearby housing grew. Though near the chicken plant, it was miles away from the center of Carthage, isolating renters and marginalizing them from public life. An early renter recalls his unsuccessful

Figure 10. Trailer park flanking the chicken plant in Canton. Photo by John Fiege. Courtesy of FiegeFilms.com.

efforts to move out of the trailer park and into town: "In the beginning they didn't rent houses in town to Hispanics. I saw a house with a 'For Rent' sign. We asked the local [Catholic] Sister to call, and they told her that we should take a look. But when we arrived a few minutes later, they said the house was already rented."

Until the turn of the millennium, residents in the decrepit trailer park next to the chicken plant in nearby Canton were mostly African American. Today, Black families occupy only a handful of the 130 trailers, and white law enforcement officials claim that drug use and crime have decreased as a result. "There has been very little crime from Hispanics," a deputy tells me. Suggesting that the trailer park has exchanged one "problem" population for another, slightly less problematic group, he continues, "Now you just see a whole bunch of public drunks sitting around. Don't they realize that if they're gonna drink they should go inside instead of sitting around on the side of the road?" But "it isn't really that bad," another white resident tells me, because "they mostly stay in the trailer park."

Rapacious Landlords

When planning my move to Forest, I stopped by the largest rental agency in Scott County, adjacent to the Michoacana Mexican store in downtown Forest and owned by the businessman who acquired B. C. Rogers' residential properties following its bankruptcy. Greeted in Spanish, I inquired about rental housing but didn't get far. I learned that all properties are rented by the week, and rent payments are accepted only in person, and in cash. There was no option to rent by the month. Moreover, I couldn't sign a lease in advance; my only option was to show up ready to move in and see what was available.

As I found, rental housing in central Mississippi is in short supply and dominated by individuals making a living off of the area's newest residents. In Scott County at the turn of the millennium, $30,000 homes were regularly rented for at least $600 a month, representing a near 25 percent annual return on the total value of the home. Chris Thompson once received a call from someone who wanted to sell a three-bedroom trailer for $14,000. "Here's the upshot," the owner told him and went on to explain that he was renting it to twelve Latino men for $2,800 per month. Each renter was paying approximately $60 per week. Asking the owner, "How do you sleep at night?" Thompson refused to list the trailer for sale.

While some residents feel that such arrangements are unjust or inhumane, others assume that migrants elect to live in close quarters because of cultural norms. Complaints about Latinos "urinat[ing] in clear view of everyone" on their lawns pathologize Latinos' "cultural difference" instead of recognizing landlords' failure to maintain minimal living conditions, such as working toilets. "Perhaps they don't care," says a middle-class white woman. "We can't force those people to adopt a higher standard than what they're used to, even if it lends itself to a very unsanitary living situation."

Thompson explains that some landlords use such arguments as a justification for not maintaining their properties: "We white people here in Scott County think that they come from a dirt floor, no indoor plumbing–type environment. So some less-than-scrupulous landlords have an attitude where if the renter does not mind sharing a house with eight or ten other single men, and if the hot water doesn't work and nobody's really complaining that loud, he will take advantage of the situation. It's unfortunate, but it goes on, probably more than we would like to acknowledge."

While predatory landlords come in all shapes and colors, I found that Latino and African American residents had very different analyses of the causes and effects of such housing conditions than those expressed in these observations of white Mississippians. As my acquaintances in the Green House underscored, close quarters are driven by economic necessity, not by cultural norms or personal preference. "We live together in order to share the bills, so we don't owe as much money, and because we want to save," one of the housemates mused. "We buy groceries together, too, because it's more affordable to share the cost of food." Low wages, coupled with the need to send earnings to family members back home, require many immigrant workers to self-subsidize, most often in the form of sharing the costs of overpriced and insufficient housing.

Keisha Brown, an African American single mom in her forties, sees the problem clearly as one of abuse. "I feel that some people try to use 'em because, now, why would you let nine or ten people live in a house and charge each one $100 a month for rent? That's more like you getting over on them or something. That's $1,000 for something that's probably not even worth $200." In her former neighborhood she has seen rental prices increase dramatically since immigrants began moving in: "They got a lot of Mexicans living over there by Tyson. They start to call it 'Little Mexico.' Now, when I stayed there, my rent was $440 a month. When the Mexicans moved in, my rent went up to $600 or $700."

Immigrants' insertion into the rental market in small-town America has effectively lowered the housing standards and raised the cost of living for all working families, disproportionately disadvantaging people of color. To make matters worse, landlord-tenant laws are virtually nonexistent in places like rural Mississippi, and renters have little recourse for contesting their living conditions or cost.

Residential Dispersal and Racialized Homeownership

In the ten years since I left Mississippi, Latinos have been expanding to neighborhoods beyond the chicken plants. On a return visit in 2014, I saw that Latinos in Carthage had all but abandoned the trailer park, thanks to more diverse housing opportunities: "One day the first person managed to rent in a neighborhood in town. After that, when an apartment came open word would travel fast, and now that neighborhood is full of Hispanics." In Canton, a collaborator in law enforcement drove me through several neighborhoods Latinos now call home. "They've found their way into some of the other Black neighborhoods and have figured out which are safer with lower crime. Oh, they're everywhere, now."

In Forest and Morton, too, Latinos have moved into new areas of town. Black families have borne a significant financial burden with the influx of migrants into their communities, but immigrants are also joining historically white neighborhoods. "Today Hispanics are much more spread out than they used to be," comments Mary Townsend, who conducted extensive outreach in the Latino community in the late 1990s. "Before they were all in one little pocket. Now, I'd have to go all over the town, and I wouldn't know which doors to knock on!" Across central Mississippi migrants are pushing at the boundaries of locally engrained patterns of spatial segregation, which has given rise to tensions as well as opportunities.

Some white residents have taken steps to minimize Latinos' incursion into their neighborhoods. Because of perceived cultural differences, deeply seated racisms, concerns about property value, and lack of enforcement of federal antidiscrimination laws, at times they have succeeded. Chris Thompson reveals the lengths to which some individuals go to ensure their neighborhoods remain white: "I'll list a house for sale, and I'll have a neighbor say, 'You're not gonna sell this to a Black or a Hispanic, are you?' I know of instances where neighbors have purchased houses so they can manipulate who goes in and out of 'em." More commonly, however, white folks have adapted to their surroundings or moved out, making room for newcomers, sometimes immigrants, to move in.

Some Latinos have succeeded in buying homes. These tend to be more upwardly mobile, lighter-skinned migrants, often South Americans, who have decided to call Mississippi home. Some have become friends with white residents in positions of relative power who have helped them navigate the system. Others have successfully gotten mortgages from the Bank of Morton with Tito Echiburu's help. The process is not without obstacles. In addition to potential interference from wary new neighbors, immigrants without Social Security numbers must request an Individual Taxpayer Identification Number from the IRS to apply for a mortgage, and doing so exposes their undocumented presence to the federal government.

One Argentine family's request for an identification number was denied. Upon receiving this news, Thompson, who served as their realtor, agreed to owner-finance the home. He purchased it with their down payment, and the family paid him rent each month until they had bought the home outright. While this arrangement put both parties in a precarious financial situation, Thompson went out on a limb. "When a Hispanic person is interested in some of the properties I have for sale," he says, "my first inclination is that I should treat them as being very credible because, in my experience, they have been excellent customers." In addition to his positive perception of Latino buyers, the fact that these customers were a likable, light-skinned family trying to learn English likely played an important role in brokering the arrangement.

Cases such as these suggest that race, class, gender, and family composition all play significant roles in determining immigrants' (and nonimmigrants') housing options in Mississippi today. Moreover, these mutually constitutive identity markers are important factors in influencing economic and social relationships between local people and the new immigrants living in their midst. On one hand, immigrant men who are single or left their families back home are particularly susceptible to exploitation by predatory landlords. On another, this exploitation has disadvantaged poor Mississippians, especially single mothers of color, who have seen their costs of living rise due to increased demand for rental housing.

Finally, while housing has been heavily policed to uphold white supremacy and has been widely successful at keeping towns residentially segregated to date, some immigrants—in particular those with lighter skin, increasing English proficiency, and family status—have begun to break through these barriers and forge entrance into the privileges of whiteness. Examining the evolution of Latinos' housing options in central Mississippi's, then, offers some evidence suggesting that certain classes of newcomers may be gaining a foothold in the category of whiteness. At the very least, they appear to be entering residential spaces that are still largely closed to African Americans.

LOCAL RECEPTIONS, RACE, AND THE IMMIGRANT WORK ETHIC

Just as a look at how low-income housing options have shifted suggests immigrants' insertion into a social space between whiteness and Blackness, an exploration of the most common discourses Mississippians of different backgrounds have adopted to make sense of the changes happening in their communities also indicates that the area's newest residents are implicated in the making and remaking of racial categories. This section considers some of the most common discourses around immigration and work and their relationship to their holders' subject positions as raced, classed beings. After introducing two views espoused by white Mississippians on opposite ends of the ideological spectrum, I focus in on various inflections of the tropes of immigration and work to illustrate how individuals' and communities' racial identities shape opinions regarding immigration.

They're Taking Over Our Town!

"They're taking over our town," a white bag boy at the Piggly Wiggly muttered as he motioned toward a van of "Mexicans" in the parking lot. As in other parts of the country, some in central Mississippi crudely see all immigrants as "illegal aliens" who are taking over and abusing the system. This discourse is heard most vociferously from white men with political clout. Each year the Mississippi legislature considers dozens of anti-immigrant bills, most of which fail to get out of committee.

While I lived in Scott County, the local circuit clerk refused to grant marriage licenses to undocumented immigrant couples, claiming "It's my opinion that I should not give someone legal documentation if they're an illegal alien."[11] When I attended a state-required training for ESOL teachers, I was left speechless when a facilitator, echoing this sentiment, aggressively asserted his belief that immigrants are lawbreakers who should all be sent home. "If these people," he continued, "who are all here illegally, don't want to follow our rules, they shouldn't be here in the first place."

During the same time, in an attempt to leverage voters' fears to capture votes, a Scott County candidate for state office accused immigrants of unfairly drawing down Americans' Social Security benefits.[12] Consistent with the neoliberal state's interest in curtailing costs of social reproduction, we are told that immigrants are disproportionately usurping local, state, and federal resources. Such accusations are often gendered, aimed particularly at women and children who are seen as the principal users of public benefits, including schools and hospitals.[13] "All the women are having babies, and we're the ones having to pay for it," a Scott County neighbor reminded me. As a result of this perception, policy makers and service providers are making it more and more difficult for immigrants to get access to basic health care and education. Many doctor's offices in Mississippi require a Social Security number just to schedule an appointment. Similarly, laws regulating the use of narcotics require pharmacists to obtain a Social Security number to dispense some types of pain medication.

While public schools in Mississippi are required to enroll all children regardless of immigration status, administrators are often unsure how to proceed when a child cannot produce a U.S. birth certificate. Numerous undocumented teens have reported that school administrators advised them to attend free community-based ESOL classes instead of enrolling in high school.

Anti-immigrant sentiment is repeated in an endless loop in the media, creating a hostile and sometimes dangerous environment for newcomers. Immigrants' analyses push back at this rhetoric, however. "They think we are invading their territory, and I think this causes the anger they feel toward us," one Guatemalan poultry worker suggested. "But it's not just a one-way street. I think that the country is also benefiting from us." A man from Uruguay shared a similar analysis, explaining that immigrants come because of the inequalities of the global political economy, not to abuse local resources: "They think that Hispanics come here because we want to. They don't understand that in our countries there aren't the same possibilities as there are here. They need to understand that we come simply out of necessity. We come only to work, and we want to do it well. We don't want them to see us as criminals, as terrorists. We are the terrorists of the tomatoes, the oranges, the chickens. Nothing more."

The rhetoric that blames immigrants for America's economic and social ills continues to be on the rise, fueled in large degree by white Americans' fear of becoming a minority. This theme's circulation in public discourse increased greatly after the 2000 census results were released, demonstrating growth in the Latino population in nontraditional receiving areas such as the South and predicting that the United States would become a "majority-minority" country by 2042.

Now It's a More Interesting Place, and other Benefits of Immigration

At the other end of the spectrum, some white Mississippians feel that immigration has brought positive changes. Among these are volunteers and service providers who have gotten to know individual migrants on a personal basis, as well as entrepreneurs who have economically benefited from the new population. While limited in number, these residents play an important role in helping new immigrants navigate their new environment.

Some feel Latinos have brought greater cultural diversity to the area, making it a "more interesting place."[14] Becky McCrady, for example, began volunteering at a local mission center in Forest in 1994. Spending time with new immigrants made her rethink some of her own biases: "I really hadn't experienced poverty. I only associated with people who had money. So I grew up thinking people are poor because they're stupid or they're not hard workers. Spending time with immigrants made me see there are other things besides stupidity and laziness that cause poverty. I met a lot of good, hardworking people who were poor, and most faced circumstances beyond their control."

Similarly, another volunteer told me that learning Spanish "did wonders to lower [his] prejudices." Yet in reflecting on the Mississippi Freedom Struggle, he still believes that "Blacks pushed things too quickly," suggesting that African Americans should have agreed to more gradual social change and given white Mississippians "more time." Thus, while proximity to immigrants has broadened people's horizons, some continue to harbor deep-seated prejudices against Black Mississippians. While seemingly incongruous, championing Latinos may effectively enable white individuals to discount their own anti-Black sentiments. After all, goes the logic, how could they be "racist" given their advocacy on behalf of the area's newest minority?

Most white people in Mississippi and beyond have learned the lessons of the Civil Rights Movement without having to think critically about their own privilege or address the workings of structural racism in the present.

Instead, they prefer to put "race troubles" behind them. By understanding racism in terms of discriminatory acts perpetrated by the isolated "redneck," middle- and upper-class white Americans ensure that any reparations for racism do not impinge significantly on their own privileges.[15] With racism relegated to the past or to a few bad apples, dominant society expects that racial justice can be achieved without disruption of the status quo.[16]

Others appreciate the influx of immigrants because of the positive economic impact it has on the local economy. Immigrant policing through traffic enforcement incentivizes the undocumented to shop locally.[17] As a result, local retail has flourished. "Hispanic" stores sell magazines, rent movies in Spanish, and effect hundreds of international wire transfers each week. Service stations and grocery stores have more customers. Sales tax revenues have grown, increasing cities' income.[18] Walk-in health clinics are busier than they've ever been.[19] And, as Thompson and others point out, used-car sales have skyrocketed: "They're working, contributing to the tax base, and buying things, and collectively they've had a *huge* positive economic impact. I mean, look around. These car lots do a *tremendous* business." Boasted the owner of one of these lots, "I probably know more Hispanics by face than anybody else in Forest."[20]

A community center in Morton offers Spanish classes for professionals in the area, and students have included teachers, nurses, police officers, insurance agents, pharmacists, and used-car salesmen. I mentioned these classes to Thompson, who was sold on the idea before it even got out of my mouth: "That's a great example of economics. Not that I'm not benevolent and love my fellow man, but business-wise, it would make good sense. I could increase my income and grow my business by learning Spanish. So why not? You don't have to force me into that!" Despite any initial misgivings they may have had about the newest members of their community, business-minded people with economic power quickly realized that immigration had a positive side.

White Mississippians on the Immigrant Work Ethic

Between these two extremes of love and hate, appreciation and fear, lies the most common reaction of white Mississippians to Latino immigration: "The majority of the people just kinda kept a little distance." Many recognize that "it'll never be just Black and white anymore." They accept the reality that immigrants are not going away anytime soon and welcome them at arm's length. A white neighbor explained to me, "They're here to stay, and they're not necessarily a bad thing, you know, so people are just getting over it." Such was the sentiment of a Latino pastor who suggested that the white community's attitude toward his churchgoers is generally, "I love you, but stay out of my yard."

Steve Carr, an elderly white man who complements his mission trips to Central America by helping immigrants in Mississippi, complicates this notion. He matches up immigrants needing work with his acquaintances who could use help for odd jobs around the house, like "raking leaves or cutting grass or changing their plants." And, he explains, "Every time they call me and just can't believe what a good job the guy did in spite of the communication problem." In other words, "Stay out of my yard unless you're here to manicure it!" And Carr insists, "It's always a positive ending, and they always want to use them again."

This attitude extends beyond lawn care. Most white Mississippians recognize that Latinos are here to work and are willing to accept their presence as long as "you do your job and leave us alone." Moreover, most people of all backgrounds see the area's newcomers as dedicated workers. No one, white, Black, or brown, disputes the immigrant "work ethic." That said, people's racial identifications can hold great weight over the ways in which they explain this reality.

White Mississippians generally accept the poultry industry's justification that Latinos were recruited to address a labor shortage. The national discourse that immigrants are doing jobs "Americans don't want" circulates widely and is echoed in local spheres with a twist. Because immigrants in central Mississippi work alongside African Americans, dominant white sentiment suggests that "if Blacks had worked harder in the first place, they never would have had to bring the immigrants in."[21] When I asked Becky McCrady about the prevalence of this discourse, she told me, "I have heard a number of people say, 'Well, you can say one thing for the Hispanics. They're not lazy like the niggers.' Excuse me for using that word 'cause I hate it, but that's what they say. They're not lazy like the Black people." McCrady was quick to clarify her remark, explaining that she didn't mean to imply that white folks are *embracing* immigrants either:

"Not that they're inviting Hispanics to their homes, but they seem to be much more accepting because they see them as industrious people. And there's this huge feeling that Black people are lazy and wanna live off the government. So a lot of the people don't seem to hate the Hispanics the way they hate the Blacks. I'm not saying they like 'em. They don't like 'em, but they consider them more white, closer to them." Under the neoliberal framework that demonizes Black Americans for the perceived cultural roots of "their" problems, in Mississippi "hardworking" immigrants are lifted up by whites.[22] This serves to further justify dominant racialized discourse and enables white society to turn a blind eye to historically rooted structural ills that persist in the present. Moreover, McCrady's comments suggest that, as Latinos are understood by whites as an answer to African Americans' presumed disinterest in work and success—in essence in opposition to Black Mississippians—the very nature of immigrants as hardworking may be seen as an initial step toward whitening, even while the extent to which this is ultimately possible or desirable remains unclear.[23]

Mississippi's Latinos on the Immigrant Work Ethic

Latinos are acutely aware of the operations of whiteness and Blackness from the moment they set foot in Mississippi, if not before. While they bring varying degrees of anti-Black sentiment with them from their home countries, most report being struck by the sheer concentration of poor African Americans in Mississippi.[24] They soon discover—and typically naturalize—the dominant belief that Blackness equals powerless and undesirable. They even set African Americans apart from the nation, referring to Black people as *morenos,* or "dark ones," while calling white folks simply *americanos,* or "Americans."

With few exceptions, Latinos echo white society's assertion that they work harder than their Black counterparts, commonly making claims such as, "the work of Hispanics is—it's probably bad for me to say this—a little bit more reliable than the work of the *morenos* in the chicken plants." At a regional union meeting, a Latino organizer celebrated this notion, asserting, "If there's one advantage we have, it's that we're good workers. That's why I want to ask for a round of applause for us, because we are the Hispanics." Applause abounded.

Figure 11. Guatemalan immigrant exhibits the spoils of hard work. Photo by John Fiege. Courtesy of FiegeFilms.com.

Despite their general embrace of their identity as "hard workers," however, unlike most white Mississippians, immigrants sometimes disagree with the notion that this comes "naturally." They point to the structural inequalities that shape their work ethic, as did a former student of mine from Chiapas, who noted, "As immigrants we are all here because of the ways our governments have handled the economy and because the United States drives the economies of the world. The consequence is that we come here with one goal. We find ourselves obliged to work however we can, wherever we can." Hard work, in this view, is driven by necessity, not by an innate desire to toil.

Black Mississippians on the Immigrant Work Ethic and Competition

While one occasionally hears Black Mississippians reiterate dominant society's notion of immigrant workers stepping in to compensate for lazy African Americans, this is not the norm. To the contrary, while Black

Mississippians are quick to recognize that immigrants are hard workers, they rarely pair this sentiment with the suggestion that Black workers are not. "I don't believe in that," said Walter Glover, an African American poultry worker in his early forties. "It's an insult to say that African Americans don't want to work for a fair wage."

Some Black residents explain that their misgivings about immigration are not personal, but due to a sense that newcomers are unjustly cutting into the slice of pie Black folks have been fighting for over many years. They express skepticism when reflecting on the numerous services that have popped up to help immigrants adjust to life in Mississippi, particularly those run by churches. This seems particularly unfair to one Black man who is certain immigrants don't pay taxes (they do). Another person indicated her displeasure when a priest introduced some Spanish phrases into an English-language Mass, noting, "Well, I'm sure at the Spanish Mass he never speaks English." Keisha Brown, a poultry worker I met through our mutual involvement in the workers' center, clearly articulated many African Americans' concerns: "You have some people that feel intimidated because Hispanics is coming getting new places to live and brand new cars. You know, they had an agreement with this country that they would help them to get them a place to stay. I'm gonna be honest. You have some people that's done *been here for years,* but white folk won't even work with you to give you nothing. I can't even get a house, you know?"

Brown was skeptical when I explained that most of today's immigrants come without permission to work or assistance from the government. Perhaps this belief was fueled by the Hispanic Project's recruitment of Cubans or its efforts to provide new immigrants housing and transportation. While the sense that the government has special programs to help immigrants get settled is largely erroneous, the notion that locals, particularly whites, have gone out of their way to enable immigrant success is based on people's everyday observations of what is occurring in their communities.

Competition over scarce resources and African American concerns about displacement are a central focus of the literature on immigrant–African American relations, much of which focuses on job competition. Scholars disagree regarding the extent to which immigrants displace Black workers. Some assert that displacement is relatively limited because immigrants fill new niches that have emerged in the neoliberal economy.[25]

Others argue that Black displacement is a very real phenomenon.[26] The most convincing studies suggest that displacement, while real, is localized and industry-specific.[27]

In central Mississippi, on one hand, the poultry industry expanded rapidly, increasing the number of low-wage jobs in chicken plants for native-born and immigrant workers alike. New work opportunities also appeared in car-parts manufacturing, fast food, and the construction of Super Walmarts in these counties. Some African American former poultry workers found employment in these industries, if not for substantially higher wages, at least in less dangerous conditions. These events suggest that there may have been room for immigrant workers to enter the poultry industry without dramatically displacing African Americans.[28] This conclusion is supported by Jamie Winders's research in nearby Tennessee, which suggests that "the general economic context of immigrant reception was relatively good in new destinations in the South."[29]

On the other hand, my own ethnographic data suggests that an available and eager pool of Black labor did indeed exist in central Mississippi in the early years of the new millennium. When the Tyson Plant in Carthage fired its Latino workforce en masse, the company quickly recovered production by hiring African American workers. Over the subsequent decade the plant has largely continued to operate by relying on a majority Black workforce. But no research to date has definitively measured the extent of immigrants' displacement of African Americans in the context of Mississippi poultry.

Regardless of any "objective" measure or the lack thereof, personal experience and perception matter.[30] Some Black poultry workers do believe that immigrants are taking their jobs. More often, however, resentment of immigrants has less to do with job loss and more to do with a recognition that wages, working conditions, and a sense of dignity are declining along with the increase in the Latino presence. "I tell you what," says Yolanda Goodloe, a veteran poultry worker. "Black people is kinda jealous 'cause the Mexican will work, okay? And they is making all the overtime that you can throw at 'em. We're thinking all this time that the Mexican is taking our job away from us, but that's not true. They're not taking our jobs, but they is working nonstop, raising expectations. Sometime they be there a couple of days, like from one shift to the other one, without even going home."

The arrival of immigrant labor seems to have restricted U.S.-born workers' strategies for coping with harsh working conditions and lack of benefits such as vacation or paid sick leave. In Laura Helton's research, some workers reported that prior to the influx of Latinos it was relatively easy to quit a job one day and then find work—at the same or a different plant—whenever they were ready to return.[31] This flexibility provided individual workers with a minimal level of control over their working lives in an industry that otherwise thwarted their efforts to collectively determine working conditions and benefits. It disappeared with immigrants' arrival and the fully staffed production lines that followed.

Brenda Turner, a leader in her plant's union, elaborates that the sense of bitterness expressed by Goodloe is shaped by Black workers' sense that they are losing what they have fought for over the years:

> See, the whites don't want Hispanic *or* Black to go too far up the ladder. Our problem with the Hispanics is, you know, we done went through all of this—killings, and hangings, and *all* of this—to get where we *are*. We got some power now. And then they comes in, and say, "I'll do that." And you say, "Wait a minute, we're using that as leverage to get up the ladder further." And the white people turn around and say, "Well, hey, I ain't got to pay. I ain't got to do this or that because I can get him to do it." And there goes your power, right out the window. So I think that's where a lot of the hostility's coming from.

"Why do they have to recruit immigrants in the first place," another Black worker leader deliberated one afternoon as we sat at his kitchen table. "So they can show that African American people don't wanna work. That's their whole game. But it's not a true statement. We came to this country, and we built this country. We worked from sunrise to sunset. From three years old to the time you died, you had a job." He later continued, "This country became a superpower on our backs, and we did not inherit one penny. What we inherited was America's ghettos, slums, and liquor stores. That's what we inherited, okay?"

It's More Like They's Using Them

A number of Black Mississippians express compassion for new immigrants, suggesting that "they's going through what we went through before." This sort of structural analysis is encouraged by advocates for racial justice, who believe that drawing linkages between the global present and the Jim Crow past opens up more possibilities of mutual understanding. Such was the argument of labor organizer and civil rights legend Rev. James Orange when a group of local and regional advocates and organizers met in 2004 to plan a training for participants of the national New American Freedom Summer that would take place in Canton: "Here we are, forty years later and we're still fighting the same battles we thought we had already won in the Civil Rights struggle. But now we're fighting for the rights of our immigrant brothers and sisters. Some of these laws being proposed against immigrants in Mississippi are just as oppressive as the old Jim Crow laws."[32]

A poultry worker leader who participated in the workers' center shared what she tells people who suggest immigrants should go back where they came from: "Excuse me. White folks used to tell us we need to go back where we come from. So it's vice versa. They have the right to be here like everybody else. Don't you say they should go home! They trying to better themself with their families, and they want to better their kids' lives."

Similarly, African Americans express concern that newcomers are manipulated by white society to further the goals of the powerful. As opposed to immigrants being brought to do work "Americans don't want," some see that companies bring them to have an ample supply of cheap labor and to maintain a low standard for wages and working conditions. One woman Helton interviewed called it a "conspiracy," while another I spoke with said, "I think when they first was coming, plants and other people was helping them out. But it's more like they's *using* them." Similarly, a prominent leader in Scott County's Black community assessed that "some African Americans are concerned that the Latino community is driven by whites as slave labor, and some pity Hispanics because they work 'em to death." Such empathy was echoed by several long-standing Black poultry plant worker leaders I got to know through the workers' center.

DIVERGENT SUBJECT POSITIONS AND THE EMERGENCE OF A THIRD SPACE

A review of the different discourses about immigration circulating in Mississippi, coupled with an analysis of who buys into and perpetuates them, suggests that individual and group subject positions play important roles in determining people's relationship to the topic of immigration. We interpret our surroundings—in this case new immigration into the Deep South—using lenses that help us understand ourselves in relation to those around us. In Mississippi's poultry region, long-standing structures that govern the political economies of race become such lenses for Black and white Mississippians to understand the changes in their community. These ways of seeing are also rooted in diverging historical memories about the area's racialized past. A historical memory of oppression and a shared recognition of its impact on the present shape the subject position of many Black southerners, while white folks tend to remember the past in ways that understand racial strife and inequality as legacies of previous generations.

The spaces and contexts in which people of different backgrounds interact with one another are influenced by these same structures and memories, and such interactions (or lack thereof) play a part in molding people's understandings and opinions. While locals of all backgrounds have struggled to come to grips with their changing surroundings, middle-class white residents, who typically do not face grueling work in the chicken plants, see Latinos most often at Walmart, in grocery stores, or walking on the side of the road. From this vantage point, they have the luxury of comparing "hardworking" migrants to "lazy" Black men and women. They can usually choose to keep their distance or interact with migrants in "safe" community spaces. Working-class African Americans, on the other hand, mostly relate to immigrants in the context of chicken plant work. This not only limits the types of interactions they have with Latinos but also provides a critical vantage point from which to understand the presence of immigrants in relation to industry and power. Ultimately, while uniquely positioned, Black, white, and Latino residents in central Mississippi understand the experience of migration in large part through discourses about work. Racial positions and historical relations to the poultry industry play critical roles in locals' understandings of and experiences with immigrants.[33]

Immigrants' experiences with local people, too, are shaped by positions of race and class and their relationship to the industry that brought them there. Their relationships with local people outside of work are often in the context of social outreach programs that support immigrants—ESOL classes, food pantries, clothes closets, churches, and so on—and these services have been provided, more often than not, by middle-class white women. Meanwhile, their experiences with locals at work tend to be with working-class Black women and men. Given Mississippi's social structure, the racial, class, and gender differences in these cross-cultural interactions are significant.

The extent to which migrants bring anti-Black sentiment with them or anticipate the racial categories of Mississippi before arriving can be debated and depends on the national, regional, and individual experiences of migrants from different countries and cultures in Latin America. What's clear, however, is that they very quickly internalize the categories around them and buy into notions of Black criminality and laziness and the immigrant work ethic. In doing so, they nearly unanimously assert a position vis-à-vis Black and white Mississippians that attempts to carve out a third space.

This space, I argue, is not at the bottom of the racial hierarchy of the South, but rather occupies a nebulous and mutable position between white and Black.[34] Such positioning appears to be facilitated by white support of the creation of this additional layer, which serves to keep Blackness at the bottom and further distance white from Black. White Mississippians' limited acceptance of some categories of Latinos into their neighborhoods, for example, as well as the broadly held belief that exalts hardworking immigrants in juxtaposition to the denigrated category of Blackness, facilitate an opening for Latinos to enter somewhere in the middle of the social hierarchy.

I opened this chapter by asking how the growing presence of Latinos is transforming social hierarchies of race in the South. Will this uneasy middle position—currently marked in Mississippi by the placeholder "Hispanic"—become cemented over time, disappear altogether, or fracture into multiple or more nuanced categories? Which individuals and communities will transcend a "Hispanic" identity, which will eventually whiten, and will any "darken"? What I saw in central Mississippi suggests that the category of whiteness may already be expanding to include those Latin American immigrants with lighter skin, higher class standing, and greater resources, particularly families. For others, the trappings of white privilege remain out of reach, but both immigrants' and white Mississippians' discursive work distances them from Black Mississippians, despite some African Americans' efforts to acknowledge and articulate their affinity with new Latino immigrants. All of this ensures that the fundamental location of Blackness at the bottom of the pyramid of structural racism endures. Yet social positions are always contextual, and we'll see in the next chapter that racial hierarchies forming inside the chicken plants may defy this trend. It is to the grit of poultry production that we now turn.

6 A Bone to Pick

"Welcome to the penitentiary!" a thin Black man bellows energetically through his beard net as we step through the front entrance of the chicken plant. After several years of hearing workers' horror stories about this work, I can appreciate his humor.

"Management couldn't have planned a more appropriate greeting," I chuckle silently as I look around. I've managed to join a plant tour as part of the Super Chicken Road Show, which aims to entice graduating college students to work in poultry production.[1] Recruits start out on the production lines, learning every aspect of chicken slaughter before moving into management. It's a hard sell, and this welcoming committee can't be helping his employer's cause.

The blue concrete-block break room bustles with activity—booths of beleaguered workers eat their lunches, visit, and rush to "doff" and "don" damp and greasy safety equipment. At one table a Black woman sits with a Latino couple, communicating mostly with animated hand signals. They are the exception. In general, the Black and Latino workers keep their distance. A lone group of white women in one corner concentrates intently on their food. Poultry processors take advantage of and encourage such divisions by segregating manufacturing tasks along lines of race and gender, a strategy that increases their control over the workforce. But I've learned that despite different experiences on the plant floor, workers of all backgrounds complain of exploitation, injuries, and abuse. They just don't always recognize these commonalities as grounds for coming together.

My anthropological gaze breaks as our group is whisked into the "laundry room," where we suit up with hairnets, smocks, earplugs, goggles, and shoe covers. Our guide, Diane, proudly announces that our smocks are made of recycled chicken feathers before warning us about what we are about to witness. "Just let me know if you need a break, and we can step out, okay?" If only workers needing breaks encountered such empathy. We walk through swinging metal doors and down a concrete hallway.

We begin our tour where the live chickens arrive for slaughter. "Down there, that's where it all begins. The live hang room. Can you see them live chickens comin' in on the belt?" I press my face against a thick, scarred glass window and peer down into a dark room one floor below. Human figures, draped in white smocks and hairnets like the one I currently wear, move frenetically, elbow to elbow, in two parallel lines. By the dim light of the bare red bulbs hanging above them, I make out the faint white forms of chickens flooding the work area. At a pace of perhaps a bird per second, each worker is snatching up chickens and hanging them upside down on metal shackles that motor past at an alarming speed. Diane explains that the darkness keeps the chickens calm, but to me the red lights evoke the hellish conditions under which the mostly Latino men below us are working. I'm not alone, as someone else on the tour marvels, "It looks like the underworld in *Mad Max beyond Thunderdome!*"

The wall where the chickens enter the building is partially open to the ninety-eight-degree heat outdoors. I can't see the workers' arms from where I stand, but I know from my time with the workers' center that they are covered in raw scratches and hardened scars from thousands of birds' futile attempts at self-defense. Similarly, their lungs are filling with dander, as they often remove their face masks to get enough oxygen in the summer heat and humidity.

There's a large ventilation fan sucking hot air out of the room, similar to the one that caught a Guatemalan worker's smock and sucked him in several months ago at a nearby plant. By instinct, he pulled back with all his might, and his thumb and forefinger were nearly completely severed

Figure 12. Hanging birds for slaughter. Photo by Earl Dotter.
Courtesy of EarlDotter.com.

from his hand. I've been translating for him at doctor and physical therapy appointments ever since, as part of my collaboration with the workers' center. Live hang is the most difficult and undesirable job in chicken processing, but those who elect to work here earn near the top of the pay scale for line workers.

Our tour guide moves us along. We reenact the path of chickens for slaughter, following the production line into the "kill room." Here birds are submerged in a trough of hot water with electric current, which loosens their feathers and knocks them unconscious. The steam in here makes it difficult to see. The birds enter a narrow passage, where their necks are sliced with a sharp blade, and they pass through a fork-shaped apparatus that tugs heads from bodies. Heads fall into a chute and disappear. Bodies double back across the room as blood drains into a long metal gutter. A lone Black man stands holding a knife, dressed head to toe in a uniform reminiscent of yellow rain gear. He manually slaughters those birds that miraculously escape the automated blade. Both he and the floor beneath him are spattered in blood.

The birds enter a large metal box—Diane says it has rubber belts on the inside—and exit featherless in a matter of seconds. They quickly pass over a flame that burns off any remaining quills and begin a steep climb toward the ceiling. The production line here reminds me of a roller coaster, and birds now hang directly above our heads. As they traverse another blade, "paws" are effortlessly separated from legs. The bald, footless, and headless carcasses, quickly beginning to resemble grocery store broilers, speed past us toward the evisceration room. We duck our heads to avoid being hit by the newly dead and speechlessly follow our guide.

As we enter evisceration, or "evis," the heat and noxious odor overwhelm us. It smells like the air in my Forest neighborhood on a summer day, only more potent. No wonder Spanish-speaking workers call this area *pollo caliente,* or "hot chicken." In English it is known as "straight line," and while the line is certainly straighter than in the fantastical kill room, it still bends and twists with apparent ease.

This department is staffed almost exclusively by Black women. In one swift automated motion, a machine appears to turn the birds inside out. Entrails now dangle outside the carcasses. Wearing white hairnets, purple aprons, and green rubber gloves, women stand on a metal platform along the production line above us and, using scissors, snip away at the organs with incredible speed—the line stops for no one. There's no time to glance up to rest their necks, even for a second. Livers, gizzards, and hearts each fall into separate water-propelled gutters and chutes, and they end up in plastic crates in one corner of the room, where more Black women package, weigh, and label them. The unusable innards are swiftly removed from the carcasses and discarded.

In the "salvage" area of the room, workers glance at the meat as it whizzes by and pull bruised, infected, and damaged chickens off the line. These are inspected, and any edible parts are reclaimed—salvaged—for consumption. Diane doesn't tell us what happens to the "condemned" mountain of yellow and purple, oozing and bloody meat that remains, and no one asks. A woman who worked in salvage is the only plant worker I ever met who told me she no longer eats chicken. After witnessing the job she did, I can fully appreciate her decision. At the end of the straight line the birds, still hanging from their shackles, pass through a machine that squeezes their middle and slices them in two—the line takes the legs in one direction while the top half drops onto a conveyor belt that takes the ribcage somewhere else.

We follow Diane through a series of doors and stand before the "chiller." This apparatus looks like a series of large steel cylindrical drums turned on their sides. They are open to the air, and we glimpse what looks like a sea of legless chicken carcasses floating downstream. The water smells strongly of chlorine. A corkscrew-like contraption moves the chickens from one end of the chiller to the other. The machines remind me of a woman who once told me that she and her coworkers would throw soap in the chiller to catch some rest on difficult days: "They have to stop the line to clean out the chiller and they have to throw all the soapy chickens away," she said with much familiarity.

Diane's voice brings me back, and she describes that the chickens are warm (still at their living temperature, just minutes after slaughter) when they enter the chiller and cold by the time they reach the end a few minutes later. Cooling the meat, she explains, makes it easier to slice through. At the far end of the room workers retrieve the birds and dump them in large wheeled containers so they can be taken to "debone."

Debone is loud, chaotic, and chilly. Diane shouts that we should keep our body parts and questions to ourselves until we get through. A warehouse-sized room is full of a dozen—maybe more—parallel lines of workers. As soon as they notice our group of mostly young women walk through the door, cat calls and dog howls ensue. We look at one another uncomfortably but dutifully follow our guide to get a close-up view of a debone line. At one end, two men—one Black, one Latino—take turns grabbing chicken halves from a bin in front of them and thrusting them onto "cones" rolling past. Each man is responsible for filling every other cone, and at this pace the work can cause permanent damage to workers' shoulders.

It takes only seconds for a chicken to pass through the entire debone line, and the birds are spaced with less than a foot between them. Because each position is so specialized, debone workers make the same repetitive motion up to sixty thousand times per shift.[2] Producing the most profitable commodities, they bear great risk of repetitive motion injuries, paying the highest cost despite their relatively low compensation.[3] Working quickly with slippery meat and knives that are rarely sharp enough makes lacerations another common injury.

The "skin pullers" are the first to attack the chicken halves, removing the skin in one swift tug. While their hands are veiled under multiple pairs of rubber and cotton gloves, skin pullers' fingernails often turn black and fall off due to the force they must exert to get a grip on the greasy chicken skin. Some complain that their gloves tear easily and instead of replacing them, managers tell workers to provide their own.

The "shoulder cutters" are next on the line, followed by the "wing rounders." Taking one cut each, they loosen a wing and pull it from the body. The following workers remove the breast meat in just two slices of a knife. After them, two more workers remove the "chicken tenders" with even fewer cuts. Finally, at the end of the line the remaining muscle is scraped from the skeleton—it is, after all, precious white meat. As the cone reaches the end, it dumps the tiny rib cage into a plastic tub and returns to the beginning of the line to commence the process anew. The carcasses are eventually ground up along with other chicken parts in the room next door, producing a pink foam used to make foods like bologna and potted meats.

This area of the plant, at least during the day shift, looks more diverse than others—men and women, Black and Latino, young and older. The night shift is made up nearly entirely of Latino men and women. Indeed, the vast majority of new immigrants in Mississippi poultry starts out in debone. This is one of the largest and most populated areas of production, and third-party labor contractors are sometimes used to ensure ample labor.

As we weave between the debone lines toward the exit, a middle-aged African American woman leans down from her post and asks me, "You wanna work here?" "Do *you* wanna work here," I respond. She looks at me in earnest and says, "Baby, I ain't got no choice. Sometimes you just ain't got no choice. You still have a choice, so don't make a mistake."

The tour picks up pace as Diane walks us quickly past "cut-up," where chicken breasts are butchered but left with bones; "IQF," where deboned meat is "individually quick frozen"; "further processing," where meat is injected, marinated, or breaded; and "CVP," where fresh and frozen chicken parts are "controlled vacuum packed" for retail consumption on trays and in bags. When I encounter the "bag sealer" machine my stomach drops. Lorena, who came to the workers' center from Chiapas, lost her index finger on her eighteenth birthday when the hot sealing metal press closed on it. All around, retail packages are crowded into larger atmosphere-controlled boxes and crates for wholesale. Packaging containers from fast food chains, big name poultry corporations, and wholesale companies litter the vast room.

The plant has gotten colder the farther we advance in the chain of production. As if to emphasize the point, Diane takes us into the freezer, an enormous warehouse with pallets of chicken products stacked floor to ceiling, awaiting shipping. Every worker here is a young Black man wearing padded blue overalls and winter jackets. They use jacks and forklifts handling massive amounts of weight, but because they can move around and communicate with one another with greater ease than in the areas we have passed through, the mood feels less oppressive.

The worker Diane recruited to show us around the freezer pauses when he sees a Latina hurry by on her way to the bathroom. He whistles, leans to grab her hand, and says, "Hey, Mama!" She offers a forced smile but doesn't stop. The exchange reminds me that my perception of this "less oppressive" area of the plant is relative, and that this space, too, is governed by gendered and raced hierarchies of oppression.

At the end of our tour, Diane opens the floor for questions. I ask which line position Diane would work at if she had to pick one. She looks at me like I'm crazy. "None! I didn't go to school to do this stuff! If I had to work on the line, I wouldn't be here at all." I leave thinking about the disproportionate privilege Diane and I have enjoyed that allow us to choose to do something other than slaughter chickens for a living. As I drive away, I hang my fluorescent orange earplugs over the rearview mirror, as the reflection of the "penitentiary," a hulking brown, windowless complex encircled in razor wire, shrinks into the distance.

.   .   .   .   .

Twenty-first-century chicken slaughter is horrific work. This chapter draws on my experiences working with the Mississippi Poultry Workers' Center and poultry workers' dramatic recounting of their own workplace struggles to demonstrate why this is so. Workers' health and safety are jeopardized on a daily basis, and injury rates are among the highest of any industry.[4] But poultry work causes more than bodily pain. Chronic abuse at the hands of superiors also injures the spirit, threatening workers' sense of dignity, self-worth, and justice.

A glimpse inside a poultry plant makes clear that the industry relies on a sort of plantation capitalism with a twist. I use the term "plantation capitalism" to describe the neocolonial relations in the chicken plants, which are owned and managed by a majority of elite white men and staffed almost entirely by working-class people of color.[5] These workers are controlled through bodily discipline; employers wield power that treats workers' bodies as exploitable, expendable machines.[6] It could be argued that the worker who welcomed me into a plant by comparing it to a penitentiary reflected a similar analysis.[7] The "twist" is the role of neoliberal globalization in shaping these work relations. In Mississippi's chicken plants, labor control is driven by new technologies of production and facilitated by the influx of "hardworking" immigrants—workers the Black community is presumed to have been incapable of producing.

In this chapter I show that poultry plant management not only takes advantage of divisions such as these but also actively works to augment workers' perceptions of difference and incompatibility. Race, ethnicity, gender, and citizenship serve as the primary identities through which people's days and nights in the chicken plant become embodied. Plants use these identity markers to stratify work shifts, departments, and job duties, and they organize production regimes through practices of plant-floor segregation, uneven privilege and opportunity, discipline and exclusion, individual and collective discrimination, bodily punishment, and the cultivation of difference as a dividing factor.[8] Thus, while many of plantation capitalism's dehumanizing conditions cut across lines of difference, they are experienced in distinctive ways by different groups. Even when people do experience oppression similarly, relations are structured such that they may not recognize the similarities they share or respond to their lived experience in the same ways.

DISCRIMINATION IN HIRING, FIRING, AND JOB ASSIGNMENTS

Discrimination in hiring, firing, and job assignments runs rampant in the poultry industry. At Peco Foods in Canton, a former office assistant reported to the workers' center that the night manager didn't hire a Black worker for six months. She claims that he instructed her to drop African Americans' applications straight into a trash can under her desk. At other plants dozens of Black applicants have complained to union representatives that they were turned away while Latino workers continued to be hired. These reports support Black workers' claims that it has become more difficult to get hired in the chicken plants since Latinos arrived.

Other scholarship similarly found that employer preference for immigrant workers is real and not just a perception of the economically disadvantaged.[9] Yet, paradoxically, while these stories suggest that the undocumented may be the poultry industry's preferred class of workers, they are also acutely vulnerable to abuse related to hiring, firing, and job assignments. In 2004, for example, immigrants reported that the quickest way to secure a job at Peco Foods in Canton was by paying a few hundred dollars to a Spanish-speaking office employee, who in turn shared a cut with a higher-up manager to ensure an expedient hire. Those who rejected this route were forced to return to the plant gates night after night in hopes that they might get lucky, a long tradition with roots in the southern plantation system.[10]

In other plants immigrant workers have reported having to pay supervisors $400 to change shifts, $100 each week just to keep their jobs, and smaller amounts to get time off to take their children to the doctor. One

Mexican woman recalls that every time she requested time off to go to New Orleans for appointments with federal immigration authorities, her supervisor insisted she bring him a bottle of tequila. When she stopped complying, her requests for time off were denied.

Almost universally, Latinos agree that they do the hardest jobs in chicken slaughter and are expected to work without complaining: "When they see that you're Hispanic, they want to take advantage of you." Immigrants are reprimanded for sharing their grievances with supervisors and are quickly silenced by threats like, "If you don't want to be here, just leave. There are twenty, thirty people outside that want to work." Many feel intense pressure to do their jobs perfectly, claiming that it takes only a small mistake for an immigrant worker to be terminated. This treatment, they say, is vastly different from that of U.S.-born workers: "They always demand more of us, and we realize the difference in treatment that exists between us and the American workers." Latino workers tend to resent such perceived differences in job security.

But they are not alone. Black women are also particularly vulnerable to job insecurities. The common policy that line workers cannot be hired more than three times puts women, thanks to their common role as primary caregivers of children and elderly parents, at a disadvantage. Because the federal Family Medical Leave Act does not protect those who have been employed under a year, and others who are eligible may be unaware of FMLA protection, many women report having been encouraged by supervisors to quit their jobs in preparation for childbirth or when they needed to care for a sick family member. One had to quit a job she had held for less than a month just so she could attend her brother's funeral. When she reapplied for the job, she learned company policy barred her from rehire in the six months following her last date of employment. Over time, situations like these result in workers being temporarily or permanently locked out of the only jobs in town. In comparison with U.S.-born workers, undocumented workers are less frequently confronted by the "three-strikes" rule because they may seek rehire using a different set of identity documents and are more often hired through third-party labor contractors. Thus, the three-strikes policy disproportionately affects women's and work authorized individuals' opportunities for work in the chicken plants, which can cause interpersonal resentment and conflict.

ABUSIVE SUPERVISORS

The previous statements corroborate accounts that supervisors regularly mistreat workers.[11] In fact, both Latino and Black workers point to abuse at the hands of their immediate supervisors as one of the most egregious problems they face in the plants. Immigrant workers complain that supervisors are unfair toward Latinos and preferential toward African Americans. Grievances abound about supervisors who are more strict with Latinos than African Americans regarding food safety rules (such as the use of beard nets), who allow Black workers to submit requests for vacation time before permitting Latino workers to do the same, and who yell or swear at immigrants in ways they would not dare to act toward U.S.-born employees. "It's difficult to work with the *morenos,* really," says Baldomero Félix, "because the supervisors demand so much from us. Any little thing, they send you to the office. But with them, the supervisor goes by and doesn't say anything. They form their little group; they stay there chatting, telling jokes, laughing. The supervisors run us back to work, but they don't do that to them."

Fidel Briceño recalls the time his supervisor referred to him as "that fucking Mexican" when he complained about his working conditions. Others share that they feel disrespected, reporting, "They treat us like we're stupid." Disparate treatment of immigrants has been so bad at times that even Black workers comment on it. "Supervisors cuss them *out,*" Brenda Turner murmured. Yolanda Goodloe agreed, noting, "They really degrade Latinos. They think they don't understand when they curse them."

Often Latinos blame African American superiors for the harshest treatment. "Some people feel like they have more rights than the Hispanics," one Mexican worker told me. When I asked him what people he was referring to, he clarified, "the *morenos,* of course." "They are very aggressive," Mariana Paz fretted one evening after work. "The worst supervisors in the plants are the Blacks, who treat whites and Hispanics poorly. I have been stuck with really bad Black women. They see that we're new and they want to order us around, but I don't let them."

I shared this observation with African American worker leaders, asking for their reflections. A few suggested Hispanics' perceptions were spot on, explaining that white supervisors are particularly conscious about race issues, concerned that "if they mistreat you, you will call it racial. Black supervisors sometimes treat you worse because of that." But another disagreed strongly: "A lot of Hispanic people have been taught that they're better than African Americans. They feel obligated to respect white America. That's whose face they see on the dollar bill. But they don't think they're supposed to respect us. It's nothing to do with a Black supervisor being more hard toward Hispanics. That's really not true." In the first analysis, the area's legacies of racial struggle are thought to differently shape white and Black supervisors' behavior. In the second, structures of white supremacy are seen to condition Latinos' differential expectations and interpretations of supervisors' actions. Both explanations, though expressing different points of view about the role of race in a supervisor's treatment of workers, reflect deeply on the racialized nature of power relations in the United States and suggest that dealings in the chicken plants are shaped by these larger structures.

Despite immigrants' experiences with discrimination and abuse in the plants, they are rarely aware that their Black coworkers have equally disturbing complaints about supervisors. One African American woman who received a call at work about an emergency that landed her child in the hospital wasn't notified until nearly an hour after the call took place. Another reports that her supervisor commented that her skin color was ugly. She replied, "You might be white, and I might be Black, but you ain't no better than I am. Your blood is red; mine is red. Your blood ain't white, and mine ain't Black."

Women bear the brunt of supervisors' abuse of power, sometimes in the form of sexual harassment. While this is not a new problem—in the chicken plants and beyond, women have faced gender discrimination and sexual come-ons from male coworkers and superiors for decades—it is a persistent one.[12] A grandmother in her fifties revealed she was fired from her job in a chicken plant in the early 1970s when she refused to sleep with a supervisor. Another remembers her days working at R&R Processors: "The supervisors mistreated us. When a young lady would come in looking for work, they would tell her they had to examine her in order to get the job." I gasped, but she continued, unfazed. "Yes, she would have to sleep with 'em. That's just how bad things was back then at R&R."

Many Latin American women share more recent stories of harassment, reporting supervisors demanding sexual acts in exchange for promotions, perks, or other types of workplace power. At Koch Foods in Morton, a

Figure 13. Inspection, supervision, and gender dynamics on the plant floor. Photo by Earl Dotter. Courtesy of EarlDotter.com.

group of women eventually filed a discrimination claim against their employer with the U.S. Department of Justice. The complaint led to a large class action race, national origin, and sex discrimination case against Koch Foods, representing more than 115 employees from the Morton plant.[13] While plants have policies that supervisors who get written up three times are supposed to be terminated, workers claim this rarely happens, even after repeated grievances.

Such unchecked wielding of power over workers wears them down, despite their best efforts otherwise. "We had twenty-something new workers last month," says union steward Onita Harvey. "Fifteen just didn't come to work last night. They quit because of the treatment, the way the supervisors are talking to 'em. And the plant is wondering why they lose so many workers."[14]

Those who do stay in their jobs despite ongoing abuse often refuse to do so quietly. Keisha Brown is accustomed to repudiating supervisors' abuse:

Tyson send management to a school, it seem like to me, to *train* people to mistreat you. That's why I don't get along with 'em, 'cause they're not gonna talk to me like that. One supervisor came over and yelled at me recently, "Woman! I told you!" I told him, "Your best bet is to get out from behind me and quit hollering at me." He kept on trying to talk: "You heard what I said. You are going to take that right hand, you're going to catch that meat off that line, and you're going to hang them legs." I looked at him, and I turned around, and I wouldn't say another word. I just set there like this, and I balled my fists up. Finally he said, "Fine," and he died down. When I got down off that line I had tears in my eyes. He had me pissed off. Because anytime you do that close up to my face to where your saliva can hit me in my face, you're too close up on me.

In another example, at a workers' center event Patrick Herring, a Black man in his sixties who had worked in poultry for decades, shared that a supervisor had told him the fans he had been sanitizing weren't clean enough. Patrick defended his work, asserting, "I spray 'em down every day." The supervisor replied, "Well, they're looking kind of dirty," to which Patrick responded, "I don't shine 'em! I just spray 'em down." The group gathered at the workers' center roared with laughter as Herring explained, "It's always been like slave stuff in the chicken plants, you know. It's always been Afro-Americans doing the work, the labor work. You've just gotta stand up for yourself, and we can do that now because we have a union."

Experiences of mistreatment at the hands of abusive supervisors in the chicken plants is one of workers' top complaints. As this section shows, these are often conditioned by individuals' subject positions as raced and gendered bodies. While workers of different backgrounds share some similar complaints, they tend to overlook the similarities. And despite commonalities, a key difference lies in workers' sense of their own power to resist such abuses. In the case of Mississippi poultry, Black men and women often feel more secure in their ability to speak back to and report abusive supervisors than do Latinos.

WAGE THEFT

Patrick Herring's assessment that chicken plants are places of "slave stuff" is valid in other ways, too, considering that violations of federal wage and hour laws run rampant in the poultry industry. The federal Fair Labor Standards Act (FLSA) states that workers have a right to be paid for all hours on the job, earn at least minimum wage, and be paid "time and a half" for overtime, calculated as all hours over forty worked in a week. Despite these protections, poultry companies regularly and systematically cheat workers out of pay.[15] In 2007, for example, Koch Foods agreed to pay 174 workers in Mississippi over $325,000 after a Department of Labor investigation revealed that the company had failed to pay them overtime.[16]

Workers of all backgrounds report being underpaid. Complaining to management sometimes fixes the problem; more often it does not. "They never pay us for all the hours we work," complains a Peruvian woman who has worked in the plants for five years. "It doesn't matter if we report it or not; they never do anything about it." Being paid piece-rate wages exacerbates many workers' underpayment. They report imprecise scales that miscalculate the weight of the chicken they produce, misclassifications of job level, and violations of pay rates as determined by their union contracts.

Despite the FLSA's regulation of paycheck deductions, violations run rampant. Plants often deduct the cost of protective equipment from workers' paychecks, though employers are responsible for providing them. Other times deductions are taken for employer-provided housing, transportation, and food, which can reduce pay to below legal limits. Few immigrant workers know their rights under FLSA, and still fewer have access to the resources necessary to demand employer compliance.

While immigrants tend to face more regular and egregious violations of federal wage and hour protections, U.S.-born workers also complain of being cheated out of pay. For example, at a workers' center FLSA training, Onita Harvey shared a grievance she was filing for repeated underpayment of workers on the night shift. Her own story was exemplary: "Last month I got a $19.97 paycheck for forty-three hours of work. I received another $45.00 for a full week of work. They said I had bought $171 worth of chicken and deducted it from my paycheck!" Harvey was fighting back to recover her unpaid wages and those of her coworkers.

Workers of all backgrounds lose hundreds or thousands of dollars in income annually due to poultry companies' refusal to pay for time spent waiting while broken machinery gets fixed, as well as for "doffing" and "donning," or taking off and putting on protective equipment. At some plants the long wait to receive and turn in equipment at the supply room requires workers to arrive early for work and leave late, resulting in hours of unpaid time each week. Workers' rights advocates argue that because employees are required to be at work for these activities, such time should be fully compensable. Most courts agree.[17]

Despite systematic wage and hour violations that affect workers of all backgrounds, in few plants are Black and Latino workers aware of one another's problems, let alone in dialogue or empathetic. At a workers' center training about fair pay, maintenance worker Walter Glover declared, "I think minimum wage should be at least ten dollars! But for these undocumented people, six dollars is fine. They could never make that kind of money at home. We haven't been given that kind of opportunity to jump *that* far ahead. We had to fight to get paid what white workers was getting paid, but Hispanics have just walked straight in."

While Glover's comments echo some Black workers' concerns that immigrants are "cutting in line," he raises another important point. Low wages go further when sent "back home" to Latin America, and immigrants often send money to support family members they've left behind. By earning in the United States but spending in their countries of origin, immigrants are better able to bear the costs of social reproduction. While this observation does not justify payment of unlivable wages, it does point to a key difference in how some U.S.-born and immigrant poultry workers manage to make ends meet with the minimal earnings they receive.

DENIAL OF BATHROOM BREAKS

I'm not trying to be funny, but he don't like Black people. I stood on that line for thirty minutes and held myself. I was like this [bent over], I was hurting so bad. Finally I took off running, and I like to fell over my apron. When I got to the rest room a lady in there said, "Baby, what's wrong?" I said, "Please help me!" I couldn't even get my equipment off. I had been waiting for a break for thirty minutes, and the lead person was just steady telling me, "Wait a minute. Wait a minute. Wait a minute."

Keisha Brown's humiliating experience is far too common; the denial of bathroom breaks is a chronic problem for poultry workers of all backgrounds.[18]

To compensate, workers often put their health at risk, drinking little liquid during their shifts and holding urinary and bowel functions as long as possible.[19] The Occupational Safety and Health Association (OSHA) states that workers have a basic right to use the bathroom and employers cannot "impose unreasonable restrictions" on bathroom breaks, but such regulations are rarely enforced.[20] In one plant, workers in evis were categorically denied bathroom breaks as part of department policy. After several women urinated in their clothes on the line, the union filed a complaint with OSHA. This fixed the problem in evis, but the abuse continued in other departments and at other plants.

While a common concern among African American women, the abuse may be even more egregious among Latinas. Immigrant workers sometimes attribute this inequality to the racial allegiances of Black supervisors: "It makes me so angry because we're all working equally, we all have the right to take a bathroom break," says Mariana Paz. "But most of our supervisors are *morenos,* and they give other *morenos* up to fifteen minutes. Us? They give us two minutes, if they let us go at all." But even more frequently, Latinas place blame on the perceived "laziness" of their Black coworkers, who they perceive as taking advantage of the system during long bathroom breaks, for which they are rarely disciplined. In this way, Latino workers commonly attribute their own oppression to Black workers' abuse of privilege.

Latinos aren't the only workers complaining about abuse of bathroom breaks. Black workers, too, identify this as a problem: "Mike don't know how to run the line. He act like he scared to tell his employees what to do, so he got people walking off the line, and they are going to take bathroom breaks for an hour or an hour and a half! The line get backed up. Then they gotta cut the line off. Chickens, I mean, girl, just falling everywhere! One time we had so much chicken on the floor, leg quarters everywhere." This perspective helps us see that, whereas Latinos tend to blame Black workers broadly (or sometimes Black supervisors specifically) for denied or limited bathroom breaks, African Americans may point to particular individuals, including Black and white line workers and supervisors, who make the situation worse for others.

While the problem is easily blamed on coworkers and immediate superiors, the restriction of bathroom breaks is an industry-wide problem that points to failures in management at higher levels. At a workers' center "listening session" a line worker who had previously worked as a supervisor framed the problem in structural terms: "When someone goes to the bathroom and leaves a shackle empty, that's a loss for the company. The general manager is going to complain to the superintendent, the superintendent is going to complain to the supervisor, and the supervisor has to do something. Because if not, they're going to suspend the supervisor. I mean, it's a chain. If there was more personnel, there would be more time for people to go to the bathroom." Indeed, the deeper problem lies in management's failure to implement a signaling system whereby workers who need a break can be temporarily replaced by "floaters." Were there sufficient floaters, bathroom breaks would not be such a problem for workers, supervisors, or others up the chain of command. While recommended by OSHA, unions, and occupational health scholars alike, floaters require remuneration. Because this affects the company's bottom line, most chicken plants are loath to comply.

REPETITIVE MOTION INJURIES

Workers in the United States suffer nearly two million repetitive motion injuries each year, and the poultry industry is one of the largest single perpetrators of this trend.[21] Though women make up less than half the U.S. workforce and under a third of total workplace injuries, they are disproportionately affected by repetitive motion injuries, accounting for approximately two-thirds of all carpal tunnel and tendinitis cases.[22] This points to the types of work women do, unduly exposing them to these risks.

In addition to carpal tunnel and tendinitis, poultry's other common chronic injuries include rotator cuff damage, muscle strains, back injuries, and trigger finger.[23] Many midcareer Black women and men shared their stories with me about when their hand "just shuts up and goes to sleep." In conversations with unions in poultry plants throughout the South, representatives commented on the industry's crippling effects on entire communities. "When they are done with you, they'll crumple you up like a piece of paper and throw you out and reach back for your kids," one observed. Another spoke of a town full of African American families with "three generations of cripples," all of whom had worked in poultry. In her analysis, the Latino workforce is growing because "they've crippled all the African American workers."[24]

Such high rates of injury are exacerbated by the ever-increasing speed of the processing line. "They just put the new lines in, and shoot! They sped it up," Keisha Brown exclaimed. "I clocked it at 110 birds per minute. It was going so fast that you couldn't look at them unless you do like this." She moved her head back and forth as if she were watching a tennis match in fast forward. "And when it's going that fast, you've got to be dead on the money." Vicky Reed, an injured mother of seven, agreed:

> Yesterday they had to keep stopping the line because I couldn't keep up. Normally there's a woman on the scale. She is supposed to pull the bags up. Another woman at the end of the scale is supposed to check the meat and fold the bag over. Then I am supposed to put in the ice, put on the lid, and send it on down. Yesterday I was doing it all. I was even lifting thirty-three-pound boxes off the line all day. I told my supervisor, "I can't do it no more. I just can't. My hands is swelling and I'm really hurting." I was nauseated in my stomach. Them pains was hitting me in my hand and was going all up my arm.

Although OSHA has recommended that the industry slow the speed of the processing line, it has implemented no specific standards. Instead, companies are encouraged to voluntarily comply. Meanwhile, line speeds keep getting faster. In 2014 the Obama administration proposed a 25 percent increase from 140 to 175 birds per minute, making the 110 that Brown counted in 2005 seem humane in comparison.[25] Ironically, the government regulates line speed only as it affects "food safety," or the USDA's ability to control meat quality.[26] Reed said that in her experience, "The only way they cut the line down is if they start to get a lot of bad birds coming through and the inspector tells them to slow it down. But not because people are getting hurt."

Poultry plants push their employees until they can work no more. Brenda Turner was shocked when she first started working in a chicken plant: "I had never seen so many women that had had operations, and they still out on the floor working! It was unbelievable. You could see the

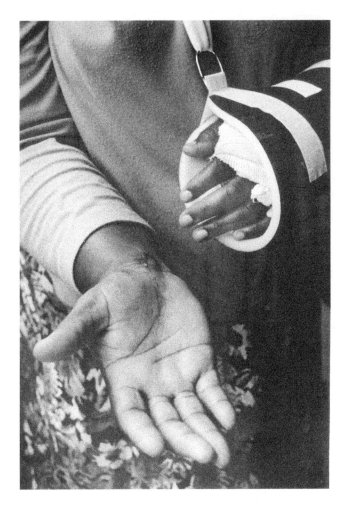

Figure 14. Repetitive motion injuries cripple poultry workers.
Photo by Earl Dotter. Courtesy of EarlDotter.com.

pain in they face and you could see the swelling in they hands." Workers'
compensation benefits in Mississippi are paid at two-thirds of a workers'
average weekly wage. For women earning poverty-level wages, this reduc-
tion in pay doesn't allow them to cover the most basic costs of supporting
a family. For these reasons, despite ongoing medical treatment and
numerous surgeries, many women in the poultry industry find themselves
forced to work in pain.

Workers and advocates suggest that a rotation system, in which workers are moved to a different position every few hours, would significantly cut down on repetitive motion injuries. But in the absence of OSHA regulations, few companies have adopted rotation policies voluntarily. "They'll tell you that you supposed to rotate, but they won't rotate you," Yolanda Goodloe shared during a workers' center workshop. "They will leave people in the same spot all day long. Then when you get hurt, they don't want to take care of you. They just wearing people out." An impassioned cut-up worker implored the group, "A lot of people is asking for rotation. Rotate these people out if that's what it's going to take to get them well! Don't treat them like they dogs! This is not slavery days anymore!"

OBSTRUCTION OF WORKERS' COMPENSATION

While injuries to African American poultry workers fall heavily on women suffering from the hazards of repetitive motion, some of the most egregious problems Latinos identify concern chicken plants' obstruction of their basic right to medical care when they are injured. Their vulnerability as undocumented workers, limited understanding of English, and unfamiliarity with workers' compensation create additional barriers to addressing emergent and often life-changing workplace injuries.

Despite the fact that the majority of poultry plant injuries are musculoskeletal problems caused by repetitive motion, Latino workers often report acute lacerations, amputations, falls, and other gruesome accidents. These injuries usually require immediate medical care, and injured immigrants are typically sent to a "company doctor" with questionable impartiality. This is important for two reasons. First, in Mississippi financial compensation for a worker's permanent disability is determined entirely by the treating physician's professional opinion. Many workers have been poorly compensated for their disabilities when doctors underestimate the extent of injury. More important, some doctors with close relationships to poultry companies have been known to misdiagnose and aggravate injuries. For example, the plant's preferred doctor in Morton improperly set a Chiapan worker's bones after his hand was mangled in a machine. A month later his bones were rebroken by a hand surgeon in

Jackson, followed by multiple surgeries to fix the problem. Adrian Vera from Argentina stepped into a drainage channel on the floor that was missing its protective grate and landed on his tailbone. The "plant doctor" sent him back to work. After a month of excruciating pain, a specialist in Jackson diagnosed Vera with multiple vertebrae fractures. Years after spinal surgery, he continued to live in constant pain, unable to work.

The plant nurse and translator can also impede medical treatment. Plant nurses often rebuff requests to see a doctor. "It doesn't matter what problem you report," lamented Perla Jacomé about the nurse at her workplace. "She always does the same thing. She rubs you down with Bengay and gives you a Tylenol. If the problem persists, she tells you buy another Tylenol from the vending machine. If you don't have a dollar, too bad." The "Bengay and Tylenol" treatment has become a dark joke among many Latinos in the area.[27] She also pressures workers to sign paperwork in English waiving their right to medical treatment. Immigrant workers often have trouble communicating about the extent of their injuries. They are forced to rely on a plant translator, whom many believe poorly interprets and diminishes the severity of their complaints. On other occasions, injured workers attend appointments with no translator whatsoever, making even basic communication a challenge.

To avoid reporting a lost work-time injury to OSHA, chicken plants regularly require injured workers to report to work and sit in the break room during their shift instead of recovering at home.[28] While some U.S.-born workers face this problem—one reported being "punished" with a day-long assignment to sit in the plant bathroom—it seems to affect Latinos at a higher rate, and many tend to view it as a practice that discriminates particularly against them: "They let the *morenos* go home when they are injured, but not us."

Employers often go out of their way to discourage injured immigrant workers from retaining a lawyer. One was picked up for doctor's appointments in a shiny black limousine. Another was offered money. He rejected the plant's $1,000 and, with the help of an attorney, eventually recovered $45,000 for his permanent disability. A third, a teenager who lost half his hand, contacted the workers' center in fear after an employer's representative showed up at his home on three separate occasions trying to talk him into firing his attorney.

When these "friendly" tactics fail, poultry plants have been known to threaten undocumented workers with job termination should they hire a lawyer, and they often make good on this promise. Mississippi's workers' comp law does not protect injured workers from retaliation by employers, making these practices legal. While injured workers have the same rights to workers' compensation benefits regardless of whether or not they lose their job, immigrants rarely know this, so termination of injured workers effectively reduces the number of workers' comp claims poultry plants must process.

Flora Ramos, a young mother of two from Arequipa, has been unable to work since being fired for requesting medical treatment after her thumb turned purple: "They always demand so much from Hispanics. But when we have an accident, we really see how they treat us differently. When we're injured they don't care about our health at all. They simply fire us." Her experience is common, and immigrant workers are often subject to termination once disabled at work. Because immigrants are less aware of their rights, more vulnerable due to their citizenship status, and often unable to defend themselves in English, they disproportionately fall victim to intimidation and retaliation following workplace injuries, often with devastating consequences.

PUSHED BEYOND THEIR LIMITS

Despite Black and Latino workers' different concerns regarding workplace health and safety, their experiences often converge in pain and abuse following a debilitating injury. Testimonies suggest that the poultry plants often continue to put them in difficult jobs despite their physical limitations. Vicky Reed recalls that when she returned to work following carpal tunnel surgery the doctor had advised restricted use of her hands. "They put me right back on the line, doing the same thing. And I'm trying to use my hand, but it's swelling up; it's not working. And my supervisor tells me, 'Well, use your good hand.' I'm there thinking, 'You fail to realize this one's really not good because it needs surgery too. I just didn't do both of 'em at the same time.'" Similarly, when Moisés Rivas injured his left hand in an accident, he was "accommodated" and continued to work with just one hand. When a repetitive motion injury crippled his other arm and he could no longer work, he was fired.

"I think it's just so wrong," deplored Reed, "that you go in there and you slave and you work, and then when something goes wrong, they just knock you down to the ground. If you don't go in there and work until you pass out and die, then it's, 'Oh, you don't want to work.'" Despite the intimidation, African Americans are much more likely to report problems, seek medical treatment, and advocate for themselves following an injury than are immigrant workers. This is due to their greater (though still limited) knowledge about workers' comp, ability to express themselves in English, U.S. citizenship, and group history of struggle and survival. At the end of a six-day stretch of working with one hand, when her supervisor ordered to stay overtime, Reed had had enough. "Look," she told him, "you can do what you wanna do, but I'm not going to another line. My hand is hurting me. If you overwork it, I'm gonna be right back up in [the hospital] again, and I'm tired of people cutting on me. So if you want to give me a [disciplinary] point, you go ahead. I'm going home."

"What I gather," conjectured Onita Harvey, "is that once you get hurt you are a liability and they want you to quit. They act like, 'So what if you had an operation? So what that you're not capable of doing your job like you used to? Go back to work.' They don't care how you do it; they don't care if you fall over. All they want is they product out." Despite some workers' protests, if they can't get the product out, and if they're not terminated, supervisors can make work so difficult that they leave in pain and exasperation. Desperate to support their families, most injured workers continue laboring in pain until they can stand it no longer, often with permanent disabilities. Once out of a job, they are forced to look for something less strenuous or depend on their families for support. While U.S. citizens can sometimes qualify for Social Security disability benefits, without this option some immigrants return to their home countries in search of medical treatment. Speaking at a workers' center press conference about his double injury and termination, Moisés Rivas courageously denounced this treatment: "They say that we are team members, but really they consider us machines. As long as we can work 100 percent, everything's fine. But if we ask for medical attention, they get rid of us. They should treat us like human beings, not like machines."

Poultry-processing workers face bodily harm every time they clock in to work—mostly predictable and preventable injuries and illnesses that the industry could curb. Employers could also ensure that injured workers have swift and fair access to independent medical treatment, evaluations, and disability-wage replacement. But decreasing injury rates and increasing access to workers' comp benefits would cost corporations millions. Instead, the industry treats workers as expendable machinery, replaced more cheaply than they can be "fixed." The lengths some chicken plants go to in order to decrease their liability for these broken Black and brown bodies—and the sheer lack of respect shown toward the people to whom they belong—is truly remarkable.[29]

MAKING SENSE OF IT ALL

Workers on the processing line face an onslaught of daily threats to their well-being. The breadth and intensity of these abuses are much too commonplace to be inadvertent. To the contrary, they have developed hand in hand with the industry itself. As poultry production picked up pace, so did corporations' attempts to keep labor costs at their lowest, and over time they have developed strategies that work. First, they have invested in new technologies that minimize their reliance on skilled labor and make workers literally disposable. Second, they have established far-reaching networks to bring an interminable supply of immigrant workers to fuel the production lines. Third, they have sped up the production line to superhuman rates that take advantage of the fact that now all workers are replaceable, disposing of injured workers as quickly and quietly as possible. Fourth, they have segregated the processing lines by race, ethnicity, and gender, using people's prejudices and misunderstandings about one another to their greatest advantage and discouraging worker communication and solidarity. Finally, they have allowed abuses of workers' basic human rights to run rampant inside the plants, creating an atmosphere of racialized and gendered hostility and fear.

Scholars have repeatedly found that food production relies on the strategic wielding of difference in the name of labor control.[30] David Griffith, for example, argues that today's labor regimes are achieved, at least in part, by employers who "marshal myths and symbols toward justifying the labor process. The ways employers draw upon myths of ethnicity, gender, and nationality to justify hiring, job allocation processes, etc. can be extremely subtle."[31] Similarly, Deborah Fink's work in pork processing suggests that ethnic division has been so beneficial to companies that "a powerful functional argument can be made for the capitalist class as instigators of racial oppression."[32] Indeed, while the advantages of a split-labor market have been shown time and time again in different spaces and eras, the recent transportation, communication, and production technologies fueling globalization have created an environment in which such divisions are heightened and the resulting abuses amplified.

The stories in this chapter illustrate that, while both African American and immigrant workers face abuses in the chicken plants, these can be experienced in very different ways. For example, processors' preference for undocumented immigrant workers produces a large class of Latino workers highly vulnerable to intense exploitation. While this predilection disadvantages Black workers at the time of hire, those who do enter the plants typically have more room to stand up for their rights than do their immigrant coworkers. Women of all backgrounds are particularly vulnerable to supervisors' abuse of power, while some workers, particularly Black men, have had more success at garnering positions in relatively less oppressive areas of the plant, such as in packaging, shipping, and sanitation. We also see that these groups' different job positions and average time working in the plants make new immigrants more susceptible to acute injuries and African Americans prone to longer term, chronic ailments. Both can be debilitating and demoralizing, yet U.S.-born workers are somewhat better equipped to seek medical treatment and workers' compensation. Immigrants suffer from greater rates of job termination as a result of workplace injuries, while African Americans are more likely to be retained but pushed to their physical limits in the hopes that they will quit on their own.

Close examination of racial hierarchies inside the chicken plants suggest a potentially interesting departure from what we are witnessing in communities. In chapter 5 we saw that Latinos appear to be entering Mississippi society in a position between the categories of whiteness and Blackness, with Blackness persisting at the bottom of the racial hierarchy.

Inside the chicken plants, however, African American workers generally have higher standing than their Latino counterparts. There, their privilege as U.S. citizens and English speakers, coupled with their collective seniority in the industry and their local history of struggle for civil and labor rights, provide them with a level of status rarely granted to immigrant workers. This relatively higher status often results in better work schedules and assignments, higher wages, somewhat less hazardous work, a sense of conviction in standing up to abusive supervisors, and a basic level of access to workers' compensation protections. New immigrants are more likely to work less desirable shifts in more demanding and dangerous areas of the production line, to be paid piecework, to put up with harassment without speaking up or reporting it, and to be denied their rights and benefits in cases of workplace injury.

Of course, such general observations are also mediated by gender, and both Black and Latina women are highly vulnerable to exploitation and abuse. Whiteness remains located at the top of the hierarchy, such that there exist few white line workers in Mississippi poultry, while upper management remains largely white and male. Thus, "privilege" as I use it here is a relative term. While workplace hierarchies of race may place Latinos below African Americans on several measures, poultry workers of all backgrounds are working in some of the most difficult and dangerous jobs in the country. These jobs are also often demeaning and demoralizing, thanks to the industry's categorical disregard for basic workplace rights and dignity.

Despite the differences workers are quick to see among them, workers would benefit from sharing their experiences of labor conditions (dismal), wage theft (rampant), abusive supervisors (omnipresent), injuries (avoidable), and the like with one another. But language barriers, prejudices, and fears of management scrutiny inhibit this communication, creating serious challenges for organizing workers in the context of neoliberal globalization. Identity-based difference in the plants has become so normalized and hierarchies of race so naturalized that few can envision a broader class-based alliance from which to affect change in their places of work. The implications of this finding, and attempts to address it, are the focus of the following chapter.

7 Sticking Our Necks Out

CHALLENGES TO UNION AND WORKERS'
CENTER ORGANIZING

It is July 2002, and two Interfaith Worker Justice interns and I are taking our time assembling packets for an upcoming meeting of the Laborers' International Union of North America local, which represents three chicken plants in Mississippi.[1] Part of our sluggishness may be due to the summer heat. A small air conditioner is working overtime in the far window, but the only cool ones in the room appear to be the flyers fluttering in its breeze against the adjacent wall. We also work slowly because we are distracted, engrossed in the stories we're eliciting from Bobby Robertson, the local's business manager, who sits near the AC unit at his desk fiddling with some papers. An oversized, mustard-hued, button-up shirt drapes over his sizable frame. Glossy black curls and heavy glasses frame his dark face. Behind him hangs a photo, in which he wears a formal red suit and matching felt hat while accepting an award at church. In it, he beams his unforgettable smile.

Robertson tells us that he had worked in a chicken-processing plant for many years when, in the mid-1990s, his coworkers began to organize and sought to find union representation. Robertson joined in the successful campaign, became an active union member, and eventually became its chief representative.[2] He recalls that not much time had passed when the

147

plants began to heavily recruit Latino workers, weakening the union's membership and bargaining power. Robertson's initial response was to organize an intense union campaign to force the plant's management to stop hiring immigrant labor. He even called federal immigration officials and implored them to deport the "illegals" at his plant.

He soon realized, however, that while he might succeed in getting one immigrant fired or detained, another person, speaking a language he didn't understand, would soon be toiling in that worker's place. With the passage of time, Robertson eventually acknowledged—as did the union movement more broadly—that he and his mostly African American membership could do very little to keep new migrants from arriving. Despite his inability to communicate in Spanish, he recognized that for his union to survive, it would have to embrace the new Latino workers in its midst: "'I need someone who can help me speak Mexican,' I told a representative from the International, and the help started coming." He gestures across the room toward us with a warm chuckle. I have heard this folklore before. In fact, it was precisely this statement that piqued my curiosity and led me to Mississippi this summer. But despite Robertson's easy smile, the humor (horror?) in his choice of words escapes him completely. This stuff— speaking "Mexican"—represents completely new territory for him.

The interns and I are here to help him increase his capacity to represent Black and Latino workers alike. He's letting me hang around because of my language abilities; on several occasions this summer and again in 2004 I will accompany him into the plants' break rooms and interpret for Spanish-speaking workers who want to communicate with their union. For tonight's meeting the local is hosting a barbecue, and we're hopeful a diversity of workers will come to learn more about the union and the Know Your Rights workshops we'll be offering throughout the summer. Though we will end up disappointed by the evening's low turnout, we'll keep trying. Robertson says he's newly inspired by our energy.

·   ·   ·   ·   ·

As I look back, I see we certainly did have energy—a youthful, hopeful, and at times too hasty energy. Over ten years later, I am astounded by Robertson's perseverance in Mississippi's incredibly difficult organizing climate. As earlier chapters have shown, the South has never been labor or union friendly, consistently shortchanging working people in the hopes of sustaining industrial investment. Industries have long worked to defeat union organizing attempts for fear that an organized workforce could interfere with profit. The geographies that increasingly entice the poultry industry to Mississippi—rurality; state incentives for investment; Right to Work and other antilabor policies; a disempowered, low-wage, and racially stratified workforce with few options; and an increasingly undocumented migrant labor pool—are the same ones that present serious challenges to worker organizing.

But the barriers to building worker power go beyond these alone. In this chapter I discuss some of the others that come into play: difficulties communicating, workers' divergent ideologies about unions and resistance, Latinos' investment in structures of white supremacy, and unions' uneven and sometimes contentious approaches to organizing in the globalized present are highlighted here. I introduce some of the unions' attempts to incorporate Latino workers into their membership since the area's transformation began in the mid-1990s. I also discuss the growing workers' center movement and the Mississippi Poultry Workers' Center's collaboration with unions beginning in 2002. This discussion highlights some of the reasons why organizing for justice in the chicken plants is some of the hardest organizing in the world. It underscores the need to move past a universal politics of class as well as beyond identity politics toward a recognition of how overlapping oppressions affect workers' lives. Ultimately, these lessons have grave implications for the possibilities of collectively organizing Mississippi's poultry workers in the twenty-first century.

LANGUAGE BARRIERS

As Bobby Robertson now famously noted, language barriers present a major obstacle to organizing in the chicken plants today, and poultry operations count on them to keep workers divided. Both on and off the line, communication between English- and Spanish-speaking workers is limited. When I first got to Mississippi there were few bilingual people there,

Figure 15. Chicken plant break room. Photo by Earl Dotter. Courtesy of EarlDotter.com.

and even fewer working on the lines in the chicken plants. While this is changing with time, the pace is remarkably slow. Moreover, because work on the processing line is loud, earplugs make it hard to talk even among coworkers who speak the same language. In the break room Black and Latino workers tend to keep to themselves. When they do share a table, it's nearly impossible to have a meaningful conversation: "We might say, 'Hi, how are you?' or something like that," Efrain López from Guatemala shares. "But when we sit together, basically the *moreno* is just looking at us, watching us eat. He eats, finishes, and we each get up and leave."

Workers express frustration with trying to communicate. Learning English mostly from middle-class white women teaching ESOL at area churches becomes a handicap for immigrants trying to communicate with African American coworkers in the plants, for example, as they often have a hard time understanding one another's accents and speech patterns. At times, immigrants interpret this as an unwillingness to communicate: "A lot of times even if they understand your little bit of English they act like they don't. Like, 'I don't know what you're saying.' It's a form of discrimination, I think, because if I go somewhere else and say the same thing, with the same words, with the same accent, they understand me." These concerns are shared by Black coworkers, some of whom believe that their Latin American coworkers "pretend not to understand" English, particularly "when they get in trouble." Union stewards who took Spanish classes at the workers' center reported that Latino coworkers would laugh at them or act like they couldn't understand when they tried to practice their Spanish at work.

Helton interviewed a Black man who had learned from a Mexican coworker how to say "lazy" in Spanish. The word was *huevón*, common slang for "lazy" in Mexico, used particularly among men. Little did he know, it is literally translatable as "big balls," and when he practiced his new phrase on a woman from Peru, she was terribly offended. He learned the hard way that language varies considerably among Spanish speakers from different parts of Latin America.[3] Beyond misgivings about one another's sincerity in communication, then, the proliferation of Latin Americans from different regions, countries, and ethnic backgrounds can also make cross-cultural communication even more complex.

IMMIGRANT DIVERSITY

As introduced in chapter 4 and underscored by the humbling case just mentioned, Latin America is home to many different peoples. In Mississippi, divisions and inequalities among immigrants along lines of nationality, race, and ethnicity run deep and represent several added layers of complexity for organizers. For starters, indigenous migrants often face a stigma in the eyes of their *mestizo* and Euro-descendant Latino coworkers. "I'm an Indian even if I wish I weren't," a young Mam-speaking Guatemalan told me. Another explained, "Many Mexicans make fun of us. 'You're a little Indian' or 'you're indigenous.' They say that we don't know how to speak Spanish, that we are ignorant. Racism still exists against our people."

The "Mexicans" some indigenous Guatemalan migrants see as discriminating against them, in turn, are often stigmatized by South Americans: "The problem is with the Mexicans. They don't plan to stay here, and if they get sent home it's easy for them to return. They will bear being treated badly because it's not a permanent situation for them, and they know they will eventually go home." This typical comment reflects what migrants from places like Argentina and Peru see as key differences between themselves and their Mexican and Central American coworkers. The former have mostly brought their families to the United States for what they hope is a permanent move, and they point out how much more difficult it is for a deported migrant to return to Mississippi from places in South America than from Central America or Mexico. Vicente Suárez from Argentina made a further distinction around the issue of legal status: "Look, you know that I am illegal, but it's one thing to be illegal and another thing to be undocumented. The United States knows that I live here because I came in through customs. I didn't come on rafts like the Cubans, I didn't come 'wetback' like the Mexicans, through the river or over the mountains. I came through customs and they stamped my passport. I am not undocumented."

So even while most Argentine and Peruvian poultry workers I met recognize the similarities they have with their Central American and Mexican counterparts—particularly their shared inability to communicate with English speakers, their vulnerability as unauthorized workers, and the exploitation suffered in poultry—many believe, just as many U.S.-born workers do about Latinos in general, that Mexican and Central American migrants are too willing to submit to employer abuse. I have heard South Americans compare these coworkers to "machines" and "gypsies." "They are more humble and submissive than we are. They do what they are told without arguing," explained Suárez. Racial stereotypes inform much of what South Americans in Mississippi think about their typically darker-skinned Mexican and Central American coworkers, and comments about lack of education, illiteracy, and even structural explanations for difference often take on the form of assumptions of "ignorance" and the inherent gratification of physical labor.

Mississippians tend, quite problematically, to lump all Latin Americans into one category, typically that of "Mexican" or "Hispanic." Even in Carthage, where the vast majority of immigrants are indigenous Guatemalans, their Mississippian coworkers generally don't know what country they are from, much less their identification as Mam. A visiting scholar from Guatemala quickly found this out when he attended a workers' center workshop in Carthage and asked African American union steward, Walter Glover, "What do you think of the Guatemalan people here?" Glover responded, "There is not that many, but we in America don't know the difference between Guatemalans, people from Latin America, Mexico, Puerto Rico. We see them all as Hispanic. I can't say that they Guatemalan because I'm not skilled in perceiving the difference between people."

"So do you think all the Spanish people are the same?" the scholar asked. "More or less. Similar. There are a lot of similarities," Glover replied. "But do you know the difference between a Mexican and a Guatemalan?" the visitor pressed on. "Not much," the steward responded. "They are all very hard workers." Paradoxically, just as countries in Latin America are beginning to recognize indigenous communities as holders of rights within the neoliberal state, these indigenous migrants now find themselves in Mississippi, where such political gains back home go unrecognized and intense homogenization begins anew.[4]

Despite some immigrants' distaste for the homogenization they experience when coming to Mississippi, where they are all lumped together as "Hispanic," when asked to reflect on the term a group of Central Americans and Mexicans came to a consensus that it may be advantageous: "I think it's a good term because it gives us a bigger group," stated one participant. Another added, "If we all work together, we can't be singled out for defending ourselves." And while discourse linking race and nationality with outdated social evolutionist ideas about submission and work leads some lighter-skinned South American workers to seek to distance themselves from their Mexican and Central American colleagues, others seem resigned to the reality that "the *morenos* and the *bolillos* think we're all Mexican anyway."[5] Together, these comments affirm the claim that the stigma associated with undocumented Mexicans "as a people reducible to the disposability of their labor for a price" affects the racialization of Latinos in the United States generally.[6] Yet while many Latin American workers agree, at least in theory, that there is strength in unity, the national, ethnic, and racial divisions between groups often keep them from realizing this collective potential.[7]

WHAT GOOD IS A UNION?

Language barriers and immigrant diversity are among the reasons poultry workers struggle to organize amid globalization; these are compounded by workers' diverging ideas about unions. Latino immigrant poultry workers' attitudes toward labor unions are shaped in large part by their experiences with unions in their home countries. For example, Argentina has a long history of organized labor, and many Argentine immigrants are quick to buy into the idea of unions in Mississippi, as well as to criticize the efficacy of those that exist. In contrast, a corrupt political party long controlled labor unions in Mexico, and as a result Mexicans in Mississippi typically express more skepticism of unions. During Guatemala's thirty-six-year armed conflict, membership in a labor union was at times reason enough for one's murder, and this bloody history may begin to explain some Guatemalan immigrants' apprehension. Regardless of these national differences, for complex and myriad reasons, many immigrant workers are reluctant to join unions in Mississippi. "I always suggest my students go talk to the union representatives about their problems at work," ESOL teacher Mary Townsend insists, "But I almost never get a positive response."

U.S.-born workers can also be skeptical of the unions. Among younger African American workers I have documented general recognition that unions can be useful, but perhaps more so in theory than in practice. While union stewards eagerly point to the job security, higher salaries, seniority, and grievance procedure outlined in their collective bargaining agreement as evidence of its value, many members are more likely to view the union as an outside party that stands up for them when needed: "Companies know that if you're in the union, you got something to stand behind you for all those tricky things they do to you. 'Cause you can just tell [the union], and then you got that big union rep coming in that knows what they're doing and ain't afraid."

Of course, many U.S.-born workers refuse to join the union altogether. These workers are disproportionately younger and newer to the industry. The main reasons they cite for not becoming union members include that they can stand up for themselves, they can better use their limited funds on things other than union dues, the union misspends its members' dues, the reps are not available when needed, and the union works against the people. "Why should I give them my hard-earned money when they never even here?" asked an acquaintance I queried over lunch one day. "What are they doing for us?"

Many immigrant workers hold these same critiques, but typically have additional concerns, including insufficient provision of Spanish-speaking representatives, lack of clarity about what a union is or what it can do for them, and fear that joining the union will trigger employer retaliation or limit job opportunities. In evidence of this last point, I was sitting in a plant's break room, serving as an interpreter for Bobby Robertson and talking with a woman from Mexico when the man next to her leaned over and told us that we should have our conversation at another time and place. "We have lots of problems, and we do need the union, but it's not safe for us to talk here. We are being watched," he said quietly.

Veteran workers who have been in the chicken plants longest tend to be unions' strongest champions. They often remind coworkers of what the plants were like before they were organized. When I asked Onita Harvey, who helped unionize the Choctaw Maid plant in Carthage in the early 1990s, to explain in a workshop why unions matter, she had a lot to say: "The union matters a lot because back in the old days we didn't really have no rights. We couldn't speak out; supervisors could do whatever they want to a team member; they could fire you for any reason; you didn't have nobody to represent you. The company paid you what they wanted to pay you; they hired who they wanted to hire; they wouldn't move you up. They could hire somebody off the street and move them up into positions ahead of you. But with the union we are being covered."

Alma Díaz, a Nicaraguan immigrant who had been at another union-ized plant for over a decade, echoed Harvey's position: "All the people who are there now, the new people, let's say, who've been here less than three years, don't want to do anything because they think the plant has always been like this. So they're always saying, 'No, the union doesn't do anything. We would get our raise, or have this, that, or the other with or without the union.' And I tell them, 'You can't say that because you didn't work here before there was a union. We fought for all of that.' They don't know what it was like before."

Long-standing union steward Brenda Turner stepped forward: "Our union reps are just our representatives. But the union, it's *within us* as the people. We got to stick together. Black, white, red, Mexican, anything, I tell 'em all, 'If we join together we can make a difference in the plant.' And we *have*. Because I have been there ever since '73." Fervent unionists like

Harvey, Díaz, and Turner gained this appreciation through bitter struggle, organizing to bring the unions in despite threats, lockouts, and violence. As a result, they strongly believe they *are* the union and spend countless hours trying to help others appreciate and share their perspective, often to their disappointment.

WEAPONS OF THE WEAK VERSUS THE BOOTSTRAP MENTALITY

Clearly, workers do not agree on the comparative costs and benefits of unionization. Along with the distinctions in their attitudes toward unions come equally stark differences around notions and forms of resistance. Mississippi poultry workers recognize that alternative employment options outside the industry are limited. This is particularly true of African Americans, who are comparatively less geographically mobile, have a longer history in the area's chicken plants, and often have a greater awareness of local histories of struggle than do their immigrant counterparts. To emphasize this point, an area pastor once suggested, "You can work full-time and still qualify for food stamps. The Black community senses that the pay rate in the plants is low and that they've been shafted. Their motivation to work is robbed. They are not a human resource. They are seen as chattel."[8]

Over time, African American poultry workers have developed varied and nuanced forms of covert resistance to their employers' abuses, which James Scott famously termed "weapons of the weak."[9] These include slowing down the processing line; jamming equipment; pulling debone cones off their tracks; taking longer breaks than permitted; and throwing, stealing, spitting on, or otherwise ruining the product. These "everyday acts of resistance" do not merely have utilitarian aims such as providing much-needed rest breaks or sabotaging employer profits; they also empower downtrodden workers to exercise power over the production process and reclaim their dignity in the face of an otherwise dehumanizing job.

In contrast, when asked about their work in chicken plants, Latin American workers regularly talk about the need to put up with poor conditions and treatment *(aguantar)* for the opportunity to get ahead *(salir adelante*). Helping family members improve their future life chances is the main factor motivating immigrant workers in Mississippi. Fear of retaliation, a desire to eventually go home or move on, and the immigrant "bootstrap mentality"—the idea that immigrants can and should pull themselves up by their bootstraps or succeed on their own without external help— shapes the ways in which migrants prioritize and make decisions that affect their lives. It also discourages many from expending energy on workplace organizing. While Latin American poultry workers endlessly gripe to one another about aspects of their work, they are often willing to sacrifice health, safety, and happiness for a chance at the American Dream. "Since we all come here to work, we don't care how they treat us," shared Efrain López. "There are people who say, 'I need this job, so I'd best just put up with all this humiliation,' and that's what most of us do."

With the exception of some forms of sabotage on the debone line that allow them to take a break, Latin American workers generally fail to appreciate their U.S.-born coworkers' acts of resistance. Without an analysis of the systemic causes of shrinking job opportunities for African Americans or the ways in which employment, education, and justice systems continue to fail people of color in the United States, immigrants are bound to misinterpret their coworkers' resistance in ways similar to those of plant management and dominant society—as laziness, poor manners, and lack of education. Similarly, Black Mississippians who have been facing the same bleak job prospects for generations will likely fail to identify with some new migrants' willingness to bow their heads, work as hard as they can, and put in uncountable hours of overtime with the hopes of "getting ahead."

WHITE SUPREMACY

As evidenced in earlier chapters, anti-Black racisms that permeate society incentivize many immigrants to distance themselves from Blackness, just as they encourage white Americans to do the same. Moreover, the notion that Black coworkers are lazy and unwilling to work is both widely and deeply held. "I think they're all a bunch of bums," Artemio Murrieta from Veracruz asserts impassively. Reflecting on his personal experience,

Baldomero Félix notes, "Back in Guatemala people have the idea that the Blacks are people who are made especially for working. But when we get here we realize that it's not really like that. When they see hard work that has to be done, they leave. Not one stays." Echoing this sentiment in defense of immigrant workers losing their jobs at Tyson (see chapter 8), another Guatemalan noted, "Where are they going to find that many people who will do the work of the Hispanics? I haven't met anyone. I can assure you that no person or color is going to do that work. Much less a white person. They don't want to get their hands dirty."

In the course of my work with the workers' center, I often asked Latinos to reflect on the experiences of African Americans and imagine what their coworkers might be going through at work. Sometimes I received blank stares in return. The concept was so far beyond many newcomers' familiarity that they seemed unequipped to even take a guess. Often they suggested that Black workers "have it easy," that they have no problems at work whatsoever. In this scenario, "problems at work" became equated with not having work authorization: "If a *moreno* is fired from the plant tomorrow, he can go apply wherever he wants to work, while the Hispanic, if he doesn't have papers, where is he going to look for work? It's going to be hard for him to find a job." One worker answered my question with her own: "You mean, Blacks and whites complain about work like we do?" Others postured that Black workers must have complaints about work, "but they don't talk to us about it." And, overwhelmingly, immigrants' comments suggested a widely held belief that Black Americans resent Latinos: "They think that we come here to steal their jobs, to take away the opportunities that they might one day have, that the opportunities are being given to the Hispanics, but it's not like that."

While some African Americans may hold a measure of resentment toward new migrants and often misunderstand their reasons for coming to Mississippi, their long history of struggle equips them with the critical consciousness necessary to begin to relate to Latino troubles in communities and chicken plants in the South (see chapter 5). A much bigger problem hindering poultry worker organizing in Mississippi is overcoming Latinos' buy-in to white supremacy. Thus, if immigrants disagree about the advantages or disadvantages of being lumped together under the category of Hispanic, they are even less likely to acknowledge a sense of collective struggle with Black Mississippians, despite the many valid reasons work in the poultry plants gives them to cooperate.[10]

UNION OUTREACH TO LATINO WORKERS

It is within this context of misunderstanding and divergence that poultry workers are today struggling for their dignity, basic rights, and a living wage. In 2014 just under half of Mississippi's poultry plants are covered by union contracts. Workers are represented by one of two different unions, the United Food and Commercial Workers' Union (UFCW) Local 1529 and the Retail, Wholesale, and Department Store Union (RWDSU) Alabama Mid-South Council. This number is down from twice as many union locals a decade ago. One disappeared when one UFCW local absorbed another, inheriting its contracts. But farther south, amid some legal turmoil the Laborers' International Union of North America (LIUNA) walked away from its Mississippi poultry contracts, leaving three plants—including the one Bobby Robertson had organized over a decade before—without representation.[11]

Each union local has a unique and compelling organizing history that is beyond the scope of this book. But one theme they share is that after successfully organizing African American poultry workers, they each had only very recently secured collective bargaining agreements at the plants they represent when immigrants began to appear in the area. In this sense, Bobby Robertson's story is not unique. Other unions in the area observed a similar shift in the workforce, which became more and more prominent as Latino immigrant workers reached a critical mass in the chicken plants by the early 2000s.

Some unions have been more proactive than others in responding to this challenge. For some, basic communication with Latino workers has been—and remains—a struggle. As this chapter's introduction suggests, LIUNA connected with Interfaith Worker Justice and other organizations in 2002 and, for a few years before its collapse, relied entirely on occasional bilingual student interns and activist researchers as translators both in and outside the plants to communicate with its Spanish-speaking constituents.

Around the same time, the UFCW recruited a young Panamanian American from Nashville who, together with a more established African American union representative, serviced the union's poultry contracts.[12] He left in 2004, and despite attempting to recruit and train up to a dozen others in the ensuing decade, the union has been unable to replace him. Latino members often complain that they have no way of communicating with the union. In fact, some workers don't even know they have a union. The turnover of Spanish-speaking staff has led to inadequate representation and poor follow-through. This has left many workers without the support they need, which has not helped the UFCW's credibility among immigrant workers.

In contrast to other Mississippi poultry worker unions' struggles to retain Spanish-speaking staff to recruit Latino members, the RWDSU took a slightly different approach. The organizing battles that led to the union's chicken plant contracts in the mid-1990s consolidated a solid group of African American worker leaders who continue to serve as union stewards today.[13] One of these, Onita Harvey, recognized the need to reach out to her Spanish-speaking coworkers and began cultivating a relationship with a young Mexican worker she knew as Jorge Morales. After overcoming his skepticism, Morales began recruiting Spanish-speaking coworkers into the union as members and stewards, and he established a relationship with the workers' center in early 2004.

Interestingly, while Morales was Mexican in a plant where most immigrants were Guatemalan Mam, he crucially recruited key members of the Guatemalan community, including long-standing leader Baldomero Félix, to join him as stewards. The union reports that thanks to the dedication of its old and new stewards, coupled with the early success of its partnership with the workers' center to contest unjust document reverification (see chapter 8), its Latino membership skyrocketed. Soon, the union boasted hundreds of Guatemalan members.

The RWDSU prioritized building the capacity of Latino poultry workers in Mississippi and elsewhere in the region to recruit more Spanish-speaking members, and in 2004 the union held its first annual Latino Stewards Conference in Montgomery, Alabama. Morales, Félix, and other Spanish-speaking organizers and workers led the event entirely in Spanish while the union's white and Black English-speaking leadership sat in the back of the conference room. These long-standing union staff members had no interpreter and were unable to understand much of what was being said, but they were visibly in awe of the contagious enthusiasm in the room among those present. Yet while it was innovative in its focus on building unity and enthusiasm among Latino workers and considerably ahead of other Mississippi poultry worker union locals in its outreach to this new constituency, the effort brought criticism from Black poultry workers who expressed concern that the union was showing favoritism toward immigrant workers. The union continued to hold its regular annual stewards conference, which was heavily attended by Black stewards, but few Latino workers participated there.

In the case of both the Latino and non-Latino stewards conferences, the gatherings consisted largely of rallying participants around the labor movement, sharing their work and union experiences with one another, and celebrating those attendees who had signed up the most members over the course of the year. There was little in the way of nuts-and-bolts training about the job of a union steward or about the organizational structure of and opportunities for advancement within the union itself. Moreover, while the conferences were framed by their participants' identity (Latino/Spanish-speaking vs. U.S.-born/English-speaking), there was almost no discussion of the changing face of labor that might help members come to terms with the differences among them or begin to understand how the chicken plants were using this to their advantage. By late 2005 a union representative wondered aloud if the separate meetings were causing more harm than good. He questioned if the union should work toward bringing the two groups together for future conferences, but said the idea was met with skepticism from some others in the union.

PARTNERING WITH THE WORKERS' CENTER

Just a decade ago, labor scholar Janice Fine broke ground when she documented the rise of workers' centers across the United States.[14] She and others characterized this as a new movement in response to a growing immigrant workforce, an increasingly informal and service-oriented economy, and a deterioration of wages and working conditions brought about by neoliberal globalization.[15] Fine catalogued 137 centers around the country working with and on behalf of low-wage and immigrant workers in recognition of these groups' heightened vulnerability to exploitation and discrimination and limited institutional support.

Workers' centers do a wide range of work, from providing social and legal services to education, advocacy, and organizing functions in order to help workers respond to abuses, improve opportunities, and organize to challenge structural barriers.[16] This variety makes them difficult to categorize, as they represent a unique hybrid that blends the work of social service agencies, labor market intermediaries, and social movement organizations.[17]

Unlike most unions, workers' centers are "profoundly local organizations, arising in response to specific conditions in particular locations," and tend to be independent from larger institutional affiliations.[18] On one hand, this gives them the potential to be more directly accountable and responsive to their members. On the other, it means they are typically underfunded, understaffed, and undernetworked and often constrained by the funds and programming priorities of private foundations.[19] Ten years ago only a small portion of workers' centers belonged to formal networks encouraging the sharing of knowledge and resources, though Héctor Cordero-Guzmán and colleagues suggest the number may be growing.[20] The Mississippi Poultry Workers' Center joined the Interfaith Worker Justice workers' center network when the latter was established, which aided the center in securing financial and human resources, opened spaces for sharing best practices with other centers, and served as an institutional anchor during periods of organizational restructuring.

While most workers' centers recognize the importance of identity, scaffolding their work explicitly on members' ethnic, racial, gender, and linguistic solidarities, they also often focus their efforts on a particular industrial sector.[21] They have grown especially in industries historically overlooked by unions, such as restaurant work, domestic work, and day labor, and in locations where workers have grown frustrated with their unions and are looking for alternatives.[22] Fewer work in close collaboration with unions, and some even arose through explicit critique of existing union efforts.

Despite, or perhaps in response to this criticism, as the workers' center movement was building, the more traditional labor movement was also realizing the need to expand its base to better incorporate a growing immigrant workforce. In this climate, while some workers' centers emerged where unions had failed or in industries that unions had largely ignored, others were founded in partnership with organized labor.[23] In Mississippi, due to its genesis in dialogue with unions (along with other actors), as well as its focus on an industry with an established—if beleaguered—history of union presence, the workers' center set out to collaborate with existing unions to multiply the labor movement's potential for growing poultry worker power.

The workers' center sought to amplify the unions' efforts and address the gaps in their service by providing them with the legal, cultural, and linguistic expertise necessary to better engage and support immigrant poultry workers. The unions learned that they could depend on the workers' center to provide translation and interpretation services, increase meeting turnout, offer technical assistance, and foster relationships with local immigrant rights advocates, community leaders, and immigrant workers. Similarly, Spanish-speaking workers realized that the workers' center would help them communicate their grievances to the unions and try to ensure union follow-up. They also quickly learned that the workers' center would step in to help them when the union couldn't.

It was thrilling and fulfilling when it worked well—when injured workers received the benefits they deserved; when workers spoke out about their struggles and were heard at community forums, press conferences, and the state capitol; when union stewards felt empowered by workers' center programming; and when immigrant workers felt acknowledged and incorporated more fully into the unions' membership, for example. The relationship between the workers' center and the RWDSU at times resembled an ideal strategic collaboration. The union relied on the workers' center for advice on employment and immigration law and encouraged its members' participation in workers' center initiatives beyond the union. Moreover, the union invited workers' center representatives to speak at regional steward conferences and gatherings of its international staff, where the collaboration was championed as an example of a successful union-community partnership.

But the problematic moments outshone the positive ones. Union representatives sent immigrants with all sorts of issues to the workers' center for help. Understandably, they couldn't spend their limited resources helping someone get their utilities connected, their children enrolled in school, or their brother out of jail. But the workers' center resisted being reduced to a support role for the unions and their immigrant members and struggled with how to build more strategic, collaborative relationships that would advance workers' abilities to stand up for themselves. Whereas the center was motivated by a commitment to building worker power, the unions were often focused on consolidating their membership, and they tended to value the workers' center primarily as a means to this end. Despite repeated conversations about the mission of the workers' center to improve conditions in the chicken plants, some union partners continued to promote it as the place union members could go for assistance with nonworkplace problems.

Serving as a liaison between immigrant workers and their union representatives—and even as a strategic adviser to the unions—was trying for all involved. The unions at times felt hassled by the workers' center, which had high expectations despite limited resources and made repeated demands on their time, while the workers' center often felt frustrated by the unions' lack of response to worker grievances. Problematically, workers began seeing the workers' center as an (often ineffective) arm of the unions. Under these conditions, trust was elusive, the potential power of a union–workers' center partnership was underrealized, and the collaboration often proved unfulfilling for all involved. Meanwhile, the workers' center leadership found itself at times prioritizing its shaky partnership with the unions over helping workers build power or supporting their efforts to hold their union accountable (see chapters 8 and 9). This dynamic led to fissures within the workers' center itself. By 2006 the unions and the workers' center had taken a step back from one another to evaluate the terms of their engagement.

My narrative of the workers' center has focused mostly on its partnership with unions. Indeed, some of our most successful movement building happened in collaboration with them. But it is worth mentioning that our efforts at the workers' center were not bound by that collaboration. In fact, much of our work happened beyond the confines of our relationships with unions. Our Workplace Injury Project, for example, helped approximately fifty poultry workers access medical treatment they needed, assisted in the recovery of over half a million dollars in disability benefits for injured workers, and educated hundreds of individuals about their rights to a safe and healthy workplace and to workers' compensation in the event of a plant-related injury or illness. In Canton we assisted law enforcement in apprehending a corrupt police officer who extorted upward of $100,000 from Latino immigrants during traffic stops, orchestrated the testimony of over fifty individuals to ensure his conviction, and helped the victims apply for and receive U-Visas to legalize their immigration status. In Morton we facilitated the connection of long-aggrieved poultry workers with legal aid attorneys, which resulted in a class action lawsuit against Koch Foods to end aggression, discrimination, sexual harassment, and other abuses at the hands of company supervisors. In sum, the workers' center's efforts resulted in many important accomplishments for and with poultry workers independent of these workers' unions. Nevertheless, I believe that the promise for change is greatest when workers' centers and unions come together in support of poultry worker justice.

REFLECTIONS ON THE STRUGGLE

Organizing such a diverse cross-section of workers in the poultry industry in today's Mississippi is a daunting task. At its most basic, people don't speak the same language. This hinders workers' communication with one another as well as with their unions. Beyond linguistic differences, racial, ethnic, and national stereotypes trouble relationship-building efforts. The label "Hispanic" obscures the incredible diversity present in Mississippi's Latin American population. Hailing from over a dozen countries, these new immigrant workers can easily identify more differences among them than similarities, inhibiting collective action. Moreover, the deep-seated anti-Black racisms outlined in earlier chapters and reinforced by everyday life and work in Mississippi stand in the way of their recognition of the common struggle they share with Black coworkers.

Workers also disagree about the benefits of unionization. While there is considerable variation on an individual level, these differences are compounded by workers' vastly divergent backgrounds. African American and immigrant workers utilize different "yardsticks" when assessing the costs and benefits of organizing in response to workplace exploitation.[24] While the former draws on everyday forms of resistance as a means to reclaim their humanity within a racialized legacy of labor exploitation in the South, the latter arrives to Mississippi in hopes that work opportunities, however painful, will allow them and their families in the United States and back home to "get ahead" and better their social standing. Thus, while I've suggested dozens of reasons that Black and Latino workers might identify to unite in defense of their rights in the chicken plants, their divergent ideologies surrounding the potential (or lack thereof) for backbreaking work to lead to financial and social prosperity in the United States remains a serious obstacle to collective organizing.

While differing in capacity, approach, and outcomes, all of Mississippi's poultry worker unions recognize the need to bring new immigrant workers into their membership to stay viable in the twenty-first century. Whether their strategies include trying to service their contracts in Spanish or training immigrant worker leaders to become more effective union stewards, however, these approaches fail to address the problems that keep Black and Latino poultry workers divided. Such approaches are substantially hobbled by their fundamental orientation toward a politics of class. If only workers could recognize the benefits of uniting as workers, the labor movement suggests, they could rise up against the capitalists who exploit them.[25] This universalist Marxist approach to social movements, while romantic, has been roundly critiqued for its essentialist repression of diverse manifestations of cultural difference, subsuming all heterogeneity by championing class struggle.[26]

Even in the case of the Latino Stewards Conferences, which draw on workers' identities to build solidarity among a particular group of members, the union's focus is fundamentally oriented toward a politics of class. The emphasis is on building membership and better representing workers, and identity is leveraged only in the sense that it allows the union to bring that particular constituency more fully into the folds of union membership. This approach ignores the nuanced politics of race, ethnicity, gender, nationality, language, and citizenship that divide workers. Moreover, discussion of the problems of globalization, racism, and white privilege is absent. Education comes into play only to the extent that it helps the union reach its organizing goal, and there are few spaces for members to strengthen their critical consciousness.[27]

Of course, these are not the labor movement's only challenges. Lest I come across as leveling an inordinate amount of critique at the unions, we must recognize that the limitations I've identified in their approach stem in large part from the pressures they face under advanced capitalism and in the Right to Work South. Their resources are so scarce and staff stretched so thin that they have little choice but to focus on keeping membership numbers up in order to survive. Servicing contracts through this business-model structure keeps representatives eternally busy, leaving limited time for the luxury of education or organizing in a broader sense. Thus, while my critiques are substantial, they are not unique to these particular organizations or individuals; they are part and parcel of the climate of labor organizing under neoliberalism.[28]

But it is precisely these limitations that have spurred the growing workers' center movement across the country. Unmet challenges like those faced by worker organizers in Mississippi poultry suggest that, despite their problems, union–workers' center collaborations remain promising paths forward in places like Mississippi today. As the following chapters show, workers' centers can amplify and sharpen union efforts, moving their focus from strictly traditional "bread and butter" issues such as wages and working conditions to the broader struggle for dignity and respect at work, which is an increasingly strong motivator for immigrant workers organizing under neoliberal globalization.[29] Moreover, because of their attentiveness to the intersecting oppressions of race, class, ethnicity, language, citizenship, and other identity markers, workers' centers are poised to move worker organizing efforts beyond a class-based politics toward one that places worker difference at the heart of the conversation about a new movement for justice.[30]

8 Walking on Eggshells

ILLEGALITY, EMPLOYER SANCTIONS, AND
DISPOSABLE WORKERS

The back corner of the fellowship hall at Saint Anne's Catholic Church in Carthage is packed this morning, evidence that the crisis at the local Tyson plant is escalating. The thirty-or-so poultry workers in the room and I talk informally in small groups, enlarging our uneven circle of chairs again and again as we make room for new arrivals. The mood is somber, the buoyancy and hopefulness of our prior gatherings submerged by the weight of the current moment. Finally, as the tide of newcomers ebbs, I call people together. "If you can hear my voice clap once. . . . If you can hear my voice clap twice." A hush falls over the room before I get to three.

"Gracias por venir," I begin in Spanish. "Thank you all for coming." Most people in the room today are indigenous Mam speakers from the Guatemalan highlands, but my practically nonexistent Mam and most people's limited English forces us to communicate in the only language we share, Spanish. I briefly jostle the rubber filaments of the multicolored Koosh ball in my hand. At the workers' center, she who holds it has the right to the group's attention.

"If you're here, you've probably received the Social Security No-Match letter by now. You're probably wondering what is going to happen to you. You may have already lost your job. The purpose of today's meeting is to share our experiences, ensure we all know our rights in this situation, and figure out how we want to respond to Tyson."

As I look around the circle, I recognize many familiar faces and see at least as many newcomers. "Why don't we begin by going around the room to make sure we all know one another and share why we're here?" Folks nod and comment briefly in agreement. "I'll start us off. As many of you know, my name is Angela, and I work with the Mississippi Poultry Workers' Center. We are a small nonprofit organization that helps people learn about and stand up for their rights in the chicken plants. In collaboration with the church leadership and with the union, we have been trying to support you since this crisis began last year." After providing a brief overview of our efforts to date and explaining that I am also a researcher studying poultry worker organizing, I pass the ball to the young man on my left.

"Good morning," he greeted bleakly. "My name is Apolino. I'm waiting to see when they're going to fire me, since I already received the letter. It's been about a month now. My wife already lost her job." He hastily passes the ball.

"I'm Rigo. They also gave me the letter. I don't know if they're going to fire me or not. I just don't know." The ball exchanges hands again.

"Hi. My name is Pancho." He sounded more upbeat than Apolino and Rigo, and his tone gave me hope. "Like the others, I also received the letter. But like everyone else, I can't go to the Social Security Administration. So I'm here to see if together we can come up with a solution. I think it's great that we're all here." With a smile, he gently tosses the ball to his cousin.

"My name is Ana." She casts her gaze down at the red and yellow strands and pulls them taut between her fingers as she speaks. "I was fired along with that guy over there." She glances up and nods across the room. "I don't know if there were others. I came today to see how this can be fixed."

"My name is Odilio. I haven't received the letter yet," confesses the older man on Ana's left. "They haven't said anything to me. I don't know."

"*Buenos días.* I am Manuel. I haven't received the letter, but everyone else has, so I'm just waiting to see when they are going to call me to the office. We'll see what happens."

And so the introductions proceed for the next hour as the Koosh ball slowly makes its way around the room, each participant adding his or her concerns to the growing wave of uncertainty, frustration, and resentment.

.   .   .   .   .

This crisis was not the first time Tyson Foods, one of the world's largest poultry processors, was forced to confront the realities of its heavy reliance on immigrant labor. In 2001 the corporation was indicted on thirty-six charges that it recruited undocumented immigrants to work in its processing plants across the rural U.S. South and Midwest.[1] While prosecuting attorneys argued that the company cultivated a corporate culture that encouraged management to hire undocumented workers to lower costs and maximize profit, Tyson alleged that company policy makers had no knowledge of the smuggling scheme executed by its middle- and lower-level managers.[2] After a Mexican store owner in Tennessee admitted he had worked in concert with Tyson to get "papers" for its workers, and following the resignation of several individuals in management, a federal jury deliberated for less than a day and acquitted Tyson on all charges.[3]

My research in Mississippi began shortly following the court's decision, and over the next few years I witnessed Tyson Foods engage in a prolonged operation to purge the largest chicken plant in the country of hundreds of unionized immigrant workers. At the same time, anthropologist Nicholas de Genova was calling for a new scholarship of migration that—instead of studying the lives of the undocumented, as had often been done in the past—would take as its ethnographic object the "legal production of migrant illegality."[4] Such research, he envisioned, would critically investigate the intricacies of immigration law, including its historical production, stated aims, and effects. Instead of taking policy makers' word about the objectives of legislative and administrative actions at face value, it would scrutinize how these policies played out at the level of practice, allowing us to document not only their consequences but the very sociopolitical process of "illegalization" itself. This chapter and the next embrace De Genova's call in order to analyze and better understand the complex and often convoluted relationships between policies of the nation state, corporate decision-makers, immigrant laborers, and worker advocates.

Figure 16. Justice and Dignity campaign postcard. Photo by author.

As the Koosh ball was passed around the circle that September morning, sentiments of fear gradually gave way to those of hope, growing into a chorus committed to organizing to change the course of history. In the months that followed, I participated in a countercampaign, organized by the affected workers, their union, and the workers' center, in an attempt to stop the unjust firings. The campaign called for "Justice and Dignity" in the form of an improved corporate policy that would simultaneously serve the interests of the company, its workers, and their communities. Herein lies the story of that struggle and my assessment of its theoretical and policy implications.

"ILLEGAL" WORKERS, IRCA, AND EMPLOYER SANCTIONS

To many Americans it feels utterly unnoteworthy that undocumented immigrants cannot legally work in the United States. This is a relatively recent phenomenon, however, as only thirty years ago workers were rarely asked to show their "papers." In 1986 Congress passed the Immigration Reform and Control Act (IRCA). In addition to enacting this country's last sweeping amnesty program, which legalized approximately three million undocumented individuals, IRCA criminalized the act of hiring people without employment authorization and implemented a system of "employer sanctions" that would, through a series of inspections and fines, punish employers who knowingly hired these workers. Employers would be required to check documents to verify the identity and work authorization of all new hires, record this information on an I-9 form, and archive the completed form in their records.

While immigrant and workers' rights advocates were pleased with the path to legalization provided by IRCA, they were concerned that the power to verify workers' documents at whim would give employers a mechanism for discriminating against workers who were injured, organizing, or otherwise deemed "undesirable."[5] To mitigate opportunities for abuse, advocates lobbied Congress for strict limitations to employers' document verification powers. In compromise, the final law includes numerous antidiscrimination provisions. First, it recognizes that employers are not trained immigration officials and that their responsibility is to verify only that each document provided by the new hire "reasonably appears on its face to be genuine."[6] If it looks legitimate, the employer must accept it. Second, except for in a few limited circumstances, employers are authorized to verify such documents only within the first three days of hire. Finally, the I-9 form includes a long list of acceptable documents that can be used to verify a new employee's identity and authorization to work. Workers are permitted to choose which of the accepted documents they will present, and employers are legally barred from demanding any particular document on the list.

Advocates argue that IRCA's employer sanctions provision served to drive many workers underground, "expanding the underground economy, creating national insecurity, undermining everyone's civil liberties, dividing workers from one another, and driving conditions down for all."[7] In sum, employer sanctions served as the genesis for immigrant "illegality" in the workplace, emboldening corporations' intimidation and exploitation of undocumented laborers.

THE SOCIAL SECURITY NO-MATCH LETTER: ROUND ONE

In 2004 Tyson Foods operated five processing plants in Mississippi. Some of these were acquired the previous year, when Tyson bought out locally

owned Choctaw Maid Farms. At the time of the transfer, Tyson became
the "successor employer" of the existing—and largely Latino immigrant—
workforce at these plants. While federal law does not require a successor
employer to reverify its workers' identity and work authorization documents, Tyson began to do just that. In the spring of 2004 Tyson began
reverifying select employees' documents at its newly acquired Carthage
facility. Those whose names appeared on a Social Security Administration
(SSA) "No-Match" list or letter were told they had three days to go to the
Social Security office, rectify the problem, and present "corrected" documentation or they would be fired. The vast majority of workers on the
No-Match list were immigrants, and alarm spread quickly.

The RWDSU immediately called a meeting, and more than 100 immigrant workers showed up at a soccer field to compare notes. The union's
convocational power was palpable, as we strategized in the sweltering
Mississippi midday heat. Only two years prior, the plant of 2,200 workers
had only 270 union members. Today there were nearly 800 members, many
Latino—a huge feat in the Right to Work and largely monolingual rural
South. The union's popularity among immigrant workers was remarkable
and unmatched by other unions in the area. As described in chapter 7, its
success was due in large part to the foresight and persistence of one long-
standing African American steward, an inquisitive Mexican worker she
mentored, and the union's subsequent investment of resources into hiring a
Spanish-speaking representative and conducting Latino steward trainings.

Days into the crisis, workers were already assessing their options and
beginning to think about alternative job prospects, which were limited.
The union vowed to file a grievance should the company terminate any
employees based on receipt of the SSA No-Match letter. A union representative later recalled, "I went to Tyson and I told 'em. I said, 'This is
what we're gonna do. You can tell as many people as you want to go [to
SSA] to get this paperwork corrected. I don't care. But the first person you
fire, I'm filing a grievance and I'm carrying it to arbitration."

The workers' center sent a community sign-on letter, endorsed by
eleven local and state-level organizations supporting poultry workers, to
the local plant's head of Human Resources. The letter proposed a meeting
between Tyson and the letter's signatories to "discuss additional ways
that we can help you and your workers comply with the obligations and

responsibilities surrounding the SSA No-Match letters while maintaining a stable workforce and economic security in the community."[8] To our surprise, within days, top executives from Tyson's headquarters in Arkansas arrived via private jet to meet with the union, concerned community groups, and worker advocates.

At the meeting the workers' center provided Tyson with a binder of nuanced legal information about the No-Match letter, the I-9 document verification process, and the limits to employer sanctions in hopes of convincing the executives that it would be in the best interest of the company, the workers, and the community to reconsider the proposed termination policy. Among this information was an overview of the mission of the SSA— to "advance the economic security of the nation's people"—a charge wholly unaffiliated with the pursuit of federal immigration enforcement.[9] It also included an explanation of the No-Match system, clarifying that it exists to "ensure that employers and employees have an opportunity to correct the information in order for workers to receive proper credit for their earnings."[10] In fact, SSA began sending the letters to employers simply because its records were often out-of-date and there was a better chance of notifying an affected worker of the problem through the workplace than by mail to an outdated home address. Moreover, participants at the meeting highlighted the following No-Match letter passage:

> You should not use this letter to take any adverse action against an employee just because his or her social security number appears on the list, such as laying-off, suspending, firing, or discriminating against that individual. Doing so could, in fact, violate state or federal laws and subject you to legal consequences.[11]

Tyson's representatives agreed to suspend firings based on the No-Match letter pending their review of the materials. The workers, their union, and community organizations all celebrated and publicized this success as an example of what can be achieved through community-labor partnerships.

GREEN CARD EXPIRATION: ROUND TWO

The celebration was short-lived. Two months later workers again notified allies that documents were being reverified. Tyson was true to its word;

the new strategy had nothing to do with the No-Match letter. Instead, it had found another avenue for firing immigrant workers. This time, local management was reverifying the documents of workers whose green cards had expired. Workers felt humiliated. They reported that Human Resources was calling people off the production line in the middle of their shifts, amid their U.S.-born coworkers' snickering the word "illegal" and hollering *"Adios, amigo!"* Once in the office, management would confiscate their badges and send them home. Workers were given three days to present a green card with a new expiration date.

Affected workers formed a committee and concluded, based on legal research, that an expiration date on a green card reflects only that the card must be renewed, not that the bearer's work authorization has expired.[12] Tyson's unnecessary and possibly unauthorized reverification of workers' documents was a serious concern for workers, but even more palpable was a collective feeling of distress at the ways in which local management was conducting the layoffs. The workers' center, in collaboration with the worker committee, the union, and local churches, conducted Know Your Rights workshops on the topic of document reverification and immigrant workers' rights. At workshops and meetings, worker testimonials expressed fear, uncertainty, humiliation, anger, and worthlessness:

> The most frustrating thing is that no one knows how they are choosing who to call into the office. Some of us have green cards with dates way past expiration, and we haven't been called; others have dates that are nearing expiration and they have already been fired.

> I go to work every day wondering if today will be my day. I just wish they would tell us before or after work instead of pulling us off the line in front of everyone. It's humiliating.

> Sometimes I feel like I'm not worth anything to Tyson. I have given them all I have for the last six years, and now I'm left hanging, waiting to see when [the personnel officer] will decide she is done with me.

Stories abounded among workers about so-and-so who presented false documents with an updated expiration date within the three-day limit and was allowed to return to work and so-and-so who spent $900 to get the newer-looking *láser* green card but was inexplicably sent away. Then there was the couple who bought updated papers from the same black market vendor, and she was permitted to continue employment while he was denied.

In addition to insisting that the process of green card reverification be stopped immediately, the worker committee also demanded transparency; just, equal, and humane treatment for all workers; and thirty-day written notification of all reverifications. The workers' center contacted Tyson with another sign-on letter detailing these concerns, and eight Tyson executives returned on their corporate jet for a second meeting with twenty union and community leaders in late 2004.

All were cordial as we sat around a conference room table. Tyson's people explained that they had reviewed the SSA No-Match information they had received in the spring and found it "very helpful," yet no revised policy was forthcoming. Religious leaders expressed concern for the "ripple effect" the firings would have in the community. Union representatives stressed that there were less punitive policies Tyson could lawfully adopt. Civil and immigrant rights advocates cautioned against the discriminatory potential for Tyson's policy to shake out along racial and ethnic lines. Tyson's representatives recognized that this was a "very, very serious issue" for the company. The discussion went in circles, with Tyson insisting that it was being a good corporate citizen by carefully reverifying Team Members' work authorization and identities, and with community members and worker advocates explaining that Tyson's policy was overly castigatory because it went above and beyond the requirements of the law. The encounter ended with Tyson's executives agreeing to again review the information, take into account the discussion, and finalize company protocol.

In a rather uncomfortable irony, everyone ignored the enormous white elephant in the room—the thousands of undocumented workers who, at that very moment, were slaughtering the chicken that Tyson feeds the world each day. In my analysis, all involved in the discussions were silenced by IRCA's employer sanctions policy, which has obliged undocumented workers to purchase false papers to be hired, incentivized companies to be unaware of their employees' undocumented status to avoid legal liability, and compelled immigrant and workers' rights defenders to pressure companies to adopt more humane policies defined by the problematic boundaries of current laws. The parties in the conference room that day, and others like us, were not alone. The federal government, too, maintains an ever-escalating charade of "border security" while ensuring that lawmakers' campaign contributors—the leaders of businesses like Tyson—have an unlimited supply of malleable and expendable laborers to continue growing corporate profit.[13]

JUSTICE AND DIGNITY! ROUND THREE

Following the meeting the mass firings in Tyson's Mississippi plants again halted. By the end of the year Tyson had sent letters to the SSA, the Department of Homeland Security, and the U.S. attorney general, among others. This correspondence detailed Tyson's proposed termination of workers receiving No-Match letters, explained that "a number of third party organizations have asked us to reconsider this policy," and requested an official opinion on their proposal.[14] Tyson waited nearly nine months for a response, finally receiving one from the commissioner of the SSA herself. She wrote, "You should not take adverse action against an employee just because his or her SSN appears on the list of unmatched SSNs."[15] Nevertheless, in August 2005 the company instituted a slightly revised but equally punitive policy of firing workers appearing on the No-Match list. This time workers were given a full thirty days to correct their problems with the local SSA office before being terminated, and Tyson would implement its policy gradually over a few months.[16]

Immigrant workers' panic reached new heights as each week more were called to the office and given their notice. The union renewed its pledge to file a grievance should any worker lose a job on account of the No-Match letter, arguing that such action constituted unjust firing, in violation of the union contract. The workers' center again began holding worker meetings to educate workers on their rights and support them during the crisis. Each meeting started with a somber round of introductions, as illustrated in the beginning of this chapter.

For immigrant workers Tyson's actions constituted a disaster, which they were quick to compare with Hurricane Katrina, the devastating storm we had survived just months prior, and Hurricanes Stan and Wilma, which had recently ravaged their families in Central America and Mexico. But what seemed to upset them most was their realization that Tyson was planning to eliminate them gradually. The plant was actively recruiting U.S.-born workers, and in their thirty-day grace period, immigrants with years of experience were personally training their replacements. "They are getting rid of us little by little, and it makes me so angry! It's like they don't recognize our value to the company," one meeting participant protested. "They know it's not in their best interest to lose us," another added, "but they're doing it anyway! And they're doing it in the way that will hurt Tyson the least."

There was talk of going on strike to show Tyson the impact of its actions. Some people wanted to make it "hurt" and force the company to face running the plant without its immigrant workforce. This plan was abandoned once they understood that a work stoppage was a violation of the collective bargaining agreement and would give Tyson legitimate grounds for firing them all.

In lieu of a strike, the workers decided to carry out a postcard campaign to exert pressure on Tyson. They hoped that public outcry, coupled with the company's concern for its image and desire to stay out of the media spotlight on issues related to its immigrant employees, would encourage executives to reconsider. Workers designed a postcard to be signed by workers and community members and forwarded to Tyson's headquarters. They chose the theme "¡Justicia y Dignidad!/Justice and Dignity!" to appeal to their employer's moral grounding and crafted a logo and a statement for their supporters to sign. The logo depicted poultry workers balancing on the scales of justice opposite Tyson's big red chicken, the two sides hanging evenly in line with each other. "The message that this sends," the group agreed, "is that we are all equally valued, the workers and the company too." The accompanying statement read, in part,

> Dear Tyson Foods . . . I believe that all persons should be treated with dignity, that all human beings are equal in the eyes of God, and that employers have a moral duty to conform to these principles. . . . I call for Tyson to stop retaliating against all workers in Carthage, MS, and in all Tyson plants whose names appear on the SSA no-match letter. I stand with the thousands of Tyson workers who demand their dignity and respect.[17]

The workers' center produced a thousand postcards, and affected workers and supporters began collecting signatures door-to-door, at churches, and even in the parking lot at the local Walmart. At meetings they com-

Figure 17. Preparing to send postcards to Tyson. Photo by author.

pared stacks of completed postcards, encouraged one another, and marveled at their collective progress.

But by late September immigrant workers were losing their jobs en masse. As before, the firings were not uniform, and workers complained of the arbitrary nature and utter lack of respect they felt. Every week's meeting included a report on the latest firings and a request for an update from the union regarding the class-action grievance it had filed. But the union was often absent from these meetings, with its one Spanish-speaking representative stretched thin, responsible for servicing many other plants in the South. In his absence, workers made comments like,

"Where is the union, anyway?" "Didn't they send word with anyone?" and "Their absence speaks volumes." When the union rep was in town, workers rebuked him for not being up-to-date on the status of the grievance.

Each meeting was smaller than that of the previous week, as workers found jobs elsewhere or left Mississippi for good. Nevertheless, they would go on to collect more than eight hundred signed postcards before mailing them to Tyson's headquarters in late 2005. This time Tyson did not respond. By the end of the year, more than two hundred workers had been fired, the vast majority union members. Uncounted others quit their jobs out of fear and in anticipation of what was to come.

EXAMINING TYSON'S MOTIVES

Throughout this crisis, workers, union leaders, and advocates struggled to understand and explain Tyson's actions. Some speculated that the closing of a unionized plant nearby, and Tyson's obligation to find displaced workers positions at its remaining facilities, might be driving the new policy, but this was never confirmed. Others questioned if Tyson's actions might be related to the fact that the plant had only recently come under Tyson management, suggesting that Tyson was just "cleaning house." But, weakening this hypothesis, workers at another newly acquired Tyson plant in Forest did not face similar attacks. Some union supporters were convinced that the company felt threatened by the union's growing Latino membership. Still others believed that the actions formed part of Tyson's ongoing public response to its indictment in federal court. While Tyson's representatives framed its policy as a straightforward effort to be a good corporate citizen, looking closely at this case suggests that a series of broad pressures acted as incentives driving Tyson's termination of its immigrant workers in Carthage.

First, it is quite possible that, as some workers believed, Tyson's policy was fueled, at least in part, by its desire to weaken the workers' collective power. One union representative told me, "I always will believe that when the membership started building in the Latino community, they targeted that group." Others agreed. "See, we got eight hundred members now, and we're steady rising up, and they don't like that," asserted veteran steward Onita Harvey. "It won't affect us today, because we got the contract now," said steward Patrick Herring. "But when negotiation time come again, if you don't have the membership, you can't ask for much." I asked how the union would survive if its members were continually forced out. "In the long run," Herring worried, "it won't. See, that's what these big companies are doing. They come at every angle to destroy the unions."

Such suspicions are indeed well founded. Not only do veterans of the labor movement have a depth of experiential knowledge substantiating this fact, but scholars of organized labor have documented an array of corporate antiunion tactics over the years.[18] Tyson has been unabashedly fighting unionization for decades, as suggested by its founder's pleas to workers at a newly acquired North Carolina plant in 1989: "Why should you and I, as individuals, have to have somebody work between us? It's like hiring a lawyer, and both of us paying him, when we could have thrown him out the window. In the last few years, of the companies that came with us, five plants that were union voted them out, where they belong."[19] Whether union busting was the intent of Tyson's reverification campaign in Mississippi is up for discussion, but it was, without a doubt, a somber consequence of the corporation's actions.

Other workers and advocates believed that Tyson's insistence on reverification was part of an ongoing response to its 2001 undocumented immigrant-recruitment scandal. They argued that, as a damage control strategy, the company was positioning itself as a thoughtful and conscientious employer, carefully following federal immigration law to—and even beyond—the letter. In an interview in early 2006, a union representative with this perspective reflected on the events unfolding:

> The bottom line is, and I'll believe it till the day I die, they don't wanna fire these people. But they're so afraid of what happened to 'em [in 2001]. They're afraid that the government's gonna come in and just kill 'em 'cause they told 'em they would. So they're going *beyond* now. They may lose their case against this grievance in arbitration, but then they can go to the federal government and say, "the arbitrator *made* us put these people back to work; it wasn't our decision." So they're protected. It's cheaper for them to do that than it is to say, "Okay, we're not gonna fire 'em," and take the federal government on.

Tyson had been intensively building its brand since the late 1970s, spending millions on marketing and advertising each year.[20] Its indictment in federal court was widely covered in the press and threatened to undo much of this work. At the same time, its acquittal suggested that as long as upper-level executives maintain a clean image, buttressed by corporate policies, they can distance themselves from actions taken at a local level and thus insulate the company from legal and ethical liabilities associated with on-the-ground hiring of undocumented workers. Thus, the court's decision may have incentivized companies to adopt policies at the national level largely for public relations purposes, regardless of local realities. Indeed, in the years following its scandal, Tyson has crafted an image of corporate social responsibility, evidenced by initiatives such as its "Statement of Core Values," "Tyson Cares" program, and "Team Member Bill of Rights." "Sustainability is an important part of the culture at Tyson Foods," noted Tyson's website at the time it was purging its immigrant workers in Carthage, "and we take very seriously the company's responsibilities to customers, shareholders, Team Members, and the communities where we live and work."[21] By this logic, the uneven application of such policies at its processing facilities across the country becomes irrelevant.

Finally, Tyson may have conducted mass firings of Latino immigrant workers in this location because they were not its only source of low-cost, disposable labor. Chapter 3 details how African American workers entered Mississippi's chicken plants following the Civil Rights Movement of the 1960s, as industries yielded to Black residents' demands for equal opportunities. Unlike the white women who worked in the plants before them, however, Black workers' possibilities for upward job mobility were more limited when the industry began recruiting immigrants (see chapter 4), and unemployment rates in rural Mississippi, particularly among Black youth, remain high.[22] So when Tyson began to purge its Carthage plant of immigrant workers, a large pool of African American applicants quickly filled their places, ensuring profits would not suffer. Sophisticated in its understanding of the racialized labor markets in which it operates, Tyson likely considered this reality when implementing its reverification policies.

AWAITING RESOLUTION

As the union awaited its day in court, it struggled to rebuild. For many months in 2006, the Carthage plant ran short-staffed, and workers pulled ten- to twelve-hour shifts to make up for the lower number of bodies on the line. The union's membership dwindled. The workers' center's organizing efforts in Carthage suffered during this time too, as Tyson employees' personal time was more limited than before and worker leaders who had lost their jobs were scrambling to find new employment, driving nearly an hour to neighboring counties in search of work in other chicken plants. Several other more established union members at Tyson were frustrated by the replacement hires, whom they perceived as young, disinterested in issues of workplace justice, and "ain't gonna be there long anyway." When I asked Herring if this would be a problem for Tyson, he shrugged, "No. They'll just replace 'em. That's what they want." Indeed, high rates of attrition do more damage to organizing efforts than to company profits, and the industry has adapted production processes to accommodate extreme worker turnover.[23]

To make matters worse, turnovers and vacancies in the union's Mississippi staff at this time demoralized Black and Latino workers alike. The union promoted an African American shop steward from Tyson's Carthage plant to service its Mississippi poultry contracts, but some workers complained that they were unsatisfied with his performance, and he didn't last long in the position. The union's Spanish-speaking representative, whose dedication had dramatically increased the union's Latino membership in previous years, was pulled to Alabama to build membership in one of the union's newly acquired chicken plants with a nearly 100 percent Latino workforce. Thus, the few immigrant workers who remained at Tyson in Mississippi no longer had union representation with whom they could communicate, while the plant's African American workers faced working with a local representative they didn't fully trust.

As 2006 wore on, the union fought for a collective-action arbitration that would consider every reverified and fired worker's grievance as part of the same policy and be decided in one judgment. Meanwhile, Tyson argued for the individual arbitration of each worker's case, which would be financially untenable for the union. In addition to making the arbitration harder for workers to win, these technical maneuverings delayed resolution of the issue and further weakened support for the union. As months passed, workers lost faith in long-standing union representatives, who had advised them nearly a year earlier that the process could take up to three months. Despite the union's urging that they "stay and fight," most couldn't afford to wait for arbitration in hopes of reinstatement. When a decision finally arrived—ultimately based on the review of just one worker's grievance—it came down in favor of Tyson.

By the summer of 2007, there were only about twenty immigrants remaining in the plant, down from at least a thousand three years before. Ten years after Tyson's purge, its Carthage plant still employs remarkably few Latinos when compared to a decade before. Many immigrants formerly employed there continue to work for other poultry processors in neighboring counties. While some have moved to Forest, Morton, and Canton, others feel Carthage is their home away from home and risk long commutes to work to maintain their sense of community.[24] Moreover, today undocumented workers have been forced even deeper into the shadows. No longer able to work using a false or made-up Social Security number, they now take greater risks, spending upward of $1,000 to obtain the identity and Social Security number of a United States citizen just to make a living. Those who were fortunate enough to get rehired by Tyson under a different identity cast their eyes down and hope they won't be remembered when management inevitably asks them, sooner or later, "Have you ever worked here before? You look familiar." This is but the most recent consequence of Tyson's (and other companies') shift in labor practices in the years following its indictment, spurred by the broken immigration and labor laws of the United States.

Were the story to end here, one might conclude that this ethnography points to a sea change in U.S. employers' preference for hardworking, docile undocumented immigrants, standing in dramatic contrast to much of the established literature on immigrant recruitment. After all, Tyson's corporate policy regarding the SSA No-Match letter in 2005 resulted in its purging the Carthage plant of its immigrant workforce almost in its entirety and replacing it with local African American workers. I do not believe, however, that this case represents a dramatic shift in employer preference or labor relations, nor is it indicative of a broader move away from the employment of immigrant workers. Rather, like most employers across time and place, Tyson was responding to a set of social, economic, and political pressures that shaped its employment decisions. Though we cannot be sure which of these were most salient in the minds of corporate policy makers and local management, it appears that some combination of a growing union membership, a preoccupation with the ramifications of current laws governing the employment of immigrant workers, heightened concern for corporate image, the abundant availability of disenfranchised African American workers, and perhaps other business concerns at the national, regional, or local levels all created conditions that led to the events that unfolded in Carthage.

THE NO-MATCH DEBATE GOES NATIONAL

The arbitration decision in this case set a precedent that went against the SSA's stated procedures, and others followed suit. Advocacy groups across the country were inundated with reports of firings induced by No-Match letters, and they worked to produce materials to educate employers, advocates, and workers alike.[25] Then, in the summer of 2007, the United States Department of Homeland Security (DHS) unveiled new rules *requiring* employers to fire workers whose names appeared on the SSA's No-Match list.

In the days following the announcement, the UFCW International Union issued a scathing press release, accusing the Bush administration of promoting an immigration reform policy "that essentially mandates federal racial discrimination."[26] Before the new rules could go into effect, DHS faced a lawsuit charging that its rules violated workers' rights, imposed burdensome obligations on employers, and would illegally threaten the jobs of U.S. citizens and work-authorized individuals because the SSA's database is marred by human error.[27] The complaint's content was supported by a report by the SSA itself, citing that "of the 17.8 million discrepancies in the SSA database that could result in a no-match letter, 12.7 million (or over 70%) belong to native-born United States Citizens."[28] Two days later a federal judge issued an order temporarily blocking DHS from implementing the new regulations. In the judge's opinion, the plaintiffs "raised serious questions as to whether the new [rule is] . . . beyond the statutory authority of the Department of Homeland Security and the Social Security Administration."[29] In response to the legal challenge and mounting pressure from other community and independent groups, by the close of 2007 DHS had abandoned its proposed rule.[30] Two years later, under a new presidential administration, DHS announced a new workplace immigration enforcement policy focusing on "increased compliance through improved verification."[31]

The push to use No-Match letters as the basis for a wrongheaded national immigration enforcement policy appears to be behind us.[32] In their place, however, Immigration and Customs Enforcement began promoting an Internet-based employment-eligibility system known as "E-Verify." Prominently placed billboards tout E-Verify's speed, stating simply, "Employment Verification. Done," and DHS developed a special logo—"I E-Verify"—that companies participating in the program are encouraged to use on their products and advertising.[33] While employer participation in the program is supposed to be voluntary, bills proposing federal Comprehensive Immigration Reform introduced in recent years are attempting to make it mandatory. These proposals come on the heels of similar efforts at the state level. In 2008 Mississippi became one of the first, and by 2012 twenty states had mandated the use of E-Verify for at least some public or private employers.[34] Despite widespread enthusiasm for this system, a serious flaw with E-Verify remains unresolved: its implementation relies on the database of the Social Security Administration, the same one responsible for producing the No-Match letters.

RECONSIDERING IRCA'S EMPLOYER SANCTIONS

Tyson's indictment and acquittal, as well as its corporate policy and local actions in Mississippi in the years that followed, raise critical questions about U.S. immigration law, employer hiring (and firing) practices, and the exploitation of low-wage workers at the turn of the twenty-first century. In 1986 IRCA criminalized the hiring of an undocumented worker and instituted "employer sanctions" as an enforcement mechanism. This broken system encourages underground illicit activity by both workers and employers and gives corporations yet another handle through which to wield unequal power over a vulnerable low-wage workforce. It has had far-reaching effects on transnational corporations, on workers of different backgrounds, and on strategies used to advocate for worker rights.

Tyson's reverifications in Carthage demonstrate how corporations maneuver to unjustly regulate the lives and livelihoods of low-wage workforces, as well as how they are finding new ways to shift the risk of undocumented employment onto immigrant workers themselves. They further illustrate how exploitation of the most vulnerable of workers has been legitimated by both the actions and inactions of the neoliberal state. Finally, they highlight the limitations inherent to localized, grassroots struggle and the obstacles to labor organizing in the face of corporate greed and state indifference.

The term "undocumented worker" took on new meaning after the passage of IRCA, and corporations, migrants, their advocates, and unions have been incentivized to find new ways to operate within the system. For employers, this has often meant "unknowingly" accepting applicants' falsified documents and devising policies meant to convince the state (and the general public) that employers are in compliance with the law. More important, it has given them undue power, enabling them to turn a blind eye to their own disregard of labor and employment laws when it behooves them and then abruptly "discover" a need to reverify workers' documents in times of union activity, workplace injury, corporate restructuring, or other moments of convenience.

For migrants seeking employment, the passage of IRCA made it illegal to be hired without papers, bolstering an ever-growing black market of document falsification.[35] The proliferation of E-Verify will not fix this problem; it will exacerbate it. Instead of presenting fake papers to secure work, undocumented migrants now have little choice but to purchase the identity of a work-authorized individual, thus fueling the burgeoning underground economy of identity theft.

Worker advocates, for their part, have been forced to come up with inventive ways to continue supporting the rights of immigrants within the confines of dysfunctional state policy, including instructing them never to discuss their legal status with anyone, lest they provide their employers with "constructive knowledge" that they or their coworkers are undocumented. This broken system spurs advocates to argue for all the reasons the No-Match letters are flawed *except* the ways in which they unjustly target undocumented workers and to reason with employers about why it is in their best interest not to take actions that might provide them with constructive knowledge as to their employees' legal status.

An in-depth exploration of Tyson's practices in one Mississippi plant allows us to analyze the effects of state and employer policies on workers' lives and on unions' and advocates' attempts to better working conditions. It makes clear that "employer sanctions" is a misnomer that, rather than sanctioning employers for their illegal employment of undocumented workers, deepens these workers' vulnerability. The policy does so by making migrants' very "illegality" the condition through which corporations can exploit and ultimately dispose of them. De Genova asserts that such "illegality" is lived "through a palpable sense of deportability, which is to say, the possibility of deportation, the possibility of being removed from the nation state."[36] Yet if deportation represents the ultimate threat that renders undocumented migrants a most vulnerable workforce, the "illegality" endorsed by IRCA's joining of immigration and labor law has resulted in the more acute—if less severe—hazard of having one's status "discovered" by an employer and thus potentially losing work that is increasingly hard to come by. Together, the dual threat of deportability on one hand and job loss at the whim of an omnipotent employer on the other ultimately reduces undocumented immigrants to an expendable commodity.

In illuminating one constellation in which differentially positioned transnational actors—immigrant workers, their advocates, and corporate policy makers—navigate the dysfunctional nexus of labor and employment law in the United States, the case of Tyson in Carthage reaffirms that "the existence of a legal prohibition creates around it a field of illegal practices."[37] Chapter 9 explores another configuration of the multiple illegalities produced by IRCA's employer sanctions and their deleterious effects: the proliferation of third-party labor contractors.

9 Plucked

Emilio Hernández and I drive in anxious silence through the heavy evening air. Like his friends and roommates in the Green House, Hernández came to Forest from Veracruz, Mexico, after hearing of abundant work opportunities in chicken slaughter. In his new home for under a week, he has agreed to let me accompany him to the offices of the local third-party labor contractor to apply for a job.

Our ride is a short three minutes to Forest's downtown district. Neither of us has been to TransMundo Contractors before, but the folks at the Green House have assured us it will be easy to find.[1] I am eager to put a face to the larger-than-life image I've constructed of Bruno, a hulking TransMundo middleman and its principal liaison with workers in the local immigrant community. I'm also a bit nervous. Will he recognize me from my work advocating for workers' rights? Will he turn me away? Will my presence affect Hernández's odds of getting hired? Adrenaline pulsing, I maneuver the car into a parallel parking spot on the curb and turn off the engine. Recognizing that my companion has a lot more on the line than I do, I breathe deeply and turn to him with a smile. *"¿Listo?"* I ask. "Ready?"

We walk about two blocks until we encounter the unmarked glass door. Hernández enters the colorless, minimalist office first, and we pack in with at least a dozen other migrants seeking work at three nearby Koch Foods chicken plants. As the only woman and non-Latino here, I am clearly out of place. We sit in beat-up folding chairs lining the walls and listen quietly as Bruno calls people one by one to fill out applications. The process is remarkably brief: "What is your name? Phone number? Address? Can you start on Monday?" Bruno jots down people's responses. Still, the wait is long, and, at my urging, Hernández gets up to ask if he can have a paper application to fill out in the meantime. Hardcopy proof of TransMundo's application requirements could be valuable for worker organizers and advocates, if we could get our hands on one. He returns to his seat empty-handed.

Once his turn with Bruno finally comes, Hernández learns that he, too, will start on Monday on the night shift in Forest. No paperwork exchanges hands. No questions about work authorization are asked. No I-9 or other government-required forms are completed.[2] Hernández asks the questions we diligently rehearsed before leaving the Green House: Who will his employer be? "TransMundo," Bruno replies. Will he be compensated in the event of a workplace injury? This elicits a raised eyebrow and a one-word "no." But Bruno is unfazed, and he quickly moves on to the next eager applicant. I am relieved to go unrecognized, and my companion appears pleased to have a job. We thank Bruno and slip out into the muggy night.

.   .   .   .   .

This chapter tells the story of the efforts of TransMundo's undocumented immigrant workforce and their allies to organize for better pay, improved working conditions, and job security in the years that followed this encounter. It highlights the under-the-table practices of third-party contractors, poultry companies' evasion of employer liability, contract workers' struggles to improve their pay and working conditions, and unions' and worker advocates' roles amid systems of vast economic inequality.

There is a long history of scholarship on labor contractors' roles in structuring agricultural fieldwork in the United States.[3] Few have analyzed labor subcontracting in an industrial setting, in particular its effects on immigrant workers' abilities to organize.[4] Those who have tend to focus on moments in which organizing efforts were successful.[5] This case, however, tells a different story, one that might be deemed a partial success at best.

Figure 18. Ready for the night shift. Photo by John Fiege. Courtesy of FiegeFilms.com.

In a complex and perverse unfolding of events, the courage and exasperation of the most vulnerable catalyzed a union organizing drive that ultimately led to the ratification of a collective bargaining agreement at the
Koch Foods plants in Forest—from which TransMundo's workers were
explicitly excluded. The tale that follows illustrates how the interests of the
state, corporations, the labor movement, and individuals in relative positions of power converge in the exploitation, exclusion, and criminalization of
immigrant communities, trapping workers within a triangle of exclusion.

THE PROLIFERATION OF *CONTRATISTAS*

While contractor crews have long been utilized in the poultry industry for
chicken "catching"—the dirty job of crating live chickens in the "houses"
where they are raised in order to transport them for slaughter—the proliferation of contractors *inside* chicken plants coincides with the industry's
recruitment of undocumented immigrant workers. The rationale behind

this expansion can be traced back nearly thirty years to the passage of the federal Immigration Reform and Control Act (IRCA). As discussed in chapter 8, IRCA criminalized the act of hiring individuals without employment authorization. But rather than curbing U.S. companies' reliance on undocumented labor, the legislation's implementation engendered complex employer maneuverings to avoid the brunt of IRCA's penalties.

The use of third-party contractors has flourished as one such strategy.[6] By relying on contractors to recruit and hire workers on their behalf, employers seek to outsource the accountability demanded of them by IRCA, avoiding problems such as those faced by Tyson Foods, as told in the last chapter. But, as the story of TransMundo's workers illustrates, the benefits of the rise of contractors go far beyond enabling the manipulation and evasion of government regulations. Using neoliberal logic, labor flexibility also ensures corporations can quickly maneuver in the global marketplace, adding or shedding labor costs—such as employees—quickly as needed.[7] As we shall see, they also serve to segment the labor force, weaken worker power, and undermine unions.[8]

Most poultry operations in Mississippi have used labor contractors in the new millennium to supply portions of their undocumented workforce. In the state's chicken plants, contract workers work on the production lines alongside direct-hire workers. Both groups do the same repetitive and dangerous work. But while direct-hire workers are employed by the poultry plant, paid a set wage determined by either the company or a union contract, and receive whatever (minimal) benefits are due to company workers, contract workers are hired and paid by a third-party contractor, receive significantly lower pay than their coworkers, and are entitled to no benefits. If the plant is unionized, contract workers are typically excluded from the bargaining unit and receive no union representation. Nevertheless, they are supervised by the same plant management, which has the power to discipline and fire all workers, regardless of whether they are contract laborers or direct hires.[9]

Third-party contractors often operate under the radar. Some are informal operations that pay their workers in cash and fail to comply with state and federal regulations. Others are registered corporations recognized by the state but still avoid fulfilling their legal responsibilities as employers, such as purchasing workers' compensation insurance, paying employment taxes, or complying with the I-9 document verification process. Some charge workers a placement fee of several hundred dollars in exchange for a job. Their offices are often hidden and open mainly in the evenings after nearby businesses have closed for the day, but their locations are well known within the immigrant community. For many new migrants—who for lack of time, money, or volition have not secured papers on the black market—*contratistas* offer one of the few mechanisms for entry into chicken plant work. Immigrant rights advocate Becky McCrady articulated this catch-22: "It's twofold. The contractors do get our undocumented immigrants work. And, you know, what do you do if there's no other way for them to enter in? The problem is they just don't take care of 'em at all. A lot of abuses go on. Immigrants are just laborers, and if they have a complaint or whatever, they're easy to get rid of." During my time in Mississippi I heard many immigrants and their supporters express a similar ambivalence toward Mississippi's third-party contractors.

Poultry processors typically pay contractors by the head for each worker provided. In addition to eliminating the need for plants to locate and process a never-ending stream of new applicants to compensate for continual turnover in the workforce, partnering with contractors also effectively outsources employer responsibility and risk related to the hiring of undocumented workers. By claiming not to be these workers' employers, companies attempt to insulate themselves from state sanctions for the hiring of undocumented workers. While this transfer of responsibility has often worked well for the industry, it is a superficial fix that has increasingly been contested by workers' rights advocates.

Most contractors and chicken processors in Mississippi would legally qualify as "joint employers," despite their maneuverings. This juridical classification is based on the definition of "employer" in the federal Fair Labor Standards Act, which determines who is an employer based on an "economic reality test." The test includes consideration of the "degree of alleged employer's right to control the manner in which the work is performed," the "alleged employer's investment in equipment or materials," and "whether the service rendered is an integral part of the alleged employer's business," among other indicators.[10] Because contract workers use company equipment, follow company orders, and do the same work as direct-hire employees, poultry plants run the high risk of being found

194   PLUCKED

jointly liable for employer responsibilities and abuses of contract workers' rights in a court of law. This legal judgment has been a crucial tool for unions and workers' rights advocates seeking to hold employers accountable for abuses in the poultry industry.[11]

TRANSMUNDO CONTRACTORS

According to one of its owners, TransMundo Contractors first started providing workers to Koch Foods' predecessor, B.C. Rogers Poultry, in the late 1990s. A former B.C. Rogers administrator explained the partnership was driven by a decision that "we didn't want to deal with the papers; we didn't want to deal with taxes." For the first few years of operation, it appears TransMundo didn't register with the state of Mississippi. It was eventually incorporated by two partners, themselves immigrants from different parts of Latin America.

Unlike many other third-party contractors, TransMundo's owners were established businessmen in Mississippi's Latino community. Besides supplying processing plants with workers, by 2004 they also provided dozens of chicken-catching crews to poultry operations in the area. And in addition to TransMundo Contractors, they or their family members also owned or had owned a number of other local businesses, including "Hispanic" stores, Mexican restaurants, Latin nightclubs in Forest and other nearby towns, and an international money transfer company through which workers could wire remittances back home. They also sponsored a weekly radio show in Spanish. The diversified nature of these businesses suggested that TransMundo's owners were less likely to disappear in times of uncertainty or trouble, as their competitors had over the years.

WORK STOPPAGE

For the first several years of operation, TransMundo's new hires were rarely, if ever, asked for work authorization documents. This changed around 2003, when Koch Foods allegedly asked TransMundo to produce copies of all its employees' completed I-9 forms. Workers reported that when they went to pick up their paychecks one Friday afternoon, Bruno began advising them that they needed to bring him their papers. Artemio Murrieta nonchalantly recounted the events, telling me, "I got some fake papers. They said it didn't matter that they were fake." He purchased false documents from a black market vendor, Bruno completed the necessary I-9 form, and nothing more on the matter was ever discussed. Another worker alleges that he and five friends bought their new documents directly from Bruno, paying about $300 each. Workers remember this time as just a small shift in TransMundo policy that cost them money but came and went relatively smoothly.

According to a representative of the United Food and Commercial Workers (UFCW), which began representing workers at the Koch Foods plant in neighboring Morton several years earlier, by 2004 TransMundo was providing nearly five hundred workers to Koch Foods in Forest, almost half of the two Forest plants' total workforce.[12] The vast majority of these worked on the night shift. While not *all* immigrants in the plant were employed through the contractor, an estimated 90 percent were. TransMundo workers started out earning $6.00 an hour—$7.00 if they were in a "premium" position, which consisted of the more difficult debone tasks.[13] Typically within the first six to twelve months, workers would receive a twenty-five-cent raise, and eventually a second. Their earnings would max out at $6.50 and $7.50 per hour. These low wages were made slightly more bearable by the fact that TransMundo did not deduct any taxes from workers' paychecks.

I knew Emilio Hernández and a handful of other TransMundo workers from the time I spent doing preliminary research and facilitating workers' rights workshops in Forest and hanging out at the Green House in 2002 and 2003. But I met many more in early 2004, when Hernández and some coworkers visited me on a Friday after work, upset about TransMundo's latest actions that would lower their take-home pay. They showed me their check stubs as they indignantly explained that TransMundo had begun to deduct taxes from their paychecks. In addition, the contractor had withdrawn many workers' raises, reducing all who were making $6.50 and $7.50 back to $6.25 and $7.25. The pay stubs indicated the deductions were for Social Security and Medicaid taxes (FICA). Coupled with the pay decreases, these deductions had resulted in a substantial pay cut of approximately 10 percent—roughly $30 on a $300 weekly paycheck. "Are they

allowed to do this to us?" the workers demanded of me. "They are," I replied
as their disappointment grew. "In fact, the government requires them to do
it." This was the beginning of my baptism by fire on the topic of employer
tax obligations.

The workers wanted answers that Bruno had not given them, and I was
of little help. "Why us?" "Why now?" Frustrated by the financial impact
the changes had on their already-meager earnings, by the end of the weekend Hernández and a group of coworkers were planning a work stoppage.
They hoped it would force the owners of TransMundo to answer their
questions and reverse the new policy. When contract workers arrived at
work on Monday, they refused to go to the production line. Eventually
someone from the plant's management came to the break room to find out
what was wrong. Using a translator, they explained why they were upset,
and the administrator claimed to know nothing about the new changes in
TransMundo policies. He said they should talk directly with Bruno, but
the workers demanded to speak with someone higher up. They asked that
Koch Foods summon TransMundo's owners to meet with them on their
next break, and when the administrator agreed, they went to work.

But on the next break, neither of the owners was present. Instead,
workers were being called into the chicken plant's office in pairs. They
reported later that week that they refused to go to the office two by two,
insisting that the issue "wasn't a problem of just two of us, but of all of us.
If they have something to say, they should come here and talk to all of us
together." Upset, the contract workers decided they would not return to
work until they could speak with a TransMundo representative. Sitting
and standing on tables, they organized their work stoppage. When the
break ended, only a few workers—all direct hires—returned to their positions. One of these recalled the emotion and power of the sit-in: "That's
where you could really see the percentage of Hispanics that work in the
plant, because all the processing lines were empty."

Supervisors yelled at the strikers to get to work. They refused.
Management emerged, threatening to permanently replace them should
they fail to return to work immediately. They remained unmoving. Finally,
the plant called the local police, who soon arrived to "assess" the situation.
Intimidated, terrified, and defeated, the workers returned to their positions and completed their shift.

After work a large group of them went to TransMundo's office in search of answers. A local pastor and I also met with one of the owners that week to better understand the rationale behind the changes. On both occasions the owner explained that Koch Foods was requiring him to deduct taxes from workers' paychecks to keep his contract with the processor. "People think I'm making a lot of money, when in fact," he claimed, "I'm just one of the little guys struggling to make ends meet." Echoing others along the poultry chain of production, he asserted, "The only way we make it is volume." He had lowered the workers' wages to compensate for the employer's portion of FICA taxes he would now have to pay to match the employees' withholding. The money had to come from somewhere, and it was only "fair," he told us. But workers were incensed by this assertion and remained unsatisfied with his explanation.

The workers' center organized two workshops in the following days to answer workers' questions about their rights and their employer's responsibilities. Meanwhile, Hernández and others expressed interest in unionizing for better pay and working conditions. Unionization, we strategized, would be one clear way to either eliminate TransMundo or force it to operate in a more just and transparent fashion. The workers' center reached out to the UFCW local at the Koch Foods plant in nearby Morton, whose leadership had expressed concern in the past about the third-party contractors in the area and had considered the possibility of organizing the Koch Foods plants in Forest. The union enthusiastically sent two representatives to attend the workshops—the local's only Spanish-speaking rep and an organizer from the union's International.

The workshops were held at a church that served the Latino community—a safe space except for one detail we had overlooked: Bruno lived across the street and participants worried he might monitor their attendance. Concerned, we agreed to find a different location for future meetings. Despite this deterrent, dozens of people packed into the fellowship hall. While we helped workers understand the basics about U.S. wage and hour laws, FICA taxes, income taxes, and other paycheck deductions, the workshops became spaces for participants to individually and collectively recount the events of the week and voice their concerns, fears, and convictions. We also talked about unions and dispelled doubts made evident by questions such as, "Is a contractor the same as a union?" The

Figure 19. The union meets with Latino workers. Photo by John Fiege. Courtesy of FiegeFilms.com.

union reps spoke about their interest in organizing Forest poultry workers and the difficulties they might face in gaining representation rights for those employed by TransMundo. Participants expressed great interest in getting the union on their side, imploring its representatives to act quickly and forcefully: "We should be in the union too. We are all working for the same company."

In the following weeks union representatives met with U.S.-born Koch Foods workers and indicated their interest in organizing *all* workers, including contract employees and direct hires. "It doesn't make any difference if they work for TransMundo or TransPundo," I overheard one worker affirm at the meeting. "As a group of people, we want everyone on our line to get the same pay, same benefits, and equal treatment! We're gonna have to do something, y'all. It's the old conquer-and-divide thing. What's bad for them is bad for us; what's good for them is good for us. We are all one people—working people. We need to be singing out of the same hymnbook." Such passionate pleas were well received by the mostly African American workers present; their responses suggested they were convinced of the plan to organize all workers in the plant regardless of employer, immigration status, race, or anything else separating them from one another.

But weeks passed in which the TransMundo workers got no news from the union, and they began asking the workers' center about next steps. Could we help them encourage the union to take action through a community sign-on letter? Were we in a position to help the TransMundo workers organize in the absence of the union? We repeatedly relayed their sense of urgency to the union local, but given the delicate nature of our partnership, the workers' center's leadership was reluctant to step on the union's toes. Rather than take action, we waited. In time we, too, grew impatient with what we perceived as the union's caginess.

UNIONIZATION

By April our union partners finally had news. After several weeks of discussion, Koch Foods had agreed to neutrality in exchange for silence. The processor was willing to allow the union in as long as there was no publicity. Should the company's name appear in the media, be it positive or negative coverage, the deal was off. Eager to avoid a protracted and expensive fight, the union readily accepted the compromise. Union reps would be permitted into the plant, receive lists of all workers, and be given the opportunity to convince them of the benefits of union representation. Workers would be allowed off the line in small groups to speak with the union, which would have to gather a majority of workers' signatures, authorizing their representation to earn the right to become the plant's collective bargaining agent. Because so many workers were recent immigrants from Latin America and the union had only one Spanish-speaking representative, a workers' center colleague and I accompanied the union to the plant with the explicit objective of ensuring Latino workers' participation in the process.

We arrived around 11:00 P.M., along with a group of the union's staff who had come from across the state to support the effort. As we walked from the parking lot to the plant's side entrance, Forest's familiar pungent bouquet grew stronger. We were passing a tractor-trailer truck being loaded with chicken products when I noticed a steady stream of brown liquid dripping out the back doors into a growing pool on the asphalt below.[14] I choked back my gag reflex as we walked inside.

It was nearly midnight when we received the worker lists, only to find they were streaked with indelible ink. Looking closely, we quickly realized that all the contract workers' information had been blacked out. I was aghast that the plant's management had reneged on its word, and I implored the union to speak up about this breach of agreement. The union reps were far more seasoned and much calmer about the situation than I, and, despite my protests, the lead representative maintained that the best approach was to go ahead and start talking with the direct-hire workers, for whom we had information. Once we had signed up as many direct-hire workers as possible, he reassured us, the union would then seek access to the contract workers. "Let's just start tonight with what we've got," he concluded. It became clear there was little I could do to alter the night's course of events. I felt as powerless before the union as I did before the corporation. Disillusioned, I joined my colleagues in the "card check."

We gathered in a small gray break room at the back of the plant, and the union reps briefly explained the plan. Along with their bilingual representative, my workers' center colleague and I would talk with Spanish-speaking workers while the rest would talk to the English speakers. We would ask the workers about their biggest concerns on the job, respond with an overview of the union and potential ways it could help address these concerns, and ask them if they would like to have the union represent them.

Typically in situations like these, those who support the union are asked to sign an authorization card, which is then used in a card check to demonstrate to the employer the workers' support for the union. In this case, the union was asking workers to sign membership forms instead. These served the same purpose, but, in addition, should the union become the workers' collective bargaining agent, the membership forms gave the union permission to deduct dues from the worker's paycheck for a period of at least one year. I heard the veteran organizers explain this clearly and talk with workers about the value of their $5.50 weekly dues—"It costs less than a six pack!"—and I followed suit. I was troubled to note that the union's Spanish-speaking organizer, who was newer to this work, seemed to regularly omit this detail when asking workers to sign. But because the

TransMundo workers were excluded from the card check, most workers who came to us that night were English speakers and therefore talked with the more senior organizers. For the same reason, our help was not needed on the day shift the following morning. Apprehensive but hopeful, my colleague and I returned home to await news about next steps.

By the end of the week an overwhelming 90 percent of the plant's direct-hire workers had signed membership forms in favor of the union—a tremendous victory in a town and an industry that have long acted to suppress labor organizing. Unfortunately, the union's success appeared to weaken its drive to pursue a similar process with the contract workers. Despite their pledge, union leaders did not immediately go back and request access to those who had not been permitted to participate. And because we were working to build a relationship of trust with a union that was skeptical of our intentions, again the workers' center's leadership opted not to press the union too vigorously.[15] Defeated or distracted, TransMundo workers' pressure on the workers' center and the union dissipated, and with the resignation of the union's only Spanish-speaking representative shortly thereafter, migrants had limited paths through which to engage the union. Organizing Forest's contract workers was put on a back burner.

CONTRACT WORKERS' MARGINALIZATION FROM THE UNION

The following year the union successfully negotiated a contract for Koch Foods' direct hires in Forest. It included a clause stating that the number of contract workers at the plants could never grow beyond current numbers. The union's efforts to unionize the TransMundo workers again gained momentum. Union staff paid Bruno a visit at TransMundo to make him aware of their presence and let him know the UFCW intended to organize the contractor's workers, "At which time," they chuckled, "he forgot how to speak English." Meanwhile, a new bilingual organizer on loan from the International reported that he was getting contract workers to sign authorization cards. Union reps continued discussions with the workers' center about legal strategies for pressuring Koch Foods to transfer TransMundo's workers onto the plant's payroll, thus eliminating the contractor and bringing the workers into the collective bargaining unit. In turn, the union was in dialogue with at least one midlevel manager for Koch Foods, sharing this information with him.

A colleague and I joined a union representative for lunch with this administrator one afternoon. Over fried chicken, okra, and hush puppies, we spoke of Koch Foods' legal liability as a joint employer and enumerated the many missteps of TransMundo over the years for which the plant could be held responsible. The best action Koch Foods could take, we maintained, was to convert the contract workers to direct hires, thus becoming a "successor employer." Since the plant already had copies of TransMundo's I-9 forms, it would not be required to reverify workers' documents. This was the cleanest way to make a break from TransMundo, and Koch Foods would be able to maintain that as soon as it had learned of the contractor's past noncompliance with federal tax law, it had immediately taken steps to sever the relationship and rectify the problem. The approach, we suggested, offered a win-win solution for the poultry processor, the contract workers, and the union.

As we finished our banana pudding, the Koch Foods administrator thanked us for the information but committed to nothing. We later learned that our meeting had paralyzed him with fear that he could go to jail, and he allegedly told the union representative in hushed tones that he was "damned if I do and damned if I don't." He referenced the infamous 2001 Tyson Foods court case, in which the poultry processor was accused of knowingly recruiting and hiring undocumented workers. In that instance, it was precisely midlevel managers like himself who had ultimately taken the blame. He worried about getting caught in a similar situation.

Koch Foods took no action, and by the close of 2005 that administrator was no longer with the company. The workers' center and the union strategized over how to organize the TransMundo workers into their own bargaining unit, which would equip them to negotiate directly with TransMundo for better compensation and working conditions. But despite successful attempts at unionizing contract workers in other industries and other parts of the country in the recent past, the idea didn't gain traction.[16] What if TransMundo closed its doors in response, causing the hundreds of workers who had initially brought the union to Forest to lose their jobs altogether? Organizational fears about who would take the blame—the union or the workers' center?—discouraged action. Unfortunately, neither organization had brought contract workers into positions of leadership whereby they could help to decide whether such a risk was worth taking. Collaboration between the union and the workers' center on this issue waned.

When I left Mississippi, Koch Foods continued to dodge federal immigration and employment laws by staffing its production line with undocumented workers employed through a third-party labor contractor. But in the years that followed, the poultry processor began to reduce its reliance on contract workers. A UFCW representative reports that when the collective bargaining agreement came up for renegotiation in 2008, only fifty contract workers remained in the Forest plants. Sometime later, long after I had stopped following the daily happenings in the plants and the workers' center had closed its doors, Koch Foods relinquished its last contract worker, and TransMundo dissolved.

TRIANGLE OF EXCLUSION

Ironically and incredibly unjustly, in this scenario the most vulnerable of workers organized on their own accord, called on an international union for help, and catalyzed a massive membership drive that led to the successful negotiation of a collective bargaining agreement, and didn't gain a thing. How could this happen? I argue that Hernández and hundreds of undocumented contract workers like him were caught up in a triangle of exclusion, a neoliberal constellation in which the poultry processor, the labor contractor, and even the workers' organizations were all incentivized to look the other way.

IRCA's employer sanctions encourage corporations to outsource the role of employer to third parties to evade government regulations surrounding the hiring of undocumented labor. But in the "race to the bottom," employers recognize additional incentives in their collaboration with labor contractors, as contractors' presence segments the labor force, weakens worker power, and undermines unions.

In turn, this system encourages the proliferation of third-party contractors to fill employers' needs for cheap labor. Employer sanctions embolden fly by night contractors that fail to comply with state and federal regulations, can disappear as quickly as they arrived, and avoid fulfilling their legal responsibilities as employers. Wage theft among contractors is rampant, and often when workers try to recover unpaid wages from contractors who have disappeared, they have no records to even begin to identify who, in fact, owes them for the work they've completed.[17] Taxpayers and the workers themselves are forced to bear the costs associated with contractors' evasion of state and federal laws, while the multinational corporations benefiting from this racket enjoy record profits.

In the meantime, union locals in the Right to Work South exhaust their limited staff and resources servicing contracts, maintaining a minimal level of membership necessary to stay afloat, and attempting to negotiate with employers amid vastly unequal relations of power.[18] Organizations such as unions and workers' centers purport to hold workers' best interests at the center of their work, but where these conflict with the building of delicate and essential relationships or with the ambitions of organizational leaders, or where the question of workers' best interests is unclear, they may not receive the attention they deserve, as this case shamefully illustrates.

Spurred by the dysfunctions of neoliberal governance and economics, the proliferation of third-party contractors serves to further entrap undocumented workers within a labor regime of exclusion and exploitation. Moreover, they weaken the power of direct-hire workers by curtailing the effectiveness of collective bargaining agreements and dividing the labor force into two classes of workers. Corporations and contractors are not the only actors complicit in this regime; unions and workers' centers also find themselves caught in a web of power relations in which each prioritizes its own survival, sometimes over the needs and interests of the most vulnerable of workers.

WHAT CAN BE DONE?

In 1986 IRCA inextricably linked the questions of immigration and work when it made it a crime to hire an undocumented worker. What can be done? The state should enforce the rules surrounding joint employers by holding corporations accountable for unethically and illegally outsourcing their employment obligations. Unions and workers' centers should bring more workers—particularly those most vulnerable—into their leadership so they have a greater say in the decisions of the organizations that represent them. This requires greater transparency and more intentional efforts to help workers see they *are* the union and not simply served by it. All workers should have the right to organize, and these rights must be protected by the state not just on paper but also in practice. All people doing similar work, side by side, should receive the same workplace protections, the same benefits, and the same pay.

But these solutions—while important—are insufficient on their own. The problems presented here and in chapter 8 demand a radical rethinking of the nexus of immigration and labor law in the United States. Ultimately, the only sure way to disincentivize corporations from exploiting undocumented workers is to decriminalize undocumented work.

Comprehensive Immigration Reform has been on the horizon—or so many have thought—for nearly a decade. Whatever form this legislation ultimately takes at the time of passage, it will almost certainly restructure the ways in which we think about and verify immigrants' work authorization. Unfortunately, none of the proposals circulating today address the roots of the issue. Most remain heavily focused on enforcement. E-Verify is likely to be a cornerstone of the plan, but as we have seen in Mississippi poultry, it will drive the undocumented deeper into the shadows and encourage identity fraud. Moreover, mandatory use of E-Verify will give employers more incentive to use third-party labor contractors or pay people under the table to skirt their obligations, which could result in tax losses of over $17.3 billion.[19]

Certainly, providing a path to citizenship for the eleven million undocumented individuals in the country would help many who are currently here, but undocumented migration will continue, and the problem will grow anew. Beyond legalization programs, to ensure basic protections for documented and undocumented workers alike, U.S. policy must delink these two realms and repeal IRCA's employer sanctions.

TRANSMUNDO'S WORKERS TODAY

What happened to TransMundo's contract workers? It appears that Koch Foods' management may have ultimately been convinced by our warnings that they could be held liable as the contract workers' joint employers. But instead of following our advice that they move these workers onto the processor's payroll and effectively become a successor employer, management opted to follow in Tyson's footsteps and gradually terminated them.

Reports suggest that Koch Foods, unlike Tyson, eventually rehired some of these workers. In 2014 I found that Hernández and many of the other contract workers I was acquainted with remain in Forest and continue to work in poultry processing. Most are still at Koch Foods, now as direct hires protected by the union contract, albeit under different names and identities. A dismal few of these are actually union members, and none I spoke with were able to tell me who their union rep is. Others have been hired by new labor contractors—one that oversees sanitation at the area's Tyson plants, and another that provides workers to two small Vietnamese-owned processing plants that have opened in recent years. Alarmingly, anecdotal accounts of work in these new plants make the area's larger processors seem like model employers in comparison.

While many of the ancillary businesses run by TransMundo's owners in the early days of the new millennium have folded, research suggests that one of the partners may now own and operate a new labor contracting business in Mississippi. Bruno still lives across from the church in Forest, and his former workers say he is now employed in auto-parts manufacturing in a nearby town. Like the hundreds he helped both to secure work and to exploit over the years, he, too, struggles to make ends meet.

10 Flying Upwind

TOWARD A NEW SOUTHERN SOLIDARITY

> We not where we ought to be, but thank God we not
> where we was. We in this together, and we got a long ways
> to go.
>
> Onita Harvey, poultry worker, speaking at the Annual Stewards
> Conference, RWDSU Alabama Mid-South Council, 2005

> We, the Guatemalans, have a bible called the *Popol Vuh*,
> and it contains a phrase that says, "May everyone rise up;
> may no one be left behind."
>
> Baldomero Félix, poultry worker, speaking at the first annual
> Latino Stewards Conference, RWDSU Alabama Mid-South
> Council, 2004

My expansive, forested backyard has been transformed in festivity. Long tables line the perimeter of the cement-slab patio, and the Mississippi staples of macaroni and cheese, fried chicken, and various casseroles find a home among Guatemalan banana-leaf tamales, Peruvian *papas a la huancaina,* beef empanadas from Argentina, and Mexican *mole poblano.* Colorful streamers and balloons hang off the metal toolshed and decorate the gray gutters, doors, and window frames of the shabby one-story home. Latin rock music pulses in the background. The yard is dotted with groupings of borrowed folding chairs, and people from all walks of life have joined in this year-end potluck to celebrate and fundraise for the Mississippi Poultry Workers' Center.

My guests have come from Canton, Carthage, Forest, Morton, and the rolling hills that surround them, although, like myself, most have traveled much greater distances to find themselves here today. Everyone here sees familiar faces but is also encountering folks for the first time. I'm impressed with people's enthusiasm and willingness to interact with strangers who look and sound different from themselves. Onita Harvey, who has participated in a Spanish and workers' rights course at the workers' center over the past four months, tries out her newly acquired language skills on a few young Mexican men, who appear equal parts impressed and amused. As their teenage children look on in boredom, an Argentine family chats with a white neighbor about the bathroom they just renovated in their new home. Efrain López and a couple of Guatemalan friends gather at the far end of the yard, checking out the remains of a modest vegetable garden I attempted to grow last summer, which pales in comparison to the impressive *milpas* they've planted around their trailers. Emilio Hernández, Artemio Murrieta, and others from the Green House have found a translator and appear to be lobbying a union representative yet again.

Today is my thirtieth birthday. The close of 2005 is in sight, and in a few short weeks I will be moving away from Forest and turning to the task of making sense of all I've learned and experienced here. I feel conflicted about leaving. On one hand, I'm frustrated as I confront the reality that the exigencies of scholarly timelines map poorly onto the longer duration of the political processes they seek to chronicle and understand. Despite the commitment I made to activist research and the four years I have invested into this project, I feel like I could stay for many more and still not see the transformations we collectively seek.

On the other hand, the workers' center has achieved some important wins despite its youth. The people here tonight—nearly all of whom have demonstrated a degree of investment or leadership in the organization— are evidence of that. As I look around at all of them, I feel proud of our work and hopeful about the workers' center's path forward. I am also encouraged by the recognition that in today's Mississippi we can gather to reflect on these successes, imagine the future, and enjoy one another's company despite our many differences and without fear of reprisal.

As the evening wears on, someone turns up the music, as its beat shifts to merengue. Under my carport, by the glare of floodlights, people of all ages, sizes, and hues pair up and dance.

·   ·   ·   ·   ·

The gathering at my house that December afternoon holds a special place in my heart, as it represents the fruits of a long, steady crescendo of collaborative effort. Years of work had gotten us to that day, where people from many different walks of life could feel comfortable with one another and invested in the workers' center's vision. One project in particular, whose pilot had come to completion just weeks before, was particularly crucial in moving us to this point. Although we had been involved in a variety of campaigns lifting up workers' rights over the years, many had focused specifically on immigrant worker issues. By the end of 2004 none had put Black workers at the center. Solidarity/Solidaridad changed that, required the workers' center to focus intensely on relationship building across difference, and finally enabled it to begin moving worker leaders toward the helm of the organization.

This chapter highlights the Solidarity/Solidaridad project and its rationale, successes, and limitations. It then steps back to reconsider the larger picture—what we have learned about the past and present of Mississippi's poultry industry and communities. Finally, in conclusion, it contemplates the future of worker justice efforts in Mississippi and beyond.

SOLIDARITY/SOLIDARIDAD

By the time the workers' center became a reality in 2004, we were clear that the organization had an important role to play in helping to cultivate the leadership capacity of a diverse cross-section of poultry workers. But we didn't have a blueprint—much less organizational consensus—for how to make this happen. Our efforts throughout that year, responding to crisis after crisis, had left us spinning, with little to show for it all. Individual and campaign wins—yes; poultry workers' shared investment in the workers' center's mission—hardly.

Our work was providing us with an ever-deeper understanding of precisely how neoliberal globalization operates by constructing and exploiting difference to individualize collectivities. Time and again we saw that people's subject positions were affording them very different experiences with and explanations for the changes witnessed and abuses endured and that common ground was not easily identified. Moreover, with immigration so often explained through the lenses of race and work, we knew that the workers' center would have to address these challenges if it was to help people contest unequal relations of power at work or in their communities.

We also saw that the unions' narrow focus on people as workers was limiting what they could achieve. While we shared their belief in a universal ideal of social justice and an ethical bottom line in the face of exploitation, at the workers' center we saw the need to recognize how the other pieces of people's identities intersect with their class position (and with one another), impacting the ways they perceive and experience the world.[1] We were buoyed by new social movement theory, which calls for reaching across difference to build multiracial, cross-gender, transnational, and intercultural coalitions to contest practices of economic, political, and social oppression.[2] The call asserts that difference be not only recognized and valorized but also used as a resource in marginalized people's struggles. In my joint roles of activist researcher and workers' center staff, I began to lead the workers' center in thinking about how we might do this.

My colleagues and I had attended several trainings at the Highlander Research and Education Center since beginning our work in Mississippi. Its radical legacy supporting southern labor struggles of the thirties and forties, and the indelible memory of its role as a catalyst in the fight for civil rights in the fifties and sixties, remained alive in the new millennium, as activists grappled with the recent effects of globalization in the South. Highlander had long relied on popular education approaches in support of its "radical democratic belief in the capacity and right of all people to achieve freedom through self-emancipation."[3] Brazilian educator Paulo Freire is generally credited for naming and advancing our understanding of popular education, which sees the process as a means for raising critical consciousness that leads to transformative social change.[4]

We were particularly inspired by a conversation between Freire and Highlander's founder, Miles Horton, in which they discuss the relationship between organizing and education. Their dialogue concludes that if the ultimate goal of an organizing campaign is the resolution of a particular problem, it doesn't matter who solves it. "Whether you do it yourself or an expert does it or some bountiful person in the community does it, or the government does it without your involvement," it doesn't matter if it "leads to structural social change, or reinforces the system, or plays into the hands of capitalists," because the specific limited goal has been achieved. If, on the other hand, your goal is the empowerment of individuals and communities, popular education—"peer learning in nonformal settings free from government regulation"—can be an important vehicle.[5] It may not solve a specific and limited problem, but it can help people realize their own abilities to eventually tackle the problem themselves. At the workers' center, our work to date had been more successful at solving problems than at workers' empowerment. We wanted to develop the latter and dreamed of bringing the two together.

In conversation with poultry worker leaders of different backgrounds, my colleagues and I began to think about how we could use popular education to achieve our shared goals of bringing people together in ways that recognize and valorize difference while also identifying common ground. Around this time a group of African American worker leaders indicated their interest in learning to speak basic Spanish so they could better communicate with immigrant coworkers. Seeing this as an opportunity not only to build workers' language skills but also to bring more Black workers into the folds of the workers' center and engage them in dialogue about perceived worker difference, racism, and power in the chicken plants and in their communities, we approached the Retail, Wholesale, and Department Store Union (RWDSU). We proposed to develop and pilot a popular education program with these objectives in mind, and the union agreed to provide an honorarium to each of its stewards who successfully completed it.

Lia Ochoa and I were tasked with developing a curriculum for the workers' center to pilot. Ochoa had been a teacher in Lima, Peru, had worked in the chicken plants upon her arrival in Mississippi a few years prior, and was now an immigrant rights advocate at a community center in Morton. I brought the frameworks of popular education, organizing, and workers' rights to our work; Ochoa's education background and experience teaching languages and working on the processing line would be an asset to our team.

We began looking for models from which we might draw inspiration, but we came up mostly empty-handed. While we knew that groups in other parts of the country were grappling with similar issues and had identified a need for curricula and dialogue guides to aid them in having difficult conversations about race, migration, and work, everyone we reached out to was experimenting alongside us. Nationwide, we were able to identify only two related initiatives that we could look to as models as we developed our own.[6] We drew on these and what we had learned through our work, eventually creating Solidarity/Solidaridad: Building Cross-Cultural Understanding for Worker Justice.

The curriculum was composed of twenty two-hour Spanish and workers' rights classes and four half-day workshops. The workers' center piloted the program with ten African American union stewards from Carthage and Forest in the fall of 2005, inviting them to help us refine and improve it along the way. We sought to forefront the identities and experiences of participants throughout, as we explored the logics and effects of neoliberal globalization. Following pedagogical models from popular education, we designed learning to be informal and horizontal in nature, valuing all forms of knowledge, using hands-on participatory activities, and relying on participants' interests and strengths to guide the direction of our gatherings. Everyone in the room played roles of both student and teacher. In the end, Ochoa and I learned as much or more from the participants as they did from us.

We structured the Raising Our Voices language and workers' rights classes around ten units, each focusing on a common problem faced by chicken plant workers, such as health and safety violations, wage theft, family illness, union representation, bathroom breaks, discrimination, and communication with coworkers. Every meeting included activities in English that focused on the "rights" issues of the unit, as well as language-learning activities in Spanish. The rights activities required the participants to identify problems, discuss potential legal and collective bargaining remedies, and practice putting these to use. We designed the Spanish portions of the curriculum to dovetail with the rights content.

For example, in the unit on wage theft, participants shared their experiences and stories of being cheated out of overtime pay and overcharged for protective equipment and other paycheck deductions. We then engaged in activities that allowed us to review the union contract regulations on pay, learn federal wage and hour laws, and discuss the concept of a living wage. Using worksheets and role-play scenarios, participants practiced calculating their pay to determine if they had earned (a) at least minimum wage, (b) the wage rate in their union contract, or (c) a living wage. The Spanish-language portion of this unit focused on numbers, currency, and a simple dialogue with a Spanish-speaking coworker about his paycheck.

The four Power and Oppression workshops identified the growing diversity in Mississippi's chicken-processing communities as "both our greatest opportunity and our biggest challenge."[7] They sought to start building a common understanding of where poultry workers of different backgrounds come from, who they are, and what is important to them. Moreover, we aimed to create a space in which worker leaders could strengthen their collective analysis of how racialized and globalized power and oppression had impacted their diverse communities in unique and similar ways. Ochoa and I cofacilitated each workshop along with community allies and Latin American poultry workers, who participated in the discussion and shared their own experiences.

The workshop series began by focusing on the legacies and experiences of Black Mississippians and inviting participants to add their own family and personal histories to a twenty-foot timeline on the wall. Starting with stories that privileged the experiences of the participants enabled them to immediately engage in an analysis of how racism, white privilege, and economic oppression had affected their lives and begin to articulate a shared vision for a world in which difference is valued and respected and where opportunity is available to all.

In subsequent workshops we used videos, guest facilitators, and simultaneous interpretation to add stories of other communities to our Power and Oppression timeline, including a cross-section of nonwhite groups in U.S. history (Native Americans, Chinese, Irish Catholics, Mexican Americans, Jews) and in present-day central Mississippi (indigenous Guatemalans, Mexican campesinos, and middle-class Peruvians). One film presented cases of discrimination against racialized others in our country's past.[8]

Figure 20. Workshop participants explore shared histories of power and oppression. Photo by author.

Another featured the migration stories of three refugees of the global economy.[9] And several guest facilitators shared their painful stories of why they left their countries, perilous travels into the United States, and their experiences upon arrival in Mississippi. The final workshop focused on building a critique of neoliberal globalization so that we could begin to talk about the structural causes of migration and industrial restructuring and their effects on people's lives.

Over the course of the workshops participants began to identify similarities in the experiences of diverse communities across the Americas and started to relate these stories to their own: "I learned that it wasn't only the African Americans who was brutalized; it was also the Japanese, and the Jews, and the Chinese. They was brought here for just one intention. They were used," said one participant, while others in the room gave her "mm-hmms" of affirmation. Another reflected, "I wasn't aware of how the Irish immigrants was done like that. I was thinking only the African Americans was done wrong. See, I find out today it was also the Indians, Chinese, Japanese, Mexicans, Guatemalans, and Native Americans. . . . We don't know our own history. We weren't taught this stuff in school." In addition to building links between different experiences of oppression and survival, participants also shared their analyses of racialized power and the role of whiteness: "What makes someone white, anyway?" one asked. Another responded, "I learned that the first refugees who came to this country were running from persecution in their own country, and after getting established, they began persecuting others for the same things that they ran from theyself. They reflect they burden on others." These reflections suggest a growing analysis of the relationship between whiteness, privilege, and oppression in the United States.

When a Mam poultry worker and former bilingual organizer from Guatemala spoke about the history and culture of indigenous Guatemalans, a participant immediately commented on the commonalities he saw between these stories and those of African-descendant slaves in the United States. When a Mexican migrant told his story of having to leave his family's farm in Veracruz and shared a harrowing tale of clandestinely crossing the desert to enter the United States, participants expressed amazement at the risks he had taken so that he could work at a chicken plant in Mississippi. This sparked a frank conversation about "illegal aliens," and the nonmigrants in the room were shocked to learn that it is virtually impossible for a working-class Latino immigrant to obtain legal permission to live and work in the United States. Through conversations such as these, we began to see participants staking out a common ground for understanding and talking about the ways in which neoliberal globalization, immigration, and structural racism affect their lives and those of coworkers of different backgrounds.

Through its Solidarity/Solidaridad programming, the workers' center sought to denaturalize difference, guiding poultry worker leaders through an exploration of their own histories and experiences with white supremacy, capitalist exploitation, and Euro-American imperialism so that they might build an analysis that would enable them to see commonalities with people they had previously seen as "other." In return, we saw poultry worker leaders become better equipped to identify with one another and gain the tools needed to communicate effectively. We hoped that their identification of common points of oppression, survival, and analysis would eventually become the basis for constructing a shared vision and a broad-based coalition for workplace justice.

Upon their graduation from the Solidarity/Solidaridad classes and workshops, participants offered enthusiastic feedback, demanding that the program continue. Based on these evaluations, we doubled the number of the Raising Our Voices classes and developed a parallel English and workers' rights curriculum for Latin American poultry worker leaders. We also shared the Power and Oppression workshops with other community groups in Mississippi and beyond and used their feedback and that of the original participants to refine the content and facilitation methods. We created an outline for an analogous set of workshops for Latin American poultry workers, which would start from their experiences as immigrants from different countries and cultures of Latin America, gradually build an analysis of neoliberal globalization, educate them about white supremacy and the Black experience in the South, and encourage them to identify common points of intersection with their African American coworkers.

We had informally started this work with Latino migrants in other settings. For example, in 2004 I showed a group of new immigrants a documentary film that uses historical (and often violent) news footage and the voices of civil rights activists to tell the story of Jim Crow and the Freedom Struggle in the U.S. South.[10] Participants were visibly stunned by the images and stories they heard, and the ensuing discussion revealed that they knew very little about the histories of racialized oppression in Mississippi. Many said that they left that day with a new appreciation for the struggles of their Black coworkers. We believed in-depth treatment of these sorts of issues and the conversations they sparked held great potential for strengthening Latino solidarity with African Americans.

We also envisioned a third series in which Black and Latino worker leaders would come together to share experiences, enjoy food and music from each other's cultures, and begin engaging the analyses they built in the identity-specific workshops. Solidarity/Solidaridad left us convinced of the power of popular education, dialogic analysis, and intergroup relationship building, and the potluck in my backyard at the close of the year offered us a glimpse into the possibilities such intentional gatherings held. We were feeling energized for the work ahead.

In subsequent years we continued the Raising Our Voices language and workers' rights classes to much acclaim by recruiting bilingual language

Figure 21. Discussing language barriers at a workers' center workshop. Photo by John Fiege. Courtesy of FiegeFilms.com.

teachers and offering them a crash course in and access to ample resources on the basics of workers' rights. A workers' center staff person supported them and was available to cofacilitate when needed. Over three years we trained six additional facilitators to lead the classes, which were offered a total of eight times to both Black and Latino groups of poultry worker leaders.

Unfortunately, our more aspirational follow-on ideas for the Power and Oppression workshops went unrealized. The human and financial resources required to develop the parallel series for Latino workers, as well as to guide nuanced and emotional conversations about racism and immigration, neoliberalism and exploitation, proved too much for the workers' center to tackle. My departure left a void in this regard, one that my colleagues and I were ultimately unable to bridge.

But our popular education efforts did bear fruit in other areas. They helped us to identify and cultivate leaders who went on to play an important role in moving the workers' center toward a new organizational model. Shortly after my departure from Mississippi, a leadership council formed, and the majority was composed intentionally of poultry workers from a broad cross-section of backgrounds. This body received trainings in organizational leadership and development, and by the next year had helped the workers' center become MPOWER, Mississippi Poultry Workers for Equality and Respect, an independent, locally led and owned workers' center.

TRANSFORMATIONS PAST AND PRESENT

I was fortunate to be in central Mississippi during a time of intense community and workplace transformation. At the dawn of the new millennium, the area's dominant industry was undergoing unprecedented growth. In its quest to maximize profit, it brought people from across the hemisphere into neighborhoods and chicken plants, irreversibly changing the ways that people think about themselves in relation to others and dramatically impacting the landscape of poultry workers' collective organizing. My training in activist anthropology equipped me with a framework through which I could document and analyze these changes as well as support the efforts of people seeking a more equitable and just distribution of opportunity that such transformations produced. I like to think that through the engaged research that produced this book, I was able to modestly contribute to both.

When Latin American immigrants began to arrive to central Mississippi's poultry region in the 1990s, they entered a society indelibly marked by a century and a half of structures of white supremacy, in which Native Americans had been "removed" and marginalized and African Americans had been imported and subjected to intense labor extraction and political and economic disenfranchisement. Moreover, they entered into an industry that had grown up in and benefited from the exploitation of these very structures of inequality. These assemblages were strengthened by the area's rurality, its poverty, and its desperation to advance economically through public investment in private industry, as well as by federal policies that sought to exploit these same regional characteristics.

Poultry plants in the region relied on the largely contingent labor of poor white women practically since their configuration as a formalized industry and resisted the rising tide of civil rights struggle that demanded equal economic opportunity for African Americans. Despite organizing throughout the state for the social, political, and economic rights of Black Mississippians, in the mid-twentieth century central Mississippi pushed back forcefully against the mounting pressures of the Mississippi Freedom Struggle. I've documented that this resistance was particularly strong in Scott County, thanks, in no small measure, to the efforts of Sovereignty Commission director and local poultry entrepreneur, journalist, and politician Erle Johnston. When these barriers finally crumbled and African Americans entered the chicken plants in growing numbers, white workers fled and the processing line came to rely nearly exclusively on a Black workforce.

By the early 1970s African American workers in the area's poultry industry began to organize for better wages and working conditions, and the independent Mississippi Poultry Workers' Union arose from the smoldering embers of the Civil Rights Movement. But relying on long-engrained patterns of racial violence and subjugation, local poultry plant owners colluded with law enforcement and defeated this effort in just a few years. While this early attempt at unionization failed to achieve the changes it sought in terms of workplace improvements, it may have enhanced the politicization of Black poultry workers across the state, as additional attempts at labor organizing arose in other areas of Mississippi later in the decade.

In this context the poultry industry first experimented with immigrant recruitment, but these efforts were short-lived. Its success at squashing workers' attempts to organize amid the new economic and cultural logics of neoliberalism of the late 1970s and throughout the 1980s may have strengthened the industry's ability to control labor locally, thus negating its desire to look further afield. But by the early 1990s, despite intense corporate resistance, some efforts to unionize the area's poultry workers had succeeded. This reality, coupled with the exponential growth of the industry, its intense technological development, and the realities of globalization that created an international labor market and facilitated migration across national borders, led central Mississippi's poultry processors to revisit the strategy of immigrant recruitment.

Claiming a labor shortage, companies such as B.C. Rogers Poultry initiated elaborate schemes to recruit, house, and retain immigrant workers from Florida, Texas, and places farther afield throughout Latin America. I have argued, in collaboration with my colleague Laura Helton, that the term "labor shortage" demands analytic attention because its purported economic and race-neutral facade masks a deeper-seated reality in which corporations used Latino immigrant labor to undermine the organizing demands and resist meeting the most basic needs of their longer-standing African American workforce. By instituting a system that could replace workers as quickly as they had arrived, programs like the Hispanic Project and its successor initiatives made them literally expendable, demanding more of workers' bodies and spirits for even lower pay and thus aiding the industry in its quest for profit. Within a decade the poultry plants no longer needed to actively recruit immigrant workers. Mounting economic and political pressures in Latin America found an escape valve in these very workers' intricate social networks, which ensured a continual flow of low-wage labor out of migrants' home countries and into central Mississippi's chicken plants.

The influx of a diverse cross-section of Latin Americans into rural Mississippi's poultry communities upset the area's long-standing racial binary of Black and white, as established Mississippians struggled to locate newcomers within the area's social hierarchies of race. When efforts to place them within the only third category recognized in the area—were these new faces Choctaw?—failed, a discursive struggle ensued in which old and new residents sought to position immigrants vis-à-vis the South's entrenched "color line" in ways that made sense to them. I have argued that in this process people have understood and explained the transformations brought about by immigration using the familiar lenses of race and work. A majority of white Mississippians tend to lift the immigrant up as "hardworking," in stark comparison with the "lazy" African American that has been promulgated by the media and popular culture since at least the 1980s.

Many Latino immigrants buy into and further this stereotype at the same time they exhibit a strong structural critique of both the poultry industry's "race to the bottom" and the conditions that have led them to backbreaking work in Mississippi's chicken plants. In contrast, most Black Mississippians sharply critique the notion of an idle Black underclass, drawing on a historicized understanding of the workings of white supremacy both in society and in poultry work specifically. Surely, some resent new immigrants for reducing job opportunity, accessing (perceived) greater social, political, and economic resources than have been available to African Americans, or hobbling their efforts at workplace organizing. But I found much more prevalent a recognition that immigrant workers are exploited in ways that parallel African Americans' labor situations prior to the Civil Rights Movement, suggesting a heightened critical consciousness among Black Mississippians that could aid in workplace organizing efforts. In sum, I argue that the presence of Latinos in central Mississippi has opened up a third but contested space between white and Black. While some (particularly lighter-skinned, English-learning) newcomers appear to be pushing at the boundaries of whiteness, most are interpreted as clearly not white, but also not Black. Meanwhile, with few exceptions, immigrants exhibit attitudes and behaviors that attempt to distance themselves from Blackness to preserve their own perceived self-interest vis-à-vis the South's "color line," thus strengthening the boundary between Black and non-Black and cementing the position of Blackness at the bottom of the area's social hierarchies of race.

These discourses are wielded and reinforced inside the chicken plants, where workers are often segregated by race, gender, and legal status. But, interestingly, racial hierarchies shift inside the plant, as Black workers' collective seniority, history of struggle, and linguistic and citizenship privilege proffer them a status in the context of the workplace that is generally above that of Latino immigrant workers.

While the industry's regimes of mental and physical abuse do great damage to the bodies and spirits of workers of all backgrounds, they operate differently with respect to distinct groups of workers. Even when their workings are parallel, people often interpret their experiences (and those of others) in dissimilar terms. In this way, poultry plants' strategies of labor control under globalization effectively destroy worker collectivities, mounting the obstacles that must be overcome to organize across difference in the quest for poultry worker justice. Adding to these challenges, the speaking of different languages, immigrants' heterogeneity and their attempts to access white privilege, and workers' divergent ideologies surrounding organizing and resistance further complicate efforts to politically mobilize Mississippi's poultry workers.

Immigrant workers' undocumented legal status has also played an outsized role in hobbling workers' abilities to build power inside the plants. Drawing on my experience organizing and educating with the Mississippi Poultry Workers' Center, I've produced two ethnographic portraits that underscore this problem, one focusing on document reverification and the other on third-party labor contractors. Both point to the structural fragility of organizing undocumented workers in the neoliberal era, highlighting the dysfunctionality of current U.S. immigration and labor laws and calling for policy change that will protect the rights of workers regardless of legal status so that workers of all backgrounds—immigrant and U.S.-born alike— can negotiate the terms of their employment on a more equal playing field.

While central Mississippi's labor unions have recognized the need to include immigrants in their organizing efforts, they have met with different levels of success. Their efforts to reach out to the new Latino workforce are hampered not only by being stigmatized and underresourced in the Right to Work South but also by their narrow conception of worker movements as those framed by a universal class politics and—beyond a crude wielding of identity politics to build their membership base—their dramatic silence on issues of ethnic, racial, and cultural diversity. Workers' centers that place these identity markers at the center of their work have the potential to breathe new life into labor organizing efforts as part of a broader fight for social, racial, and immigrant justice, but their collaboration with labor unions is fraught with challenges. As the Mississippi case shows, the workers' center's relationships with unions proved tenuous, confronting constant internal tensions between improving relations of trust with union leadership and empowering workers to hold this very leadership accountable.

The workers' center's Solidarity/Solidaridad efforts, by recognizing the reality that all social actors are uniquely positioned based on their own shifting multiplicities of identity and putting this at the center of poultry workers' conversations about the omnipresent nature of neoliberal ideologies driving globalization, offered us a glimpse of a different way forward. Unfortunately, the experiment was short-lived. By 2008 the workers' center had dissolved, an institutional demise I discuss further in the postscript. Grassroots successor projects have emerged in its wake, but whether they will ever garner the resources or inclination to resume this unfinished business remains unclear.

BUILDING POULTRY WORKER POWER FOR SOCIAL JUSTICE

What, then, can this story teach us about building worker power today? It paints a rather grim picture for workers' prospects of contesting capitalist exploitation in defense of their dignity, respect, and rights. Building the power of ever-more diverse working people is not a simple proposition; the challenges are numerous and burdensome, and the pitch is markedly uphill. Broadly, these problems are not unique to the U.S. South, and in many respects the analysis of the globalization of Mississippi poultry parallels the issues workers face across the country and around the world.

At the same time, it confirms that the spread of neoliberal globalization across time and place has been far from uniform. Witnessing its unfolding in the Deep South confirms it has regional and local inflections molded by the region's historical and sociopolitical economic context. The poultry industry's historical relationship to central Mississippi, for example, clearly guides and patterns globalization's local articulations. Moreover, the area's regional and local histories of racialization, and their relationship to this industry, too, shape globalization's modulations in different ways and intensities than it assumes elsewhere.

I have cautioned us, however, from interpreting this tale as one that is exceptional to the South or even to Mississippi; rather, I've suggested that through this case we might better assess the promises and pitfalls of globalization in other parts of the country and the world and take action based on these deepened understandings. We might use Mississippi as a mirror, albeit one with magnifying properties, whose reflections encourage us to take a closer look at our own relationships to the ills of white supremacy, xenophobia, and neoliberalism and begin to address them.

Neoliberal globalization is expanding unevenly throughout the world, creating through its very existence potential pockets of contestation. It is within these complex and uneven disjunctions where culture and capital compete, adapt, merge, and repel and where opportunities for resistance emerge.[11] But these sites of contradiction can be difficult to identify and even harder to leverage. Our work in Mississippi suggests that people's different life experiences, conditioned by their multiple and shifting identities, require that they build relationships across difference as a vital first step in any struggle to equalize social, political, and economic power.

While short-lived, the Solidarity/Solidaridad experiment left us with hope for the potential of popular education and intergroup dialogue efforts to breathe new life into struggles for workers' rights and social justice in Mississippi and beyond. My colleagues and I were not alone; the ensuing years have seen a virtual explosion of such initiatives for addressing the challenges of difference and inequality in the neoliberal era. Driven by the dearth of materials Ochoa and I encountered when seeking guidance for the workers' center's efforts, after leaving Mississippi and completing my graduate studies I led another activist research project that conducted a much more thorough mapping and analysis of existing programs.[12] Intergroup Resources, an online resource center, now houses the results of this research, and members of its national advisory committee support groups in adapting the resources to their local contexts.[13]

I believe initiatives like ours in Mississippi and others that proliferated in subsequent years offer a modest glimpse into a strategy that might begin to contest racialized and other identity-based divisions upholding industry power and white supremacy in an increasingly globalized world. They are rooted in the realization that diverse groups of individuals will not naturally come together because of their common oppression as

Figure 22. "Until justice rolls down like waters and righteousness like a mighty stream." Mam poultry worker leaders visit the Civil Rights Memorial in Montgomery, Alabama. Photo by author.

workers, but "coalitions within and across identity categories can be built by open and honest discussion of the ways in which all of us have been differently racialized, gendered, and infused with complex and composite identities and interests."[14] They confront the structural and institutional nature of power and oppression exercised through neoliberal globalization head-on, seeking not to silence difference in building class solidarity but rather to embrace diversity as both a lived social problem and a resource to be leveraged in building a more just world. They hold that any sustainable worker movement must be rooted in experiences of culture, history, and identity, and that this approach is vital to the "emancipation of the whole."[15]

To reach this goal, Solidarity/Solidaridad sought to create a common language and points of connection through which poultry workers might begin to construct coalitions with coworkers and community members different from themselves. Work such as this is vital, encouraging people to see one another as deeply human and helping to build a shared antiracist and antineoliberal politics that can begin to reimagine a more equitable and participatory democracy. Only through this collective reimagination may people take action together to realize this vision.

The Mississippi Poultry Workers' Center was certainly not the first to approach social justice work in this way, but it did offer a vision seldom articulated among workers' or immigrants' rights groups in the South today. It endeavored to build a coalitional politics based on shared—but not identical—experiences and analyses of the workings of capital, race, and power in the lives of African American and Latin American poultry workers in the Deep South. Ultimately, it sought to move us from social positions to ideological ones, embracing the journey rather than the end goal, asking us to critically consider and act on the ethics we want to shape our futures.

Home to Roost

Growing up in Kent, Ohio, I was aware of but rarely paid attention to the annual commemorations of the May 4, 1970, National Guard shootings, which killed four students at Kent State University, just miles from my home. This violence was spurred by the fears of people in positions of power over student protests mounting across the country in opposition to war, imperialism, racism, and oppression. Days later, with the Kent State massacre fresh in their minds, students at the historically Black Jackson State College in Mississippi rallied against oppression they had long endured. Some historians recount that several white Mississippians drove past the campus that night and expressed concern about the congregating masses of politicized Black youth. After students began to riot, seventy-five police came to the scene armed with their service weapons, personal revolvers, and submachine guns. Shortly after midnight the law enforcement officers opened fire and emptied at least 460 rounds of ammunition on the students. Two were killed and more than a dozen injured. Around the country in the days following, millions of students protested and shut down campuses, organizing the only nationwide student strike in U.S. history.[1]

These events took place five years before I entered the world, and I wasn't aware of the connections between Kent and Jackson State as a child. My relationship to Mississippi was limited to my friendship with Latrina, whose mother had sent her to Kent to live with relatives. What little I knew of her home was framed by those stereotypes that circulate in public discourse about entrenched poverty, stifling oppression, and racial inequality in "the most southern place on Earth."[2] I, like others, envisioned Mississippi as exceptional, representing the most repressive social hierarchies in the country, to which white people in places like Ohio could point as proof that *we* had surmounted the social and economic relations of the past; *we* weren't racists. I never expected that I might one day cultivate such a deep appreciation for the South—not for its exceptionalism but for the ways it reflects back at us realities about ourselves, our country, and our world. And I never anticipated that struggles for justice in Mississippi would become my struggles too and that these would help me clarify my engagement with the discipline of anthropology and its relationship to how I want to live in the world.

When I stumbled upon anthropology in college, I was captivated because it troubled conceptions I held about the world and my place in it. It challenged me to think about others in new ways, but, more important, it pushed me to understand myself—and my privilege as a white, middle-class, U.S.-born college student—in a new light. My first anthropology course, taken when I was an exchange student at a Mexican university, focused on the legacies of a colonialist science that sought to categorize and classify the racial "other" to justify European and North American global dominance. This critical self-reflection laid the foundation for my continued study of the discipline.

By the end of the twentieth century I was a graduate student at the University of Texas, and while I was excited by the critical theoretical and methodological tools anthropology offered, I struggled to come to terms with the discipline's deep colonialist roots. How might I be part of the reconceptualization of an anthropology that charted a different path forward? I found sustenance in a new brand of scholarship that my mentors dubbed "activist." A small cohort of faculty there had begun training students, recruiting faculty, and carving out institutional space for an anthropology that drew on the field's critical history and moved it in new directions.

As introduced in this book's first pages, the Austin School teaches that activist research "begins with an act of political identification and dialogue with collective subjects in struggle for relief from oppression, for equality and betterment."³ I was drawn to the democratic and deeply committed practice that undergirds this approach because of its potential contributions to social transformation as well as its promise for decolonizing anthropology. In the years that followed, in an attempt to put these ideas into practice, I designed and carried out the research that formed the basis for this book. My fieldwork essentially became an extended experiment in the prospects and challenges of activist research.

In this postscript I consider my positioning as an activist anthropologist in central Mississippi and discuss my understandings of the genealogies, promises, and pitfalls of this approach to scholarship. These reflections highlight some of the ethical and practical challenges I faced as an activist researcher in the field and offer a concrete case through which to consider the complicated issues of power, accountability, and reciprocity in anthropological work concerned with social justice. By making my personal and methodological positioning explicit, I consider how activist scholarship can begin to respond to the notorious imbalance of power between anthropologists and the communities in which we work, how its intentional melding of theory and practice can enrich our understandings of the world, and how a discussion of both can help to elucidate our intentions, as well as recognize our limitations, as activist scholars.

While I aim for these reflections to provide readers with richer context through which to assess the claims I make in this book, I also hope they will contribute to a growing conversation on engaged scholarship and provide those who would consider this approach with encouragement and material to think more intentionally and critically about the frameworks they use to engage with anthropology and the world.⁴

THE IDENTITY POLITICS OF FIELDWORK

Critiques of the notion of scientific objectivity are now widely accepted in anthropological circles, and the discipline, on the whole, recognizes that all views are partial and situated. Activist research embraces this reality, acknowledging that all research is political, and all encounters have consequences. In the beginning of this book I provide some background on how what began as a loose collaboration with a collective of activists, advocates, and poultry workers eventually morphed into a more formalized relationship with the Mississippi Poultry Workers' Center, and later I'll discuss this in greater detail as illustrative of some of the challenges of an engaged approach. Yet while I was politically aligned with the Mississippi Poultry Workers' Center throughout my fieldwork, my positioning vis-à-vis those with whom I interacted in the course of research was not always defined strictly by this relationship. The numerous hats I wore, in addition to my race, gender, class, linguistic, and other identifications, influenced greatly the ways in which others perceived and interacted with me, as did their own identifications and politics. By sharing some reflections on how my intersecting identities shaped the research process, I position myself in relation to my various collaborators, the data I gathered, the analyses I assert, and the narrative I write. In so doing, I encourage the reader to consider the ways in which our positioning is always situated and shapes our findings and the stories we tell.

My most numerous relationships in Mississippi were with Latin Americans of different backgrounds. Most, though not all, worked in the poultry and ancillary industries. Through my affiliation with the Mississippi Poultry Workers' Center, my work as an ESOL teacher, and my frequent visits to the homes of immigrants, I became widely known as an ally and compassionate resource. My fluency in Spanish, interest in Mam, firsthand experience in several Latin American countries and cultures, and critical take on the broken U.S. immigration-labor nexus were further evidence of my solidarity with these fellow "outsiders." Immigrants were often excessively respectful toward me, and it became a joke among some that I insisted they address me using the informal Spanish *tú* or *vos* when they often opted for the more formal *usted*. Others, whom I initially met in ESOL classes, still refer to me as *maestra* (teacher), despite many interactions in other contexts over the years. Such forms of deference reflect the omnipresence of structural inequalities of power despite my best efforts at equalizing these in my personal relationships.

I met white Mississippians as landlords, neighbors, medical professionals, lawyers, local business owners, elected officials, school administrators, law enforcement officers, religious leaders, immigrant rights advocates, poultry executives, and, on only two occasions, chicken plant workers. I was always an outsider, despite my attempts to create some form of southern affinity by emphasizing my recent move from Texas. Most people, though not all, were aware of my work on issues of poultry worker justice or at the very least my relationship to the area's Latino community. Despite my political allegiances and my not being "one of them," I found that my whiteness signified an affinity that made most white Mississippians feel comfortable sharing with me opinions and feelings they would have been unlikely to share with a person of color, as evidenced by my ill-fated interactions with a potential landlord in chapter 1.

My interactions with Black Mississippians were most frequently with people who worked in the chicken plants, many of whom were active union stewards. They were also with union staff, immigrant and civil rights advocates, religious leaders, law enforcement officers, shop owners, and elected officials. Most of these relationships were forged through my connections with the workers' center. Like white Mississippians, African Americans also saw me as an outsider, but this status, coupled with the political commitments I tried to maintain evident at all times, seemed to suggest that we might be more likely to find common ground than if I had been a white Mississippian. When I worked as a facilitator of the Solidarity/Solidaridad program I cocreated for Black poultry worker leaders in 2005, for example, participants were clearly skeptical of me at first. But over a period of several months, our confidence in one another grew into relationships of mutual trust, respect, and, in some cases, friendship, based largely on our shared ethical and political commitments.

The ways in which African Americans, Latinos, and whites related to me in the context of rural Mississippi tended to shift when they met my partner, Tutu, from Equatorial Guinea, the only Spanish-speaking country in sub-Saharan Africa. He did not live in Mississippi and was usually not present, though he visited numerous times and met many of my collaborators over the years. For my African American acquaintances, meeting Tutu seemed to solidify relations of trust and deepen the significance of my political commitments. Latin Americans, on the other hand, were shocked upon encountering Tutu to hear a Black man speaking Spanish, a rare phenomenon in the rural South. I believe one Mexican collaborator echoed the unspoken sentiments of many immigrants who were aware of my interest in race relations and my work with Black and Latino poultry workers when, after meeting Tutu, she leaned toward me, looked deep into my eyes, and said, "Angela, now I understand why you do the work that you do." I smiled uneasily, unsure of how to respond to her assumption that my personal relationships were prescriptive of my politics.

Among white Mississippians the most obvious shifts in attitude came from neighbors and absolute strangers. One elderly white woman had ironically stopped by my house one day to share her concerns about how the neighborhood had changed over the years, commenting on the influx of Latinos, African Americans, and unscrupulous whites with questionable morals. She said the house across from mine had once been a "house of ill repute," with Black and white men and women openly intermixing. After the encounter I diligently took notes on her comments for purposes of documenting the exchange. A few months later, while Tutu was in town, the neighbors in the former "house of ill repute" stopped by to let me know that the woman had been looking in my windows while I was out. She never visited again. This exchange is emblematic of what I felt was a general shift in the ways white Mississippians perceived me when I was alone versus when I was with Tutu. Interestingly, I did not feel this difference when I was out in public in Mississippi with Black women, nor with Hispanic women or men. Furthermore, with the exception of an incident at a mall in Nashville, Tennessee, I haven't felt such deep alienation as a "race traitor" in any other parts of the United States.

As a young woman I encountered situations both advantageous and troublesome throughout my fieldwork that were influenced by my age and gender. For example, it was not uncommon upon visiting homes of immigrant men to encounter sex workers who were just leaving. Once when I was visiting the overcrowded apartment of a Mexican friend, a housemate emerged from a bedroom to ask if I was available and, if so, for how much. My friend quickly jumped up, insisting that I was a *mujer de respeto,* a respectable woman. I grew uncomfortable not because of the housemate's mistake, but because it was immediately clear what this definition implied about my friend's esteem of the other women—mostly of color—who regularly made the rounds to supplement their meager income in this largely immigrant and male apartment complex. While I escaped the embarrassment of marriage proposals by male immigrants desperate to gain legal status in the United States, nearly all the other ESOL instructors I worked with, including some women in their fifties, had received numerous propositions from their students. On the other hand, my gender identity also helped build relationships with women poultry workers. Despite our numerous other differences, our intersecting experiences as women were central to their sharing with me experiences of gendered violence, harassment, and discrimination at home and at work.

In earlier chapters I write extensively about the workers' center's collaboration with poultry workers' unions. Indeed, I spent many hours with local, regional, and international union staff and volunteers during my fieldwork, and these exchanges were typically framed by my collaboration with the workers' center. As such, upon meeting new union folks I had to make it a point to explain my "other" role as an activist researcher. In strategy meetings with union representatives, on more than one occasion I felt that the graying (mostly white) men in the room were dominating the conversation and taking less seriously the contributions made by the younger women (white and of color). On the other hand, not always being taken seriously as a young woman meant that I was sometimes received as less threatening, as I believe was the case particularly in my interactions with some union officials and industry administrators.

Poultry company executives I met with knew me as a researcher studying the changes brought about by immigrant workers in the industry, and I didn't discuss the politically engaged component of my work unless asked. On one occasion I was simply one student of hundreds participating in a poultry company's recruitment event. On another occasion I was an ESOL teacher needing a plant tour so that I could learn the appropriate vocabulary I should be teaching my poultry worker students. Rarely did I reveal my affiliation with the workers' center during conversations with industry representatives, though this connection was abundantly clear to two of my most key industry "informants." In these situations, where people in relative positions of power may have opened up in part because of their underestimation of a young white woman student, these stereotypes arguably aided in my data gathering.

Finally, I wrote in chapter 1 about how my status as a U.S. citizen proffered a myriad of daily privileges that granted me access to research subjects, spaces, and security that enabled me to conduct this project. Between my discussion at the book's outset and here, I hope to have illustrated that over the course of research my identities were multiple and constantly shifting. The different axes of my positionality intersected in ways that variously facilitated and constrained my fieldwork experience, often simultaneously. This is no truer for an activist researcher than for any other, but the transparency required by a more explicitly engaged approach may make it easier to recognize. I hope that what I have shared here, however partial, enables my interlocutors to more directly consider the ways in which my positioning—indeed, all positioning—necessarily shapes what we see and thus our ways of knowing.

GENEALOGIES OF ACTIVIST RESEARCH

Activist anthropology has a multistranded genealogy. One vital predecessor can be located in efforts to create an "action anthropology" as far back as the 1950s. This work, which grew out of Sol Tax's collaborative research with the Fox (Mesquaki) Indians, sought to create an anthropology that was more dialogic and practical in approach than its forebears.[5] Tax and his students strived to involve community members in identifying the problems that social science might help to solve, conducting studies, and generating more useful community-centered products. Critics disagree about the extent to which Tax achieved these ideals, but they concur that his ideas were groundbreaking for their time.[6] His work influenced a subsection of American anthropologists and marked the early formalization of the field of applied anthropology in the United States.[7]

In the wake of independence movements around the globe in the late 1960s and early 1970s, a critical mass of anthropologists and those affected by their work caught the discipline's attention. With biting critiques of anthropology's role in bolstering colonial administrations and furthering the empires of the United States and its European allies, these postcolonial voices set the stage for what is today referred to as anthropology's "critical turn."[8] Around the same time, in South America Paolo Freire's critical teachings on popular education as a tool of resistance inspired social scientists to conceive new collaborative research methodologies as pedagogical tools for social transformation, giving rise to participatory action research.[9] By the end of the 1970s these entwined efforts, in tandem with other crucial global and domestic processes of political significance (movements for racial justice and gender equality; politics of war and peace; U.S. foreign policy) had politicized a growing number of U.S. anthropology departments. Among students and newly minted faculty, the concept of "radical anthropology," a critical theory–based Marxist approach seeking to align its aims with those of the oppressed, began to emerge.[10]

In the 1980s these critiques prompted anthropology to turn its gaze on itself and begin to grapple with questions of ethnographic authority and the politics of representation.[11] Feminist scholars' scathing critiques of long-held ideas about objectivity and positivism in science had far-reaching impacts on the field.[12] Around this time increasing numbers of women, people of color, queer writer-theorists, and other scholar-activists on or beyond the margins of the discipline deepened the critical turn, engendering intense discussions over anthropology's (and the academy's) role and relevance in society and its complicity in sustaining unequal relations of power in the world.[13]

As works in this vein have multiplied in recent decades, the discipline has witnessed an increased interest in an "engaged" anthropology that "gives back" to the communities where we work and seeks relevance with broader publics. Several edited volumes and articles on the topic have emerged in recent years.[14] In 2010 *American Anthropologist,* the discipline's leading U.S. periodical, dedicated a new recurring section of the journal to anthropologists' public engagement.[15] The term "engagement," however, has as many meanings as it does users. Some focus on putting anthropology "to use," reclaiming the moniker "applied" in its broadest sense.[16] Others seek to alter understandings of important social issues through their scholarly critiques (which some dub "cultural critique").[17] Still others strive for a broader "public" impact on social change by writing for a more general audience, sometimes using new communication technologies.[18]

Activist anthropology grows out of this diverse scholarly and political lineage and intersects variously with these contemporary inclinations, yet it proposes something qualitatively distinct. Its defining feature is its emphasis on long-term collaboration with "communities in struggle" in each phase of the research process. "To be an anthropology which no longer serves the interests of the oppressors it must be one which actively serves those of the oppressed," wrote Gordon, one of its earliest proponents, in 1991.[19] Such transparent, values-driven alignment enables us and our interlocutors to more directly consider how our positioning is always situated and shapes our research and results. Failure to do so is a political act of its own, which may well be read as complicity with the status quo.[20]

Activist anthropology attempts to address long-standing power inequities in the relationship between anthropologists and their research "subjects"—in essence, democratizing our practice—while simultaneously putting anthropology to use in ways that advance struggles for justice more broadly. But calls for a more "militant" anthropology driven by an ethical bottom line only partially address the advantages proffered by activist research.[21] While it may enable some of us to be anthropologists while staying true to our deepest beliefs about the world and our role in it, politically engaged scholarship is compelling for other reasons as well.

Activist anthropology offers the potential for at least two other significant scholarly contributions to our discipline, those of enhanced methodological rigor and theoretical innovation. In terms of methodologies (how we approach and carry out our work), Charles R. Hale makes the case that because activist research demands a more horizontal, collaborative relationship between anthropologists and interlocutors from the conception of the research questions to the dissemination of its final products, it offers fertile ground for improving rigor. Moreover, our collaborators often need positivist, objectivist findings resulting from sound, defensible methodologies to inform their struggles. By exploring new or creative ways to internally validate our data and by positioning ourselves in the most transparent ways possible, Hale argues, activist researchers can enhance the precision and accuracy of our conclusions, reclaiming notions of strong objectivity in the process.[22]

Hale also suggests that activist anthropology is positioned to enrich our discipline by offering new analytic insights into social processes and relations. The argument here is quite simply that deeply engaged and collaborative research provides the researcher with a *different* partial perspective from which to examine the problems under study.[23] Our epistemologies, or ways of knowing about the world, shift. This alternative vantage point can provide novel understandings to help us complicate and advance theories of power, inequality, and social change. Shannon Speed makes a similar claim, and her work on how discourses of human rights have been wielded in the Zapatista struggle for indigenous rights in Chiapas offers a prime example of how activist research positioning can enrich anthropological theory.[24] In sum, activist research produces qualitatively different findings.

ACTIVIST ANTHROPOLOGY IN SUPPORT OF POULTRY WORKER JUSTICE

In what remains of this postscript, I reflect on my activist research trajectory in Mississippi, considering the ways in which it sustains and complicates the basic tenets of activist research: first, its ability to generate better scholarship in the form of improved methodological rigor and the creation of new and different knowledge; second, its promise of reconceiving relations of power within the research process; and, third, its potential for contributing to the movements of marginalized people toward their own liberation. I do this by considering how these goals were achieved or problematized throughout the various phases of my research.

Conception of the Research Questions and Research Design

As indicated in chapter 1 my experiment with activist research was steeped in dialogue with people and organizations with whom I am politically— though not uncritically—aligned. It is precisely these relations of accountability and reciprocity from which the greatest promises of activist research emerge. My process began with a collaborative design of the research when I spent a summer in Forest to meet partners, share the concept of activist research with them, and explore their ideas for how it might contribute to their work. The political task is not to "'share' knowledge with those who lack it," note Akhil Gupta and James Ferguson, but to "forge links between *different* knowledges that are possible from different locations and to trace lines of possible alliance and common purpose between them."[25] The exchange of ideas among differently positioned social actors, including the researcher, lays the foundation for a dialectical process of fieldwork in which methodologies, data, and analyses remain in constant dialogue with one another, as well as with their interlocutors.

Figure 23. Meeting with allies in Jackson, author in foreground. Photo by John Fiege. Courtesy of FiegeFilms.com.

This simultaneity makes it possible—indeed essential—to collaboratively reappraise and revise project questions, methods, and theoretical assertions throughout the research process.

In Mississippi early conversations between local actors, the Equal Justice Center, and activist researchers gave rise to the Poultry Worker Justice Research Project, in which we sought to partner students with Mississippi-based groups in ways that would advance these organizations' work while providing students with an introductory experience in activist research. With seed funding from the university, over the next two years our initiative enabled the participation of four additional student researchers, stipends for the organizations with which they collaborated, and minimal institution-building monies to help launch the workers' center. This modest redistribution of resources from academia to community-based organizations represents one facet of the ways in which we might begin to redress the historical imbalance of power and resources in the research process.[26] It also allowed us to expand the research questions under study to advance our understandings of the dynamics in a changing Mississippi and provide additional limited human resources to support collaborators there.

Fieldwork and Data Collection

Depending on the context, the very process of fieldwork and data collection can sometimes help our collaborators build their individual or organizational capacities. This has been noted in cases where the research process expands and strengthens existing social networks, where fieldwork entails training local partners in the conduct of research (oral histories, participatory mapping, focus group facilitation), and where it results in legal claims in support of their improved access to rights and resources.[27] In the case of my work in Mississippi, the research and emerging analysis led to the creation of the workers' center's Solidarity/Solidaridad program. What my colleagues and I were learning about the poultry industry's strategies of labor control, the union's struggles to organize across difference, and how racial positions shaped experiences with immigration informed our approach to political education with Black and Latino worker leaders, thus benefiting the center and its participants. At the same time, the Solidarity/Solidaridad classes and workshops served as informal focus groups by generating data that deepened our understanding of the very issues we were struggling with, and which I was studying.

But more often, data collection and analysis take place alongside, if somewhat separate from, other roles and responsibilities. For me these included interpreter, community organizer, fundraiser, staff trainer, strategic planner, social planner, coalition partner, logistical coordinator, photographer, and coffee maker, to name a few.[28] Given the multitude of hats I wore, few individuals primarily identified me as a researcher. As such, I had to make more careful and repeated efforts to ensure that my collaborators understood my scholarly objectives and the potential risks and benefits involved in participating in the research than would a more traditionally positioned fieldworker.

I often found it difficult to balance my participation in and commitments to the workers' center with some of the more conventional roles of ethnographer. Overwhelmed by the day-to-day demands of poultry worker outreach and education—often in the form of pressing crises:

mass firings, injuries requiring immediate medical attention, violence, extortion, detention, deportation, even death—finding time for structured interviews, archival research, and the taking of field notes proved challenging. Written accounts of activist research rarely acknowledge such hurdles and vulnerabilities, but the conversation is necessary, especially for students and junior scholars embarking on engaged research.[29]

Despite these challenges, activist researchers' unorthodox roles and the political commitments they demand are what enable us to gain privileged perspective and insight into the social processes under study. And it is precisely this positioning through which politically engaged research offers the promise of deeper, more nuanced, and arguably better analyses and results.[30] One not only learns more but also learns differently and gains access to distinctive and collaborative theoretical insights through active partnership with the people at the core of analysis.

The word "collaborative" in the previous sentence deserves more attention here. The relationships forged through activist research virtually ensure that analyses and theoretical insights represent a process of collective thinking forged in dialogue with a web of allies. Such a reality brings into question academic notions about the process by which knowledge is produced and to whom it belongs. It can create tensions for activist scholars, who are compelled to recognize the shared development and ownership of knowledge while at the same time finding themselves situated within the world of academia, which conditions rewards on ownership claims to innovations in theory and scholarship and where there exist strong systemic disincentives to recognizing collaborative knowledge production.

But we are working at cross-purposes with the decolonization of the discipline and of our institutions unless we recognize the reality of collaborative-theory production and its ultimate value for scholarly innovation. In my case, the insights I have gleaned through this project would not have surfaced were I not deeply enmeshed in our collective work for poultry worker justice. This is both because my engagement literally opened spaces to which I otherwise would not have obtained research access and because such engagement produced the dialogic and shared analyses that shaped my anthropological thinking and laid the foundation for this book.[31]

This said, the Austin School's call for research forged in collaboration with an organized collective of people working toward their own liberation is messier in practice than in its ideal type. In Mississippi I learned that the politics of organizational affiliation and critical alignment can be much more complex than the existing literature on politically engaged scholarship might lead us to believe. One reason is that scholarly timetables and the scheduling demands of academic pursuits map rather poorly onto the longer-term calendars of political and social change. Despite the fact that activist researchers' time commitments often significantly exceed those of more traditional ethnographic research, building a world in which power and resources are more equitably distributed is a collective effort with a time frame that far surpasses that of even the most committed and politically engaged ethnographic research project. Accompanying a struggle or movement from beginning to end is rarely a realistic possibility. Our accounts are therefore no more than a window into a particular time and place, necessitating that we situate them historically.

The second reason activist research is stickier in practice than on paper relates to our conceptions of an "organized collective." Collectivities can be constituted in multiple and complex ways. Moreover, they are always composed of individuals, each with their own ideas about the group's focus and strategies. Collectivities are therefore constantly under negotiation, and these processes are often contested by some members of the group who seek an alternative path. For activist researchers, recognizing the complexity of these situations can complicate questions of political alignment, raising questions such as, With whom? And on what grounds?

In Mississippi both the individuals and the collective with whom I collaborated shifted over time, and at times I struggled to define the contours of the activist research relationship. Early conversations between a loosely organized group of individuals and organizations in 2002 and 2003 birthed the idea of a workers' center. By 2004 the Mississippi Poultry Workers' Center was formed. Due primarily to questions of human and financial resources, it became a project of the Equal Justice Center, with a focus on strengthening workers' rights through more effective union representation and legal advocacy. But by 2005, as the workers' center matured and the structural issues faced by Black and Latino poultry workers came into sharper focus, the work began to shift toward community-based education and organizing. Moreover, a more locally accountable leadership council was formed, of which at least half were poultry workers, and it strived to implement a decision-making model built on consensus. These changes conflicted with the institutional structure of the Equal Justice Center, and tensions gradually mounted. In 2007 the workers' center spun off from the Equal Justice Center in the hopes of becoming its own community-based organization and changed its name to MPOWER (Mississippi Poultry Workers for Equality and Respect).

The activist research relationship that began as a collaboration with local advocates and the Equal Justice Center, and which had grown over time into a close, if complicated, partnership with the center, shifted into a third phase, in which I was most closely affiliated with MPOWER. These shifts in leadership and structure illustrate the internal struggles that this nascent organization went through as it sought to gain footing.[32] They are important to my discussion of the complexities of fieldwork in the activist research context because they illustrate the challenges in collaborating with a (more or less) organized collective. Politically engaged research with a more established organization—one with a clear constituency, vision, and plan—would likely entail a different type of negotiation between researcher and institution, resulting in a more defined relationship with specific responsibilities and deliverables. In my case, as part of a project building from the ground up, these were often amorphous and changed over time in conversation with various interlocutors at the workers' center.

Validating Findings and Writing Up

Activist research approaches the process of validating findings and "writing up" in particular ways. How can we write against inequality? What are the political stakes of publicly sharing our analyses? How do we balance accountability to our political commitments and collaborators while being self-reflexive, honest, and critically attuned to our topics of study? Who owns the knowledge produced from collaborative, politically engaged projects, and who should control and benefit from its dissemination? To begin to address some of these questions, activist research demands that we be in dialogue with our collaborators not just leading up to and throughout fieldwork but also during the lengthy stages of analysis, writing, and dissemination. It requires that we grapple with how to incorporate their critiques and concerns into the research products. Doing so increases the accountability, accuracy, and usefulness of the research, forming the crux of the argument that activist anthropology increases methodological rigor.[33] Moreover, validation, popular consumption, and critique of our analyses forces us to seriously consider who will benefit from the knowledge we produce and its utility to on-the-ground struggle.

Over the years I have shared draft chapters of this work with roughly twenty-five collaborators, including workers' center colleagues, Black and Latino poultry workers, union representatives, former industry executives, community-based advocates, local law enforcement agents, civil rights historians, and other long-standing Mississippi residents. This process was complicated by the fact that by the time I began writing about my work in Mississippi, the workers' center had become MPOWER, and many among its leadership were not the same individuals who had participated in discussions over the years about the role of activist research in furthering the goals of poultry worker justice. I found myself five years into the work starting new conversations about the politics, methods, and objectives of politically engaged research. While frustrating at times, activist research is at its best when accompanied by long-term commitment, and any sustained social justice project is subject to turnover and change that requires rearticulation of ideas and redefinition of relationships over time. Failure to take the time to retrace our steps and get critiques and validation of our findings from our partners, new and old, puts at risk the very struggles we support and can even jeopardize the livelihoods and lives of our collaborators.[34]

So, while some were baffled, asking what they could possibly contribute to my academic writing, about fifteen people took up the challenge. Some immigrant collaborators even read drafts of chapters with an English dictionary in their hand, providing me with detailed feedback despite the intense commitment of time and mental focus that this entailed. I sat with others and read them sections in which they are featured, translating from English to Spanish as I went. I have been overwhelmed by my collaborators' dedication and enthusiasm at offering constructive criticism on numerous drafts. I have taken their comments seriously throughout, and this book is testament to the collaborative writing process demanded by the activist research approach.

While internal validation helped to refine word choice, correct factual errors, and validate or question the assertions I made, it also challenged me to think about the ways in which different groups might interpret my writing. For example, when I shared drafts with workers' center representatives in 2007 and 2008, they were cautious about the ways in which I wrote about the complexities of partnerships with unions, and they encouraged me to rethink the language I was using to voice my critiques. When I met with union representatives in 2014, I again pored over the chapters in which they were featured, attentive to how they would receive these. As politically engaged researchers, we make decisions about what to make public, and in what words, in dialogue with those who are most deeply impacted by our work.

My writing has also been influenced by the movement toward a more public anthropology. These efforts seek to ask questions of relevance beyond the academy and to present the knowledge gleaned in ways more accessible for a broader public. While this trajectory has moved parallel to, but separate from, that of activist anthropology, politically engaged researchers should pay more attention to narrative and storytelling in ways that avoid jargon and translate complex concepts into common language. Doing so has the potential to reinvigorate anthropology by making it more relevant to the world. It also opens up our work to broader critique and debate, moving the dialogue about its validity and stakes into a more public realm. Like the internal validation I discussed earlier, this external validation of our ideas helps to refine them and holds us accountable to a wider cross-section of society.

FINAL REFLECTIONS

While the realities of carrying out activist research are always more complicated in practice than in theory, considering the challenges and contradictions that emerge from on-the-ground scholarship aligned with political struggle enables us to further refine the analytic frames through which we conceive our work. Moreover, critical reflection on the approach can also show us what we're doing right. What, then, might we take away from my efforts to carry out a politically engaged research project with collabora-

tors in central Mississippi, with regard to the promises of better scholarship, a more democratic anthropology, and social transformation?

In my assessment this approach lived up to its promise of producing
better scholarship. The collective theorizing and deep ethnography about
the impact the globalization of the Deep South is having on people's
understandings of one another and on their abilities to organize in the
poultry industry could not have been produced through a more traditional
approach. This is both because neutrality would have curtailed my access
to the spaces and experiences that produced analytic insight and because
it would have preempted the more committed relationships that enabled
collaborative theorizing. The activist research relationship opened up new
methodological possibilities—and demanded a high level of validation of
the study's findings—that a more traditional approach would not have
yielded.

I also think this "experiment" makes a modest contribution to the
decolonization of anthropology. It did so by affording me the epistemological and methodological tools to involve the traditional "subjects" of
research in the definition of the research questions, the design of the fieldwork, the collaborative analysis of findings, and the validation and critique of the products. Certainly, there is more work to be done here, particularly in thinking through how these very tools might be made more
readily accessible for our research participants to leverage for their own
projects, with or without our participation. More thought, too, should be
given to alternative products of the research that might be more helpful
for people in struggle than are books and articles, such as policy reports,
presentations, shorter journalistic articles, videos, popular theater, graphic
novels, a social media presence, and the like. Plenty of anthropologists
have experimented with these products in ways that could be emulated.

On the claim that activist research can help people in their struggles for
liberation, my reflections on this project are more skeptical. The cases I've
shared with the reader have been of partial and limited success, at best.
Poultry workers in Mississippi and across the world still labor in terrible
conditions, with low pay and with little respect for their basic human dignity. Locally, efforts sputtered out.

Throughout 2007 and 2008 MPOWER struggled to become an independent, locally sustainable organization. In its split from the Equal Justice

Center, it lost some of its funding and much of its institutional knowledge. A national search for a director failed, and a move toward a worker-led organization proved more difficult than the leadership council had anticipated. As MPOWER wrestled with regrouping and building the capacities of its new leadership, an interim director mismanaged its limited remaining funds. By the end of 2008 the workers' center was dormant. Local efforts to resuscitate it surfaced in subsequent years, but these too have waxed and waned.

Of the four unions that represented poultry workers in Mississippi a decade ago, only two remain. Recent years have seen them continue to struggle to represent workers without a steady Spanish-speaking staff person. The nascent community-based support that existed when I worked there, including ESOL classes, social activities, and the provision of basic services through a local religious mission center, has declined significantly. With the exception of a Catholic priest and a handful of nuns, all the advocates with whom I worked have moved away. Religious services and a few ancillary projects they support appear to be all that remain of the infrastructure that once existed.

On the other hand, immigrant children, who were mostly quite young a decade ago, have grown and are using their bilingualism to help parents navigate in ways they couldn't do before. Some have qualified for Deferred Action for Childhood Arrivals, a 2012 program that enables qualifying young migrants to regularize their status. Several have begun college; others have joined their parents in the chicken plants—mostly on the processing line but also as line leaders, mechanics, and supervisors.

At the turn of the millennium I had very high hopes. In hindsight I can see that a youthful idealism and enthusiasm about the budding national workers' center movement contributed to my formation of unrealistic expectations about the types of change we might be able to achieve toward poultry worker justice and that these hopes set me up for disappointment. Recognizing that the fight is, in fact, a long, hard struggle has helped me better appreciate the smaller wins, and becoming a professional educator has shown me the profound impact one can have on the life of another. These insights give me renewed perspective on my Mississippi experience.

My contributions there helped educate people about their rights at work, build union membership, and, at times, hold their leadership accountable. While most of my activities were not featured in the book, my collaboration with the workers' center also helped people in very concrete ways, such as to recover unpaid wages; put an end to individual practices of police extortion, sexual harassment, and discrimination; and ensure injured workers' access to medical and workers' compensation benefits. Most promising and perhaps most lasting, my involvement helped people get to know their own histories, build relationships across difference, and articulate a shared structural analysis of power and oppression in the context of the Mississippi poultry industry, opening spaces for people to step into positions of leadership in their communities and workplaces. These contributions are important, but they failed to fundamentally transform the poultry industry—a lofty aspiration, but one by which we all felt driven.

Ultimately, I worry that this case suggests activist research may do more to advance anthropology through novel methodologies and theoretical insight that push toward its decolonization than it does for helping our collaborators achieve liberation. For those of us who chose this path because it mapped onto our desires to help build a more just world, this is a disheartening conclusion. On the other hand, for those seeking a case that helps strengthen the argument for greater institutionalization of politically engaged research approaches in the academy, such a conclusion may be beneficial, because it emphasizes the promise activist research holds for scholarship while deemphasizing its more politicized goals.

This is not a comfortable resting place for me. I have wrestled with coming to terms with the workers' center's missteps and limitations. The energy around poultry worker justice in Mississippi today is not what it was a decade ago. The lasting effects of our work are seen in individuals, but not yet in collectives. Melissa Checker theorizes periods of dormancy not as failures but as moments of "quiescent politics," arguing that if we look for them, we can find active traces of efforts that sustain movements even in the lulls.[35] Taking a longer view, then, perhaps we can imagine linkages between the efforts of the Mississippi Poultry Workers' Center at the turn of the twenty-first century and others that are yet to come. That history remains to be written.

Notes

CHAPTER 1. SOUTHERN FRIED

1. With the exception of public and historical figures and a few others who specifically requested I use their names, I follow standard ethnographic practice of using pseudonyms to protect the identities of my collaborators.

2. All translations from Spanish to English are my own. Unfortunately, the process of translation tends to dilute and homogenize by filtering and "standardizing" language in particular ways. As such, the English quotes throughout the book exude the local language and mannerisms of Mississippians to a much greater degree than the translated quotes from Spanish are able to convey about their speakers from a vast array of nationalities and backgrounds. Despite this disparity, I have chosen *not* to standardize quotes in English. At least one collaborator who read earlier drafts of this work worried that this choice might reflect negatively on the individuals quoted, distract from the content, or imply disrespect on my part. While sensitive to these concerns, I chose to leave English quotes in their original form out of respect for these people's experiences, personalities, and analyses, to allow their richness to come through.

3. In this text I follow the scholarly tradition of capitalizing Black to emphasize its reference to a particular political and social identity. As explained in a 2014 *New York Times* op-ed on the subject, "Black with a capital B refers to the people of the African diaspora. Lowercase black is simply a color." Lori L. Tharps, 2014,

"The Case for Black with a Capital B," November 18. For further explanation, see, for example, Vargas (2006, 249n1).

4. "Hispanic" is both a census category and the term used in much of the South, including Mississippi, to refer to all migrants from Latin America. Naming is a political act. This term is problematic in that it homogenizes the vast diversity among people from Latin America, many of whom do not claim Spanish roots at all. In this book I tend to use "Latino" or "Latin American," reserving the use of "Hispanic" for when I refer to government statistics or want to emphasize Mississippians' viewpoints.

5. Kochhar, Suro, and Tafoya (2005, 2). Kocchar and colleagues' study focused on the southern states experiencing rapid growth of the Hispanic population from a small base: North Carolina, South Carolina, Tennessee, Georgia, Alabama, and Arkansas. Other states traditionally deemed part of the South include Mississippi, Louisiana, Kentucky, West Virginia, and Virginia. While the Confederate South technically also included Maryland, Florida, and Texas, these states are typically excluded from considerations of the Deep South because of their longer-standing histories of migration—a tradition I follow here.

6. Passel and Cohn (2011, 23). For maps of the 2000 Hispanic and Black populations in the South and the percentage of Hispanic growth by county in the preceding decade, see B. E. Smith (2001).

7. On the longer history of Latinos in the South, see, for example, Guerrero (2014) and Weise (2015).

8. L. Fink (2003); Mohl (2003). While several edited volumes have documented recent Latino migration to the region (Ansley and Shefner 2009; Murphy, Blanchard, and Hill 2001; Odem and Lacy 2009; Smith and Furuseth 2006; Zúñiga and Hernández-León 2006), fewer have used ethnography to illuminate the dynamics of these new immigrant destinations (Gill 2010; Marrow 2011; Winders 2013; Ribas 2015).

9. Lipsitz (1998, 219).

10. Since the 1970s cotton fields have given way to catfish ponds across the Delta. While the catfish industry is much smaller than poultry, workers report that catfish slaughter is even more difficult and dangerous than slaughtering chickens. For more, see Cobb (1994); Green (2000); and White (1996, 330–33).

11. Cobb (1994).

12. The South is, indeed, a global actor (Cobb and Stueck 2005; Peacock 2007; J. Smith 2004). I am indebted to a cadre of scholars who are redefining southern studies. At times referred to as the "end of southern history" or the "new southern studies," this mostly historical work rejects the southern exceptionalism promoted by previous generations and pushes the boundaries of how we think about the South as a region and as a people (Crespino 2007; G. Hale 1998; Kruse 2005; Lassiter 2007; Richardson 2007; Sokol 2007; Weise 2015).

13. Delmarva Poultry Industry (n.d.); Mississippi State University (2007); Buzby and Wells (2006).

14. Boyd and Watts (1997); Schwartzman (2013); Striffler (2005); Stull and Broadway (2003).

15. Corporate earnings rose more than 300 percent in the fifteen years between 1987 and 2002 (United Food 2002).

16. U.S. Department of Labor (2000, 3).

17. Quandt et al. (2006).

18. Ames Alexander, Kerry Hall, Ted Mellnik, and Franco Ordoñez, 2008, "OSHA Eases Poultry Companies' Penalties: Workplace Inspections at 15-Year Low," *Charlotte Observer*, February 15, 1A.

19. U.S. Government Accountability Office (2005, 7).

20. Sinclair (1906).

21. For more historical context on these issues, see, for example, Arnesen (1991); Barrett (1987); Bodnar (1985); Brody (1987); and Gerstle (2002).

22. Coclanis (2005); Trouillot (2001); Wolf (1982).

23. Appadurai (1990); Hardt and Negri (2000); Inda and Rosaldo (2002).

24. Giddens (1990); Harvey (1990); Jameson (1984).

25. Kearney (1995, 548). See also Appadurai (1996).

26. Bourdieu (1998a, 1998b); Harvey (2005).

27. See, for example, Brenner (2001); Harvey (2005); Petras and Veltmeyer (2001); and Sassen (1998).

28. Clawson (2003, 131–63); Global Exchange (2008); Harvey (2005).

29. Morales and Bonilla (1993).

30. This work builds on scholarship of the labor histories of poultry processing and meatpacking and the role of industrialization and immigrant labor in transforming these industries, including Boyd and Watts (1997); D. Fink (1998); L. Fink (2003); Gabriel (2006); Gray (2014); Griffith (1993); Keefe and Bolton (2012); Ribas (2015); Sampson and Morrison (2007); Schlosser (2001); Schwartzman (2013); Striffler (2005); Stull, Broadway, and Griffith (1995); and Stull and Broadway (2003).

31. L. Fink (2003); Griffith (1995); Kandel and Parrado (2004); Schwartzman (2013); Striffler (2005).

32. Cook (1999, 79); Kandel (2006). While immigrant poultry workers in Mississippi are to date almost exclusively Latin American, in other states immigrant poultry workers also come from the Marshall Islands, Laos, Vietnam, and Korea, among others; see, for example, Griffith (1993) and Striffler (2002). The meatpacking industry has gone through similar transformations that have fueled the growth in Latino and other immigrant populations throughout the Midwest and Great Plains; see, for example, Aguilar R. (2008); D. Fink (1998); Gabriel (2006); and Schlosser (2001).

33. Of course, other industries have also brought immigration to the region, including, most notably, foreign auto manufacturing, construction, and the growing service economy.

34. Hood et al. (2012). The industry generates nearly as many jobs in ancillary sectors, including freezers and refrigerated warehouses; trucking companies and railroads that transport feed, live birds, and finished products; sales of farm and plant equipment and packaging materials; and construction firms that build processing plants and chicken houses (Hood et al. 2012).

35. U.S. Department of Health (2014); U.S. Department of Labor (2014).

36. Mississippi State University (2007, 9).

37. While central Mississippi has experienced Mississippi's largest growth in Latin American immigration since the mid-1990s and is the geographic heart of this ethnography, it is not the only poultry region in the state. I focus on central Mississippi because of the area's historical importance for the state's poultry industry, the innovative migrant recruitment efforts that began there, and the work of the Mississippi Poultry Workers' Center, which focused its work in Scott, Leake, and Madison Counties.

38. Jerry Mitchell, 2004, "Key Suspect in '64 Killings Planning Fair Appearance," *Clarion-Ledger* (Jackson, MS), September 20, A1; "Ku Klux Klan Slates Parade in Carthage Downtown, September 28," 2002, *Carthaginian* (Carthage, MS), September 19. When the KKK tried to organize a rally in Morton, the town's elected officials changed the city's policy on public demonstrations to keep them from marching. Even among whites, the KKK is no longer a widely accepted form for enforcing white supremacy. But on one occasion while I was in Mississippi, migrants commented to me that advocates had advised them not to leave the house one weekend because the KKK would be in town. In 2008 the Southern Poverty Law Center released a report showing that Mississippi is still the state with the highest number of organized white supremacist groups in the country ("Hate Rises," 2008, *Washington Post*, March 9).

39. U.S. Census Bureau (2000a, 2010d).

40. U.S. Census Bureau (1990, 2000b, 2010f, 2009).

41. As of 2010, Forest's non-Hispanics were 42 percent Black and 34 percent white, while Carthage counted 52 percent Black and 33 percent white (U.S. Census Bureau 2010c, 2010b). Morton is a minor outlier in that its white-Black ratio is flipped, with 31 percent Black and 52 percent white (2010e). Canton represents a more interesting demographic departure, with 75 percent of its non-Hispanic population Black and just 18 percent white (2010a). This is because Canton is closer to the historically higher-percentage African American Mississippi Delta and its cotton plantations, still observed in rural areas around Canton, and because much of Canton's white population has moved out of the city, into the unincorporated areas nearby and to the wealthier white Jackson suburb of Madison, Mississippi.

42. U.S. Census Bureau (2010b). It is unclear whether this figure represents a significant undercount of the new immigrant population, if immigrants were counted but did not identify as Hispanic, or if other factors contributed to the figure of 12 percent.

43. Gordon and Hale (1997).

44. E. Gordon (1991, 2007). For a thorough discussion of the methodologies, promises, and challenges of activist research, see the book's postscript. See also Stuesse (2015).

45. In her groundbreaking work, Janice Fine defines workers' centers as "community-based and community-led organizations that engage in a combination of service, advocacy, and organizing to provide support to low-wage workers" (2006, 2).

46. ESOL stands for English for Speakers of Other Languages.

47. Vargas (2006).

48. George Lipsitz's (1998, 2011) scholarship forms part of a movement that names whiteness as a racial category that grants its holder social, economic, and political privileges, incentivizing people of diverse backgrounds to invest in the workings of white supremacy in hopes of reaping its benefits. The present work is grounded in this and other critical race theory that considers the roles of the categories of whiteness and Blackness in shaping social relations, how the power imbued in these categories influences individual and community identification, the extent to which these are self-initiated or dictated by broader society, and how these impact race relations broadly and the power of African Americans and people of color specifically. For a thorough review of this literature, see, for example, Stuesse, Staats, and Grant-Thomas (forthcoming) and Marrow (under review).

CHAPTER 2. DIXIE CHICKEN

1. Forest Area (2015).

2. Forest Chamber of Commerce, ca. 1950, "There's a Future for You in Forest," Forest file, Mississippi Department of Archives and History (hereafter cited as MDAH), Jackson.

3. Takaki (1990).

4. Jordan (1968); Takaki (1990).

5. Bonner (1984a); DeRosier (1970, 131–32).

6. Nearby is Nanih Waiya, the mother mound of the Choctaw people and the center of their creation story (Watkins 2008). The Mississippi Band of Choctaw Indians was officially recognized by the federal government in 1945. In the 1990s the tribe began actively pursuing economic development opportunities, including the establishment of industry and the development of the Pearl River

Resort and casinos. Today the tribe is the second largest employer in Mississippi (Elliott 2004; Mississippi Band 2007).

7. D. Bell (1998).

8. William B. Allison, "Scott County—General Information and Points of Interest," Scott County Historical Sketches file, MDAH.

9. Bonner (1984b, 145).

10. Historian James C. Cobb documents that in the Mississippi Delta during this decade the slave population increased almost sixfold (1994, 8).

11. Takaki (1990, 129).

12. Phil Mullen, 1962, "127 Years Ago: Terrible Fourth of July Celebrated at Livingston," *Clarion-Ledger*, July 1.

13. Some areas of the South comprised part of a large lumber industry in the late nineteenth and early twentieth centuries. See, for example, Woodruff (2003).

14. Allison, "Scott County"; Bonner (1984b).

15. Allison, "Scott County"; *Centennial Edition: Morton, Mississippi, 1866–1966*, 1966, MDAH.

16. See, for example, Tracy (1895).

17. Allison, "Scott County," 6; Phil Mullen, 1962, "Industries Welcomed: Canton among Fastest Growing State Cities," *Clarion-Ledger*, February 18, 8G.

18. Warren (1914, 87–88).

19. Cobb (1994); Foner (1988).

20. Ayers (1992).

21. Cobb (1999).

22. Using flour sacks with floral patterns was a common practice throughout the rural South and Midwest from the mid-1920s through the early 1960s. See, for example, Cummings (2007).

23. For further discussion of sharecropping as a dialectic process of domination, struggle, and resistance, see, for example, Jaynes (1986) and Cobb (1994).

24. Ayers (1995).

25. Hudson and Curry (2002); Payne (1996). The poll tax in Mississippi was implemented in 1878. Described by a former member of the Franchise Committee of the Mississippi Constitutional Convention of 1890 as "the most effective instrumentality of Negro disenfranchisement," it remained in effect until it was declared unconstitutional in 1966 (Kousser 2000).

26. Litwack (1998).

27. Payne (1996, 15).

28. For more on African Americans who chose to stay in Mississippi during this time instead of migrating north, see McMillen (1990).

29. Goldfield (1990, 27).

30. Cobb (1999, 16).

31. Green (2007, 26–27).

32. Morrow (1957). Today the Bienville National Forest covers over 178,000 acres in Central Mississippi, including all of Scott County. Logging in the national forest continues apace, and pulpwood trucks jockey with chicken haulers for space on the two-lane highways that crisscross this part of the state.

33. Jones (2006).

34. *Centennial Edition.*

35. "Legacy of B. C. Rogers" (1989).

36. Grabowski (2003, 18).

37. Morrow (1957).

38. Striffler (2005, 34). The Delmarva region encompasses the eastern shores of Delaware, Maryland, and Virginia.

39. Striffler (2005, 35, 45). "Broiler" is an industry term referring to chickens bred for meat and slaughtered while young and tender.

40. Griffith (1993); Striffler (2005).

41. Striffler (2005, 37–38).

42. Griffith (1993); Rasmussen (1951).

43. "Carthage Service Rites Are Planned for Three Races," 1948, *Jackson Daily News,* November 5.

44. Jack Hancock, 1949, "Tri-Racial Good Will Festival Slated at Carthage Is Further Proof of Harmony Existing in Leake County," *Jackson Daily News,* October 23.

45. Walter Durham, 1949, "Singing One Song, Three Races Prove Good Will Is No Dream," *Commercial Appeal,* October 28.

46. Horton and Freire (1990); Payne (1996).

47. "A Story to Tell, a Farm to Sell: Live the Good Life in Mississippi," 1975, MDAH.

48. Summary of BAWI Plan, 1963, MDAH.

49. The Forest Area Chamber of Commerce refused to grant permission to reprint the brochure here, allegedly concerned that this book might cast local industry in a less-than-favorable light.

50. For more on BAWI's role in the resurrection of the New South, see Cobb (1993).

51. Mississippi Legislature, 2002, "Senate Concurrent Resolution No. 513," Reg. sess., 02/SS01/R501.

52. Forest Chamber of Commerce, "There's a Future."

53. As late as 2005 Mississippi chickens' consumption of corn continued to surpass the state's ability to produce this key feed staple. That year, 47 million bushels of corn were raised in Mississippi, while broilers consumed more than 116 million bushels (Mississippi State University 2007).

54. "New Scott Grain Elevator to Aid Corn Production," 1954, *Jackson Daily News,* February 4.

55. Forest Chamber of Commerce, "There's a Future."

56. Morrow (1957).

57. Ramzy (1984).

58. Striffler (2005, 39).

59. "Chicken Festival Dinner Set Thursday P.M. in Forest," 1954, *Jackson Daily News*, July 21.

60. Erle Johnston to Senator Ed Henry, March 19, 1963, Forest, MS, SCR ID 99–39–0-171-1-1-1, Mississippi State Sovereignty Commission (hereafter cited as MSSC), MDAH, http://mdah.state.ms.us/arrec/digital_archives/sovcom/.

61. Mississippi Legislature, "Senate Concurrent Resolution No. 513."

62. Forest Area (2015); Morrow (1957).

CHAPTER 3. THE CAGED BIRD SINGS FOR FREEDOM

1. Gilbertson (2013); "Legal Holidays," *Miss. Code Ann.* § 3-3-7 (1972).

2. Johnston (1990, 402).

3. Mississippi Department (2008).

4. For more on the history of the Sovereignty Commission, see Irons (2010); Katagiri (2001); and Rowe-Sims (1999).

5. "Report on Canton, Madison County, Mississippi," February 26, 1964, Canton, SCR ID 2–24–2–47–1-1-1, Council of Federated Organizations; Luther O. Atkins to Erle Johnston, May 14, 1964, Forest, MS, SCR ID 2–128–22, Forest Municipal Separate School District, both in MSSC, MDAH.

6. "Informant X-Canton, Mississippi," February 25, 1964, SCR ID 2–24–2-26–2-1-1, MSSC, MDAH.

7. "Investigation of Boycott Threat in Madison County, Mississippi," January 23, 1964, SCR ID 2–24–2-2-1-1-1, MSSC, MDAH. The Sovereignty Commission closed its operations in 1973 but was not dissolved by the legislature until 1977. Its records were ordered sealed in a locked vault for fifty years, until 2027, at which time they would be made available for posterity at the Mississippi Department of Archives and History. That same year, however, the American Civil Liberties Union in Mississippi filed a class action lawsuit against the state for "illegal surveillance of its citizens." Following a court battle lasting over twenty years, in 1998 many of the commission's records were opened to the public. By 2002 they became available in their entirety online. For more on the opening of the Sovereignty Commission files, see Rowe-Sims, Boyd, and Holmes (2005); and Speer (1999).

8. Johnston (1990, xvi, 17).

9. Atkins to Johnston, Forest Municipal Separate School District; Memo, Subject: NAACP, March 21, 1960, Scott County, SCR ID 2–128–0-4-1-1-1; Memo, Subject: Rankin, Scott, Newton, and Lauderdale Counties, February 27, 1962, SCR ID 2–128–0-10-1-1-1; Erle Johnston to Luther O. Atkins, March 17,

1967, Forest, MS, SCR ID 2-128-9-38-1-1-1; Charles Evers to J. T. Logan Jr., April 15, 1965, Jackson, SCR ID 2-105-0-52-1-1-1, NAACP, all in MSSC, MDAH.

10. Johnston (1990, 7).

11. Johnston to Atkins, MSSC, MDAH.

12. This history is corroborated by a newspaper article penned by Jack Rogers, "The Voluntary Integration of Morton High School, 1967 Klan Intimidation, Part II," 2007, *Scott County Times*, Feburary 14, 8a. Rogers later noted that the article incorrectly set these events in 1967 instead of 1963 (e-mail message to author, April 21, 2015).

13. For more on the fight for school desegregation in Central Mississippi, and in Leake County in particular, see Hudson and Curry (2002).

14. Dittmer (1994); Payne (1996).

15. "Negro Called for Scott Jury Duty," 1955, *Clarion-Ledger*, March 6.

16. "Negroes' Suit Would Desegregate Madison," 1965, *Jackson Daily News*, March 11.

17. Hudson and Curry (2002, 38).

18. James Saggus, 1965, "Court Overturns Conviction of Negro in Attack Attempt," *Clarion-Ledger*, January 26.

19. Madison County Movement, *Madison County Citizen*, leaflet, 1964, SCR ID# 2-24-2-60-1-1-1, MSSC, MDAH.

20. "Report on Canton," MSSC, MDAH.

21. Madison County Movement, *Canton Liberator*, leaflet, spring 1964, SCR ID 2-24-2-28-1-1-1, MSSC, MDAH.

22. "Informant X-Canton, Mississippi," MSSC, MDAH.

23. Oral history from Barbara Devine Russell, daughter of Madison County Movement leader Annie Devine, shared with participants at the New American Freedom Summer orientation in 2004.

24. "Investigation of the Planned and Anticipated Demonstration in Canton by Negroes on Friday, February 28, 1964," March 3, 1964, SCR ID 2-24-2-48-1-1-1, MSSC, MDAH. For more on the deleterious racist implementation of the state's "literacy requirement," see, for example, Hudson and Curry (2002, 9, 38).

25. Memo to Erle Johnston Jr. and File, April 13, 1965, Canton, MS, SCR ID 2-24-3-14-1-1-1, MSSC, MDAH; "Madison Voter Registrar Asks Halt to Drive," 1964, *Jackson Daily News*, March 14.

26. Dittmer (1994, 237).

27. William L. Chaze, 1965, "Registrars Qualify over 1,100 1st Day," newspaper clipping, August, Canton, SCR ID 2-24-4-21-1-1-1, MSSC, MDAH.

28. Sovereignty Commission, [memo?], ca. August 1965, SCR ID 2-24-4-17-2-1-1, MSSC, MDAH.

29. "Investigation in the Following Counties for the Purpose of Ascertaining If Any Subversive Activities and KKK Activities Exists *[sic]* in Hinds County,

Madison County, Neshoba County, Claiborne County, Jefferson County and Adams County," SCR ID 2-24-4-16-1-1-1, MSSC, MDAH.

30. "Investigation of Possible Subversive Activities in Leake County," SCR ID 2-105-0-54-1-1-1; SCLC, SNCC, CORE, MFDP, and Delta Ministry, news release on the Madison County Movement, June 9, 1966, Memphis, TN, SCR ID 2-24-4-37-1-1-1, both in MSSC, MDAH.

31. Hudson and Curry (2002, 45).

32. Gene Dattel, 2012, "Beyond Black and White in the Mississippi Delta," *New York Times,* December 1; Mauer and King (2007).

33. Johnston (1990, 325).

34. Orey (2000, 794).

35. Johnston (1990, 376).

36. Johnston (1990, 325).

37. "Report on Canton"; "Canton Boycott," September 1, 1966, SCR ID 2-24-4-41-1-1-1; "Racial Matters and Boycott," December 2, 1968, SCR ID 2-24-4-65-1-1-1, all in MSSC, MDAH. Other successful boycotts took place in Jackson and Port Gibson, Mississippi.

38. Madison County Movement, "Don't Buy at These Stores," leaflet, n.d., Canton, Madison County Committee on Selective Buying, SCR ID 2-24-2-6-1-1-1, MSSC, MDAH.

39. Madison County Movement, "Confidential . . . to the Negro People of Madison County," leaflet, n.d., Selective Buying Campaign, SCR ID 2-24-2-27-1-1-1; Madison County Movement, leaflet, 1964, Selective Buying Campaign, SCR ID 2-24-3-78-1-1-1, both in MSSC, MDAH.

40. Visitor's registration form, n.d., Canton, SCR ID 2-24-3-58-1-1-1, MSSC, MDAH.

41. "Boycott Threat," MSSC, MDAH.

42. "Report on Canton," MSSC, MDAH; Johnston (1990).

43. "Report on Canton," MSSC, MDAH, 3.

44. "Madison County: Canton Boycott," February 14, 1964, Canton, SCR ID 2-24-2-11-3-1-1; "Investigation of a Bombing and an Attempted Bombing of Two Grocery Stores in Canton, Mississippi on Sunday, Sept. 6, 1964," September 9, 1964, SCR ID 2-24-3-60-1-1-1; "Madison County," June 10, 1964, SCR ID 2-24-3-42-1-1-1; "Investigation of a Written Statement Dated August 25, 1964 and Signed by Ernest Thompson . . . ," October 16, 1964, Canton, SCR ID 2-24-3-69-2-1-1, all in MSSC, MDAH.

45. "Canton Boycott," memo, February 3, 1964, Canton, SCR ID 2-24-2-7-1-1-1, MSSC, MDAH.

46. "Canton Boycott," memo, February 17, 1964, Jackson, SCR ID 2-24-2-22-1-1-1, MSSC, MDAH.

47. Johnston (1990, 332).

48. Erle Johnston to Ed Henry, March 3, 1964, Canton, SCR ID 2–24–2-52-1-1-1, MSSC, MDAH.

49. "Report on Canton," MSSC, MDAH, 1.

50. Madison County Movement, "Selective Buying Starts Again!," leaflet, 1965, Selective Buying Campaign, SCR ID 10–55–0-56-1-1-1, MSSC, MDAH.

51. Phil Mullen, 1964, "Canton Merchants Will Tell Facts on Boycott," *Clarion-Ledger*, January 16.

52. See, for example, "When Hughes Officials Came Calling, Scott County Met Them at the Door," 1985, *Clarion-Ledger*, October 13, K3.

53. "Bond Issues in Canton Favored by Big Margin," 1955, *Jackson Daily News*, March 26; "Sunbeam Clocks Made in Forest," 1970, *Scott County Times*, June, 2; "A Story to Tell, a Farm to Sell: Live the Good Life in Mississippi," 1975, MSSC, MDAH; "New, Current Industries Honored at Program," 1978, *Scott County Times*, June 7, 1; Sue K. Richmond, 1951, "Garment Company Plans to Locate Plant at Carthage," *Jackson Daily News*, March 1.

54. "Sunbeam Clocks," 2.

55. "Industrial Survey of Forest, Mississippi, Especially Prepared for Forest Chamber of Commerce," 1963, New Industries Department, Mississippi Power Company, Forest Vertical File, Forest Public Library.

56. Ramzy (1984, 179–80).

57. B. C. Rogers Poultry was an exception to this general rule, building a new processing plant in 1958 that increased production with two shifts, producing nearly eight hundred thousand chickens per week (Grabowski 2003).

58. Stuesse and Helton (2013). One exception to this rule was R&R Processors, which Black residents suggest always operated under a "plantation mentality," "referring simultaneously to racist attitudes among whites and perceived fear and dependency among . . . African-Americans" (Green 2007, 2). The management of R&R had hired a mostly Black workforce for as long as folks can remember, and, in small-town Carthage, "If they knew your family, you was gonna get your job." There were even Black supervisors, who former employees insist treated them no better than their white counterparts. One man compared his former supervisors to "house slaves," just one small step above the "yard" and "field" slaves doing the hard processing work. Company ownership and management had always been controlled by whites.

59. Stuesse and Helton (2013).

60. "Planned and Anticipated Demonstration"; "Cross Burnings in Forest," memo, May 7, 1965, SCR ID 2–128–0-32-1-1-1, both in MSSC, MDAH.

61. Stuesse and Helton (2013).

62. Helton (2003, 17).

63. Stuesse and Helton (2013). While I couldn't corroborate growing demands from white workers in Mississippi poultry at this time, others have documented

the entrance of Black workers into industries precisely when white workers began to organize (Boyd and Watts 1997; Chatterley and Rouverol 2000; Griffith 1993; Stull, Broadway, and Griffith 1995; Stull and Broadway 2003).

64. Helton (2003, 18).

65. Robert Analavage, ca. 1970, *GROW: A New Movement in the White South*, booklet, 331.8 A 532g, MDAH.

66. When a majority of workers vote in favor of a union during an NLRB election, the union is certified as the employees' exclusive bargaining representative, and the employer is obligated to recognize and negotiate with the union toward a mutually agreeable labor contract.

67. The federal Taft-Hartley Act of 1947, for which southern business interests lobbied intensively, weakened labor protections under the National Labor Relations Board. This legislation empowered states to determine if employees at unionized workplaces would be required to join the union. Under Right to Work legislation, enacted at the time of publication in twenty-five states in the South, West and Midwest, every individual worker can choose whether or not to pay union dues and become a member. In such "open shops," while all workers are protected by the collective bargaining agreement and unions are required to represent all workers equally, often only a fraction of these workers are dues-paying members. As a result, unions in Right to Work states typically have fewer resources, crippling their ability to sustainably organize and represent workers (Leachman 2000).

68. "Delta Ministry Report," May 1972, Charles Horwitz Papers, Tougaloo College Civil Rights Collection, T/014, MDAH.

69. Moody (1968).

70. Anecdotal evidence suggests Black workers at B.C. Rogers Poultry in Morton may have first attempted unionization as early as 1966 but were unsuccessful.

71. Lutz (2004); Moberg (1980); "Striking Poultry Workers Seek Change in State Law," 1979, *Clarion-Ledger*, June 17, 4A; "Striking Truckers Shut Down Miss. Poultry Processing Plant," 1979, *Clarion-Ledger*, June 17, 1A.

72. For national media coverage of the events unfolding in Laurel, see, for example, Warren Brown, 1979, "Unions Take Up Where Marchers Ended," *Los Angeles Times*, December 13, L18; Colman McCarthy, 1980, "Striking a Blow for Unions in the South," *Washington Post*, May 18, H2; "Little Town of Laurel Hosts Historic March," 1980, *New Journal and Guide* (Norfolk, VA), June 11, 9; William Serrin, 1980, "200 Mississippi Women Carry on a Lonely, Bitter Strike," *New York Times*, February 17, A12; and Pamela Smith, 1981, "Black Women's Struggle against Sanderson Farms Far from Over," *Philadelphia Tribune*, September 18, 11.

73. Holt (2002).

74. Milkman (2006).

75. Gabriel (2006); Keefe and Bolton (2012); Stull and Broadway (2003).

76. Ollinger, MacDonald, and Madison (2005).

CHAPTER 4. TO GET TO THE OTHER SIDE

1. Robert Schoenberger, 2000, "Chicken Catching Goes High-Tech," *Clarion-Ledger*, January 28, 1C.
2. Striffler (2005, 22, 18).
3. Striffler (2005, 20).
4. Chatterley and Rouverol (2000, 99).
5. Griffith (1993, 84).
6. More specifically, "between 1935 in 1995 the average market weight of commercial broilers increased by roughly 65 percent while the time required to reach market weight declined by more than 60 percent and the amount of feed required to produce a pound of broiler meat declined by 57 percent" (Boyd 2001, 637–38).
7. Boyd and Watts (1997); Griffith (1993); Katz (1993); Kelley (1993); Stull, Broadway, and Griffith (1995); Stull and Broadway (2003).
8. Stuesse and Helton (2013).
9. "Rogers Wins Title" (1989); "Rogers Wins Tennis Tournament" (1989); "Broiler Festival's a Fun Day" (1992).
10. "Morton Plant Gets Workers from El Paso," 1977, *Scott County Times*, September 21, 3A.
11. Helton (2003, 18).
12. Stuesse and Helton (2013).
13. Stuesse and Helton (2013).
14. Ramzy (1984); Susie Spear, 1989, "Obituary: Curtis 'Tal' Ramzy, Poultry Manufacturer," *Clarion-Ledger*, June 28, 28.
15. "B.C. Rogers' Exports" (1992, 2).
16. N. Rose (1999).
17. "Workers Come" (1995); Sid Salter, 1994, "Getting Along: Importation of Labor Is a Sign of the Times," *Scott County Times*, April 20, 4A; Chris Shaw, 1997, "Poultry Workers Hard-Found," *Clarion-Ledger*, October 19, 1C.
18. See, for example, Milkman (2006); and Parrado and Kandel (2011).
19. Stuesse and Helton (2013).
20. See also Waldinger and Lichter (2003) on the ethnic and racial stereotypes involved in employers' preference for workers with a "good" attitude over those with a "bad" attitude.
21. For more critiques of welfare reform and its racialization, see, for example, Bauer (2006); Gilmore (2002); Neubeck and Cazenave (2001); Persaud and Lusane (2000); Reagan (1987); and Vargas (2006).
22. For more analysis of PRWORA see, for example, Chang (2000); Morales and Bonilla (1993); and Painter (2002).
23. Edin (1993); Edin and Lein (1997).
24. Helton (2003, 14).
25. Stuesse and Helton (2013).

26. Such deductions violate the federal Fair Labor Standards Act by reducing workers' earnings to below minimum wage. Not surprisingly, these unlawful deductions generally went unchallenged by workers thankful to have a steady job and place to live and unaware of FLSA protections.

27. After researching various options and potential buyers, Rogers sold the company as an Employee Stock Ownership Plan to decrease the amount of taxes owed on the sale ("Employees Buy Rogers," 2000, *Scott County Times*, January 12; "B. C. Rogers Becomes 100% Employee Owned," 2000, *Spirit of Morton*, January 12, 1). For the next two years, B. C. Rogers was technically owned by its employees. In reality, the employees had nothing to do with the purchase, though on paper they had the potential to earn generous stock options and retirement benefits.

28. During the crisis Argentina defaulted on over $100 billion in debt, its GDP fell rapidly, unemployment rates were as high as 20 percent, and approximately half of its population was in poverty. Over a quarter million people left the country between 2001 and 2003, and the majority came to the United States through Miami (Marrow 2007, 600–601).

29. Arnold Lindsay, 2001, "Rogers Poultry Files Chapter 11," *Clarion-Ledger*, November 21, 1C, 6C.

30. Chatterley and Rouverol (2000, 102).

31. Arnold Lindsay, 2001, "Rogers Seeks OK to Sell Plant for $42M," *Clarion-Ledger*, December 20, 1C; Lindsay, 2001, "B. C. Rogers Poultry Sale OK'd," *Clarion-Ledger*, December 21, 1C, 6C.

32. U.S. Department of Justice (2002). The Visa Waiver Program allows nationals from select countries to enter the United States without applying for a visa. They simply fill out entry paperwork on the airplane and present it to immigration authorities upon arrival, and they typically have permission to visit the United States as a tourist for up to six months.

33. Peruvian migration to the United States around the turn of the twenty-first century was both economic and political in nature. During the 1990s the income of the average Peruvian dropped by 30 percent, and nearly two-thirds of the country lived in poverty. Furthermore, hopes that the country had surmounted its political crisis of the 1980s were dashed in 2000, when the government's highest officials were implicated in a web of corruption and fled Peru. That year 183,000 Peruvians left the country in record-breaking numbers (Marrow 2007, 599).

34. Griffith (1993, 159–64).

35. The term *coyotes* refers to the guides or smugglers of undocumented migrants.

36. In 2004 two young Comitecos left year-round work in the chicken plants to attend high school in Mississippi. With financial support from their older siblings, and by working full-time in the chicken plants every summer, these remarkable individuals pursued education despite the difficulties of being among only a handful of Latino students at Carthage High School and struggling

to identify with the life experiences of their classmates. Others, after mastering English, continued to work full time in the plants while studying in a GED program offered by a local community college. I had the privilege of teaching many of these individuals when they were still perfecting their English, and some shared with me their dreams of attending college. Thanks to the Obama administration's announcement in 2012 of Deferred Action for Childhood Arrivals, which offered legal status to qualifying young people who entered the United States before the age of sixteen, it finally became possible.

37. See, for example, Chavez (1994); Gomberg-Muñoz (2010); Levitt (2000); Nagengast and Kearney (1990); and Rouse (1991).

38. Ortiz (2002, 401); Waldinger and Lichter (2003).

39. De Genova (2002, 424); Sassen (1998, 56).

40. Griffith (1993, 28, 7).

41. Holmes (2013); Marquardt et al. (2013).

CHAPTER 5. PECKING ORDER

1. Lipsitz (1998, vii).

2. Warren and Twine (1997, 208).

3. Lipsitz (1998, 3).

4. See, for example, Alba (1990); Barrett (2012); Brodkin (1998); Guterl (2001); and Roediger (1991).

5. Guinier and Torres (2002, 31); Guinier and Torres (2002, 8–9; see also 226, 244).

6. Weise (2015).

7. See, for example, Frank, Akresh, and Lu (2010); Lee and Bean (2007); Marrow (2009); Waterston (2006); Yancey (2003); Bonilla-Silva (2004); Gans (2012); O'Brien (2008).

8. Helton (2003, 9).

9. Kruse (2005); Lassiter (2007); Lipsitz (1998).

10. Sid Salter, 1994, "Forest City Council Shuts Door on Trailer Parks in All City Zoning," *Scott County Times*, September 7.

11. WAPT (2003).

12. "Frank Herring for Representative," 2003, campaign leaflet, in the author's possession.

13. On social reproduction, see, for example, Chang (2000).

14. Helton (2003, 21).

15. Delgado (1995, 50–51).

16. Charles R. Hale (2006b) makes a parallel argument regarding structures of race and privilege in Guatemala following the armed conflict there.

17. Stuesse and Coleman (2014).

18. Chris Shaw, 1996, "Hispanic Economic Impact Strong Locally," *Scott County Times*, June 19, 1A, 9A.

19. Butch John, 1996, "Language New Health Care Barrier: State Adjusts to Needs of Hispanic Residents," *Clarion-Ledger*, December 14, 1A, 17A.

20. Helton (2003, 1).

21. Helton (2003, 4).

22. Waldinger and Lichter (2003) similarly argue that employers' perceptions of immigrants as hardworking influences hiring decisions in ways that privilege new immigrant workers over African Americans among the lowest rungs of the labor market. For more on the role of the immigrant work ethic in employer preferences, see, for example, Zlolniski (2006).

23. For more on Latinos and their relationships to whiteness and blackness in the South, see, for example, Marrow (2011); McClain et al. (2007); and McDermott (2011).

24. For studies of Blackness in different parts of Latin America, see, for example, Davis (2007); De la Fuente (2001); Gordon and Hale (2002); Greene (2007); Hanchard (1999); and Vinson and Vaughn (2004).

25. Bean et al. (2011); Borjas (1990); Johnson and Hing (2007); Waldinger (2001).

26. Johannsson and Shulman (2003); Mohl (1990); Schwartzman (2008); Steinberg (2005).

27. Alvarado and Jaret (2009); Borjas (1999); Pastor, De Lara, and Scoggins (2011); Stuesse and Helton (2013).

28. Stuesse and Helton (2013).

29. Winders (2013, 21).

30. Doherty (2006).

31. Stuesse and Helton (2013).

32. Earnest McBride, 2004, "National Leaders Unite with State Lawmakers against 'Jim Crow' Laws," *Jackson Advocate*, March 18–24, 1A, 12A. For a discussion of the development of "elite" coalitions between Black and Latino leadership in other parts of the South, see, for example, Marrow (under review) and Williams and Hannon (forthcoming).

33. Helton (2003).

34. This assertion of a developing tripartite racial order in the Deep South resonates with emerging sociological analyses of the changing U.S. color line (Bonilla-Silva 2004; Gans 2012; O'Brien 2008).

CHAPTER 6. A BONE TO PICK

1. The plant description in this chapter comes in part from the Super Chicken Road Show tour. During my time in Mississippi I gained access to various plants

as a union interpreter, workers' center representative, and ESOL teacher wanting to learn workplace vocabulary appropriate for my students. The description herein represents a composite recollection from these numerous visits.

2. U.S. Department of Agriculture (2014).

3. Linder (1995b, 1995a).

4. Quandt et al. (2006); Rick Thames, Kerry Hall, Ames Alexander, Franco Ordoñez, and Peter St. Onge, 2008, "The Cruelest Cuts: The Human Cost of Bringing Poultry to Your Table," *Charlotte Observer*, February 10–17.

5. While scholars have traditionally used the term "plantation capitalism" to refer to the historical reliance on slave labor to produce agricultural profit, I am inspired by civil rights activist Rev. James Lawson's use of the term to signal the inextricability of racism and other forms of oppression from capitalism in his analysis of globalization. See, for example, Lawson and Stelzer (2010).

6. Foucault (1978, 1979).

7. Recent scholarship has outlined the historical and structural continuities between slavery, Jim Crow, and the growing prison industrial complex (Alexander 2010).

8. For a parallel consideration of working conditions and racialized structures of labor organization in pork processing in the U.S. South, see Ribas (2015). For more on split-labor market theory, see, for example, Bonachich (1972).

9. Ciscel, Smith, and Mendoza (2003); Gordon and Lenhardt (2007); Johnson and Hing (2007); Pitts (2007); M. Rose (2008); Steinberg (2005); Saucedo (2006).

10. Ida Leachman, a union organizer in the Mississippi Delta, reports similar practices at a furniture company in the 1970s, where Black applicants had to wait outside for the boss to come out, scan the crowd, and select new workers on a whim by calling out, "Hey you, boy (or girl)" (Leachman 2000, 386).

11. See, for example, Compa (2004); Gray (2014); Striffler (2005).

12. See, for example, Gray (2014, 80–81, 108–10).

13. The case, litigated by the U.S. Department of Justice's Equal Employment Opportunity Commission (EEOC), alleges that one of the supervisors at Koch Foods engaged in various types of discrimination, including sexually assaulting and harassing female workers, physically assaulting male workers, charging workers money to obtain basic employment benefits (such as the use of leave, transfers to other positions, or the ability to take bathroom breaks), and generally threatening or retaliating against workers who complained. At the time of this writing, the case was on its way to trial. See *EEOC v. Koch Foods*, 3:11-CV-00391-CWR-LRA (S.D. Miss. 2013).

14. Union stewards are workers who have been trained to play a leadership role in their union. In addition to regular work duties on the processing line, they represent and defend the interests of their coworkers, help to uphold the union contract, and file grievances when contract provisions have been violated.

15. See, for example, Gray (2014, 120); U.S. Department of Labor (2000, 3).

16. Yezbak (2007); Tim Tresslar, 2007. "Koch Foods Hit with Safety, Wage Fines." *Journal-News* (Hamilton, OH), August 29.

17. Linder and Nagaard (1998).

18. On bathroom breaks as a persistent workers rights violation, see Linder (2003) and Linder and Nagaard (1998).

19. RWDSU (2005). While being denied the right to use the restroom affects everyone adversely, it is especially dangerous for menstruating and pregnant women, people with diabetes, and people taking medications for high blood pressure. Anita Grabowski, 2007, Poultry Industry Overview, summary for John Edwards Presidential Campaign, Center for Community Change, Poultry Worker Project, in the author's possession.

20. Linder (2003); Linder and Nagaard (1998).

21. U.S. Government Accountability Office (2005, 28). For a treatment of the gravity of workplace injuries in meatpacking that parallels that of poultry, see, for example, Schlosser (2001, 168–90).

22. United Food and Commercial Workers (2005).

23. MPOWER (2008). A recent study by the National Institute for Occupational Safety and Health shows that 42 percent of workers have evidence of carpal tunnel syndrome at current line speeds (Musolin et al. 2014, 21).

24. For treatment of the issue of line speed and repetitive motion among poultry workers in Arkansas and Louisiana, see Gray (2014, 110–13).

25. E. Johnson (2014). In response to public outcry, the increase was not implemented (U.S. Department of Agriculture 2014).

26. U.S. Government Accountability Office (2005, 32).

27. Others have reported similar practices in the poultry industry (Ames Alexander, 2008, "Judge Criticized Tyson Guidelines: Carpal Tunnel Policy Modified since 2002," *Charlotte Observer*, February 12) and farmwork (Saxton 2013, 137).

28. For more on companies' underreporting of injuries and illnesses, see Gray (2014, 113–17).

29. For more on poultry workers being pushed past their physical limits, see, for example, Gray (2014, 77, 110).

30. See, for example, Compa (2004); Holmes (2013); Jayaraman (2013); Karianen (2008); and Sen and Mamdouh (2008).

31. Griffith (1993, 205).

32. Fink (1998, 118).

CHAPTER 7. STICKING OUR NECKS OUT

1. Most national or international unions are organized into local branches that elect their own leadership. The term "local" is often used to refer to the

locally based body and "international" in reference to the larger organizational structure to which it belongs.

2. This campaign represented one of the first poultry contracts for LIUNA, a union that traditionally represents construction workers. For a discussion of the International's decision to venture into representation of workers in the poultry industry, see Fink (2003).

3. Interview with poultry worker, summer 2003, conducted by Laura Helton, Poultry Worker Justice Research Project, Morton, MS.

4. For a discussion of neoliberal multiculturalism in Latin America, see, for example, C. Hale (2006b); Hooker (2005); and Speed (2008). For a more thorough treatment of the indigenous Guatemalan community in Carthage, Mississippi, see Mandel-Anthony (2005).

5. *Bolillos* is slang for "whites." This comment echoes Striffler's quote of a poultry worker in Arkansas who told him, "Look, we are all Mexicans here. Screwed-over Mexicans" (2005, 124).

6. De Genova (2002, 433); Vélez-Ibáñez (1996).

7. For a detailed discussion of Latin American heterogeneity and how real and perceived differences among Latino immigrants impacts organizing in Mississippi, see Stuesse (2009).

8. Interview with area pastor, summer 2003, conducted by Russ Cobb, Poultry Worker Justice Research Project, Laurel, MS.

9. Scott (1985).

10. Based on her research in a pork-processing plant in North Carolina, Vanesa Ribas (2015) similarly finds that amid the South's complex racial hierarchies, new Latino Americans display an array of actions and discourses to distance themselves from their African American coworkers.

11. For a glimpse into the legal complications surrounding LIUNA Local 693 prior to its demise, see Chiem (2014) and Wickham (2014).

12. For more analysis of this bilingual representative's approach to organizing, see Grabowski (2003).

13. Linda Cromer, former organizing director of the RWDSU who catalyzed the union's efforts to organize poultry workers across the South, has written about a successful campaign that led the union to Mississippi by the early 1990s (1990).

14. Fine (2006).

15. Bernhardt et al. (2009); Fine (2006); Fink (2003); J. Gordon (2005).

16. Fine (2006); J. Gordon (1995); Jayaraman and Ness (2005); Narro (2005).

17. Cordero-Guzmán, Izvanariu, and Narro (2013); Fine (2006); Milkman, Bloom, and Narro (2010).

18. Tait (2005, 129).

19. Cordero-Guzmán, Izvanariu, and Narro (2013); Fine (2006); Milkman, Bloom, and Narro (2010).

20. Cordero-Guzmán, Izvanariu, and Narro (2013).

21. Tait (2005, 129).

22. On workers' centers in restaurant work, see, for example, Jayaraman (2013) and Sen and Mamdouh (2008). On domestic work, see Chang (2000) and Hondagneu-Sotelo (2001). On day labor, see J. Gordon (2005) and Valenzuela et al. (2006).

23. Fine (2006); Fink (2003); Wong and Shadduck-Hernández (2008).

24. Gordon and Lenhardt (2007).

25. Marx and Engels (1972).

26. Harvey (1993); Kingsolver (1998).

27. For further discussion on the differences between organizing and education, see Horton and Freire (1990).

28. Durrenberger and Erem (1999); Fisk, Mitchell, and Erickson (2000); Milkman and Voss (2004); Zlolniski (2006).

29. Milkman and Wong (2000); Zlolniski (2006, 71).

30. Tait (2005).

CHAPTER 8. WALKING ON EGGSHELLS

1. Jim Gallagher and Phyllis Brasch Librach, 2001, "6 Tyson Foods Officials Face Federal Charges of Smuggling Immigrants," *St. Louis Post-Dispatch*, December 20, A1; Kirsten D. Grimsley, 2001. "Tyson Foods, Execs Indicted," *Clarion-Ledger*, December 20, 1A; "Indictment Says Tyson Used Illegals," 2001, *Houston Chronicle*, December 20, 1.

2. Mark Bixler, 2001, "Hiring of Illegals Props Poultry 'Culture,'" *Atlanta Journal and Constitution*, December 23, 4A; Jeffrey Gettleman, 2001, "Town Not Surprised by Tyson Charges," *Los Angeles Times*, December 21, 42A; Sarah Kershaw, 2001, "Tennessee Town Loses Allure for Immigrants," *New York Times*, December 22, 12A.

3. J. Bell (2004); Brian Lazenby, 2004, "Tyson Defense Named Best of '03," *Chattanooga Times Free Press*, March 25, B1.

4. De Genova (2002, 429).

5. Unions, however, may have been divided on the issue of employer sanctions. In the 1980s many unions were still staunchly anti-immigrant, and some pushed heavily *for* the legislation in an effort to keep immigrants out of the workplace (Wong and Shadduck-Hernández 2008, 212).

6. Immigration Reform and Control Act, U.S.C. § 1324a (1986).

7. Break the Chains Alliance, 2005, Employer Sanctions concept paper, National Mobilization against Sweatshops, New York.

8. Community sign-on letter to Terry Prideaux, Tyson Foods, May 7, 2004, Mississippi Poultry Workers' Center, Carthage, MS, 3.

9. U.S. Social Security Administration (2008).

10. Mehta, Theodore, and Hincapié (2003, 48).

11. Community sign-on letter, Mississippi Poultry Workers' Center, 1.

12. National Employment Law Project (2002).

13. Andreas (1998); Chavez (1997); Cornelius (2001); Dunn (1996).

14. Kenneth J. Kimbro to U.S. Attorney General John Ashcroft, December 30, 2004, Tyson Foods, in the author's possession, 1.

15. Commissioner Jo Anne B. Barnhart to Mr. Kenneth J. Kimbro, March 8, 2005, U.S. Social Security Administration, in the author's possession, 1.

16. Libby Lawson to Mississippi Poultry Workers' Center, August 19, 2005, "Protocol for Receipt of No Match Letter," Tyson Foods, in the author's possession.

17. "¡Justicia y Dignidad!/Justice and Dignity!," 2005, Tyson Postcard Campaign, Mississippi Poultry Workers' Center.

18. Brodkin 1988; Brodkin and Strathmann (2004); Bronfenbrenner (1994); Bronfenbrenner et al. (1998); Weinbaum (2001).

19. Striffler (2005, 72).

20. Striffler (2005, 26).

21. Tyson Foods (2006).

22. Stuesse and Helton (2013). The 2005 American Community Survey calculated the unemployment rate of Mississippi's Black residents at 16.1 percent, nearly three times greater than that of the state's white population (5.7 percent) (U.S. Census Bureau 2005).

23. Griffith (1993); Striffler (2005); Stull and Broadway (2003).

24. For more on the dangers of driving undocumented, see, for example, Coleman and Stuesse (2014) and Stuesse and Coleman (2014).

25. Low-Wage Immigrant Worker Coalition (2009); National Employment Law Project (2009); "DHS Issues 'Final' Safe Harbor Rule," press release, December 27, 2008, National Immigration Law Center, www.nilc.org/safeharbor.html.

26. United Food and Commercial Workers (2007).

27. *AFL-CIO v. Chertoff*, Secretary of Homeland Security, "Complaint for Declaratory and Injunctive Relief," August 29, 2007, Northern District of California.

28. MPOWER, in collaboration with community partners, "Community Sign-On Letter to Mark Hickman, President of Peco Foods, November 27, 2007," in the author's possession, 1.

29. "Court Halts Government from Implementing Flawed Social Security No-Match Rule," press release, August 31, 2007, National Immigration Law Center.

30. Despite a 2008 "revised" rule (criticized by opponents for making no substantive changes), in late 2009 DHS rescinded the regulation altogether. National Immigration Law Center 2008; "Safe-Harbor Procedures for Employers Who Receive a No-Match Letter: Recession," 74 Fed Reg 193, 51447–51452

(2009) (8 C.F.R. pt. 274a), U.S. Immigration and Customs Enforcement, Department of Homeland Security.

31. "DHS Issues Final Rule Rescinding Controversial 'No-Match' Regulation," October 6, 2009, "Latest Developments" announcement circulated on NELP's *Employment Rights of Immigrants* listserv.

32. Following a dormant period, in 2011 the SSA resumed issuing No-Match letters, only to suspend the program again in 2013 due to budgetary constraints.

33. Neil A. Lewis, 2009, "Immigration Officials to Audit 1,000 More Companies," *New York Times*, November 19.

34. National Conference (2012). As of 2012, a few states—California, Rhode Island, and Illinois—had also passed legislation seeking to limit the use of E-Verify, with limited degrees of success (Feere 2012).

35. Chavez (1992, 169–71); De Genova (2002, 437–38); Mahler (1995, 159–87).

36. De Genova (2002, 439).

37. Foucault (1979, 280).

CHAPTER 9. PLUCKED

1. TransMundo Contractors is a pseudonym.

2. For a discussion of the completion of the I-9 form and other employer responsibilities at the time of hire, see chapter 8.

3. See, for example, Martin (1994) and Ortiz (2002).

4. See, for example, Milkman (2006); Milkman and Wong (2000, 176–80); Zlolniski (2006).

5. See, for example, Zlolniski (2006).

6. Horton (forthcoming); Sosnick (1978); Thomas (1985).

7. Emerson (1984); Wells (1996); Zlolniski (2006).

8. Griffith (1993); Griffith and Kissam (1995); Hahamovitch (1997); Martin (1988).

9. This structure of independent labor contracting in Mississippi poultry looks somewhat different from what scholars have described in other industries. For example, in custodial work in the Silicon Valley, Zlolniski documents an additional layer of "shop floor" management provided by the contractor (2006, 70). While his research suggests that the "client company" still has some level of control over workers' job tasks and performance, more supervision responsibilities are delegated to the contractor in an organizational system he calls "indirect rule." In Mississippi poultry, contractor-provided supervision is virtually nonexistent.

10. Legal memo on third-party contractors, July 2005, Mississippi Poultry Workers' Center, 4.

11. See, for example, *Heath v. Perdue Farms*, 87 F. Supp. 2d 452 (D. Md. 2000); *Castillo v. Case Farms*, 96 F. Supp. 2d 578 (W.D. Tex. 1999). As this book went to press, the National Labor Relations Board ruled that the owner of a recycling plant utilizing contract labor was a "joint employer," buoying unions' hopes that this ruling would help them organize workers in other industries plagued by contractors, including food processing. "Unions Set Sights on e-Commerce and Manufacturing Firms after NLRB Ruling," 2015, *New York Times*, August 28.

12. For a detailed history of the UFCW's organizing history in Morton, see Grabowski (2003).

13. Live hang workers were paid slightly more in exchange for doing the plant's most difficult job.

14. The liquid leaking from the back of the truck that night was a slightly more concentrated shade of brown than my bathwater in Forest, which consistently looked the color of dilute iced tea. Over the years Central Mississippi's poultry industry has repeatedly been cited for pollution of the groundwater. In 2000 Central Industries, a rendering plant in Scott County run by a conglomeration of local processors, pleaded guilty to what prosecutors called "20 years of conspiring to violate the Clean Water Act" and were forced to pay a fine of $14 million. The case represented the fifth-largest environmental settlement in U.S. history. According to a local newspaper, "An investigator was prepared to testify that, during an inspection of the area, he found the water had a brown color and a tanker truck was emptying chicken blood into the creek" (Collin Johnson, 2000, "Pollution Plea Nets Payment of $14M," *Clarion-Ledger*, November 3, 1B, 6B). Another reported that the plant "allegedly piped pollutants in the form of 'ammonia nitrogen, fecal coliform, oil and grease, suspended solids and other rotting materials'" into local creeks ("Poultry Processors Indicted," 2000, *Carthaginian*, January 27, 1A, 20A). Contamination of water and other forms of environmental degradation have become a major issue in poultry processing regions. See, for example, Sampson and Morrison (2007).

15. In the postscript I write about the ethical and practical challenges I faced as an activist researcher, politically aligned with individuals and institutions whose interests were, at times, at odds with those of the very workers they claimed to represent.

16. See, for example, Zlolniski's (2006) discussion of the Justice for Janitors campaign at Bay-Clean in Northern California in the early 1990s.

17. Milkman, González, and Narro (2010); Price, Timm, and Tzintzun (2013).

18. Durrenberger and Erem (2007, 76–78); Fisk, Mitchell, and Erickson (2000, 207–22); Zlolniski (2006, 68).

19. Smith and Cho (2013, 15).

CHAPTER 10. FLYING UPWIND

1. Radical feminists of color have encouraged us to envision a shifting grid or web, in which forms of difference, such as race, gender, nation, sexuality, immigration status, age, class, and language are placed on different axes. These axes crisscross one another at different points, and as contexts and situations change, so do these points of intersection (Collins 1998, 115–20; Crenshaw 1991). For more on how other scholars have shaped and developed this theory, see, for example, Anzaldúa (1987); hooks (1990); Kelley (1997); Lorde (1998); Pérez (1999); Sandoval (1991); and B. Smith (2000).

2. Alvarez, Dagnino, and Escobar (1998); C. Hale (1997); Jordan and Weedon (1995); Lowe and Lloyd (1997); Zamudio (2001).

3. Horton and Freire (1990, xxx).

4. Freire (1970).

5. Horton and Freire (1990, 119–20, xxi).

6. Someone gave us a photocopy of an unpublished course the Workplace Project had developed for its immigrant membership in Long Island, which provided some inspiration. More directly relevant was a recently released curriculum from the National Network for Immigrant and Refugee Rights called BRIDGE, Building a Race and Immigration Dialogue in the Global Economy, whose historical timeline became a key building block of our program (Cho et al. 2004).

7. "Power and Oppression: Valuing Our Differences, Envisioning Our Common Struggle," 2005, organizational planning document, Mississippi Poultry Workers' Center.

8. Guggenheim (1995).

9. Khokka (2001).

10. Guggenheim (1994).

11. Lowe and Lloyd (1997).

12. Stuesse, Staats, and Grant-Thomas (forthcoming).

13. AnthropologyWorks (2013); Lende (2013b); Melendez (2013); Staats (2012). See IntergroupResources.com and TheSpacesProject.org for further details.

14. Lipsitz (1998, 232).

15. Kelley (1997, 110).

POSTSCRIPT. HOME TO ROOST

1. For more on the 1970 events at Kent State and Jackson State, see, for example, Erenrich (1990) and Spofford (1988).

2. Cobb (1994).

3. E. Gordon (2007, 95–96).

4. For other cogent discussions of the theory, practice, and politics of activist anthropology, see E. Gordon (1991); C. Hale (2008); and Speed (2006a, 2008).

5. Tax (1952).

6. Blanchard (1979); Foley (1999, 1995).

7. Bastide (1973); Rylko-Bauer, Singer, and Van Willigen (2006).

8. Asad (1973); Deloria (1969); Hymes (1972); Lewis (1973); Nader (1972); Symposium (1973); Willis (1972).

9. Fals Borda (1979); Freire (1970, 1982); Kassam and Mustafa (1982). For more discussion of the development of PAR and its contemporary uses, see, for example, Hemment (2007) and Nabudere (2008).

10. Polgar (1979).

11. Clifford (1988); Clifford and Marcus (1986); Marcus and Fischer (1986); Rosaldo (1989).

12. Haraway (1988); Harding (1987, 1993).

13. See, for example, Anzaldúa (1987); Behar and Gordon (1995); Collins (2000); Crenshaw (1991); Enslin (1994); Fox (1991); Harrison (1991); McIntosh (1988); Moraga and Anzaldúa (1981); Narayan (1993); Scheper-Hughes (1995); B. Smith (1983); Trouillot (1995); and Visweswaran (1994).

14. See, for example, Beck and Maida (2013, 2015); Benmayor (1991); Craven and Davis (2013); Field and Fox (2007); Goldstein (2014); C. Hale (2008); Holland et al. (2010); Hyatt and Lyon-Callo (2003); Juris and Khasnabish (2013); Low and Merry (2010); Osterweil (2013); and Sanford and Angel-Ajani (2006).

15. Checker, Vine, and Wali (2010); see also Griffith et al. (2013).

16. Rylko-Bauer, Singer, and Van Willigen (2006).

17. For a critique of this approach and its limitations, see C. Hale (2006a).

18. Borofsky (2007, 2011); Ericksen (2006); Lende (2013a); Scheper-Hughes (2009).

19. E. Gordon (1991, 153).

20. C. Hale (2008); Vargas (2006).

21. Scheper-Hughes (1995).

22. C. Hale (2008, specifically 12–13).

23. C. Hale (2008, 20).

24. (Speed 2008).

25. Gupta and Ferguson (1997, 39).

26. Holland et al. (2010, 26–27).

27. On expanding and strengthening existing social networks, see Hemment (2007). For training local partners in research methods, see, for example, Rouverol (2003) on oral histories; E. Gordon (2003) and C. Hale (2006a) on participatory mapping; and Schensul, Berg, and Williamson (2008) on focus group facilitation. On supporting participants' legal claims, see E. Gordon (2003); C. Hale (2006a); Johnston and Barker (2008); and Vine (2009).

28. Other scholars have also reported fulfilling multiple roles while conducting activist research (Checker 2005; Perry 2013; Speed 2008; Vargas 2006).

29. Checker, Davis, and Schuller (2014).

30. C. Hale (2008); Holland et al. (2010); Speed (2006b).

31. Similarly, Speed (2008) provides a compelling rationale for why she would not have been granted the access necessary for her research if she had not explicitly aligned herself with the EZLN.

32. For a more detailed consideration of these issues, see Stuesse (2015).

33. For in-depth discussion of and models for incorporating collaborators' critiques into our final products, see, for example, Duneier (1999) and Foley (1990, 1995).

34. I learned this lesson much too closely through the follies of a student researcher who participated in the Poultry Worker Justice Research Project in 2003. He spent a summer collaborating with a union local and had dreams of becoming an investigative journalist. Despite receiving training in the politics and ethics of activist research, upon leaving Mississippi he published—without consulting either the union or his PWJRP collaborators—a scathing exposé of one of the chicken plants he had gained access to through his relationship with the union. When the plant's management got wind of the story, they contacted the union's International, which fired its local leader. Meanwhile, the student went on his way with a few shiny new lines on his CV. Despite our best efforts to remedy the situation, we were unable to help our union collaborator recover his job. Our relationship with that union, both locally and internationally, was irreparably damaged, precluding any further collaboration. Activist researchers must possess a heightened sensitivity to the potential ramifications of making knowledge public and be intentional in the ways in which we verify and validate it prior to publication.

35. Checker (2005).

References

Aguilar R., Daniel E. 2008. "Mexican Immigrants in Meatpacking Areas of Kansas: Transition and Acquisition of Cultural Capital." PhD diss., Kansas State University.

Alba, Richard D. 1990. *Ethnic Identity: The Transformation of White America*. New Haven, CT: Yale University Press.

Alexander, Michelle. 2010. *The New Jim Crow: Mass Incarceration in the Age of Colorblindness*. New York: New Press.

Alvarado, Joel, and Charles Jaret. 2009. *Building Black-Brown Coalitions in the Southeast: Four African American-Latino Collaborations*. Atlanta: Southern Regional Council. www.southerncouncil.org/pdf/BlackBrownCoalitions.pdf.

Alvarez, Sonia E., Evelina Dagnino, and Arturo Escobar. 1998. *Cultures of Politics, Politics of Cultures: Re-visioning Latin American Social Movements*. Boulder, CO: Westview.

Andreas, Peter. 1998. "The U.S. Immigration Control Offensive: Constructing an Image of Order on the Southwest Border." In *Crossings: Mexican Immigration in Interdisciplinary Perspectives*, edited by Marcelo M. Suárez-Orozco, 341–61. Cambridge, MA: Harvard University Press.

Ansley, Fran, and Jon Shefner. 2009. *Global Connections and Local Receptions: New Latino Immigration to the Southeastern United States*. Knoxville: University of Tennessee Press.

AnthropologyWorks. 2013. "Engaged Anthropology with and for Latino Immigrants." *AnthropologyWorks*, January 25. http://anthropologyworks

.com/index.php/2013/01/25/engaged-anthropology-with-and-for-latino-immigrants.

Anzaldúa, Gloria. 1987. *Borderlands/La Frontera: The New Mestiza.* San Francisco: Aunt Lute Books.

Appadurai, Arjun. 1990. "Disjuncture and Difference in the Global Cultural Economy." *Public Culture* 2 (2): 1–24.

———. 1996. *Modernity at Large: Cultural Dimensions of Globalization.* Minneapolis: University of Minnesota Press.

Arnesen, Eric. 1991. *Waterfront Workers of New Orleans: Race, Class, and Politics, 1863–1923.* New York: Oxford University Press.

Asad, Talal. 1973. *Anthropology and the Colonial Encounter.* London: Ithaca.

Ayers, Edward L. 1992. *The Promise of the New South: Life after Reconstruction.* New York: Oxford University Press.

———. 1995. *Southern Crossing: A History of the American South, 1877–1906.* Oxford: Oxford University Press.

Barrett, James R. 1987. *Work and Community in the Jungle: Chicago's Packing-house Workers, 1894–1922.* Urbana: University of Illinois Press.

———. 2012. *The Irish Way: Becoming American in the Multiethnic City.* New York: Penguin.

Bastide, Roger. 1973. *Applied Anthropology.* Translated by Alice L. Morton. London: Croom Helm.

Bauer, Gary. 2006. "The Man Who Gave Us Welfare Reform (Robert B. Carleson, 1931–2006)." *Weekly Standard* 11 (32).

"B. C. Rogers' Exports Cover a Lot of Ground." 1992. *Rogers Report* 6 (2): 1–2, 8.

Bean, Frank D., James D. Bachmeier, Susan K. Brown, and Rosaura Tafoya-Estrada. 2011. "Immigration and Labor Market Dynamics." In *Just Neighbors? Research on African American and Latino Relations in the United States*, edited by Edward Telles, Mark Q. Sawyer, and Gaspar Rivera-Salgado, 37–60. New York: Sage Foundation.

Beck, Sam, and Carl Maida. 2013. *Toward Engaged Anthropology.* New York: Berghahn Books.

———. 2015. *Public Anthropology in a Borderless World.* New York: Berghahn Books.

Behar, Ruth, and Deborah A. Gordon. 1995. *Women Writing Culture.* Berkeley: University of California Press.

Bell, Derek. 1998. "White Superiority in America: Its Legal Legacy, Its Economic Costs." In *Black on White: Black Writers on What It Means to Be White*, edited by David R. Roediger, 138–50. New York: Schocken Books.

Bell, June D. 2004. "A 'Less Is More' Strategy Clicks with Jury in Tyson Case." *National Law Journal* 26 (28): 1.

Benmayor, Rina. 1991. "Testimony, Action Research, and Empowerment: Puerto Rican Women and Popular Education." In *Women's Words,* edited by Daphne Patai and Sherna Berger Gluck, 159–74. New York: Routledge.

Bernhardt, Annette, Ruth Milkman, Nik Theodore, Douglas Heckathorn, Mirabai Auer, James DeFilippis, Ana Luz Gonzalez, Victor Narro, Jason Perelshteyn, Diana Polson, and Michael Spiller. 2009. *Broken Laws, Unprotected Workers: Violations of Employment and Labor Laws in American Cities.* New York: National Employment Law Project. www.nelp .org/page/-/brokenlaws/BrokenLawsReport2009.pdf?nocdn=1.

Blanchard, David. 1979. "Beyond Empathy: The Emergence of an Action Anthropology in the Life and Career of Sol Tax." In *Currents in Anthropology: Essays in Honor of Sol Tax,* edited by Robert E. Hinshaw, 419–43. New York: Mouton.

Bodnar, John E. 1985. *The Transplanted: A History of Immigrants in Urban America.* Interdisciplinary Studies in History. Bloomington: Indiana University Press.

Bonachich, Edna. 1972. "A Theory of Ethnic Antagonism: The Split Labor Market." *American Sociological Review* 37 (5): 547–59.

Bonilla-Silva, Eduardo. 2004. "From Bi-Racial to Tri-Racial: Towards a New System of Racial Stratification in the USA." *Ethnic and Racial Studies* 27 (6): 931–50.

Bonner, Malcolm. 1984a. "Early Days in Leake County, Mississippi, 1833–1840." In Spence and Spence 1984, 130–38.

———. 1984b. "Third Decade, 1850–1860." In Spence and Spence 1984, 143–50.

Borjas, George J. 1990. *Friends or Strangers: The Impact of Immigrants on the U.S. Economy.* New York: Basic Books.

———. 1999. *Heaven's Door: Immigration Policy and the American Economy.* Princeton: Princeton University Press.

Borofsky, Rob. 2007. *Defining Public Anthropology: A Personal Perspective.* Center for a Public Anthropology. www.publicanthropology.org/public-anthropology/.

———. 2011. *Why a Public Anthropology.* Center for a Public Anthropology, Hawaii Pacific University. www.publicanthropology.org/WaPA/r.pdf.

Bourdieu, Pierre. 1998a. "The Essence of Neoliberalism." *Le Monde Diplomatique,* December. http://mondediplo.com/1998/12/08bourdieu.

———. 1998b. "A Reasoned Utopia and Economic Fatalism." *New Left Review* 227 (January–February): 125–30.

Boyd, William. 2001. "Making Meat: Science, Technology, and American Poultry Production." *Technology and Culture* 42 (4): 631–64.

Boyd, William, and Michael Watts. 1997. "Agro-Industrial Just-In-Time: The Chicken Industry and Postwar American Capitalism." In *Globalising Food:*

Agrarian Questions and Global Restructuring, edited by David Goodman and Michael Watts, 192–225. London: Routledge.

Brenner, Neil. 2001. "State Theory in the Political Conjuncture: Henri Lefebvre's 'Comments on a New State Form.'" *Antipode* 33 (5): 783–808.

Brodkin, Karen. 1988. *Caring by the Hour: Women, Work, and Organizing at Duke Medical Center.* Urbana: University of Illinois Press.

———. 1998. *How Jews Became White Folks: And What That Says about Race in America.* New Brunswick, NJ: Rutgers University Press.

Brodkin, Karen, and Cynthia Strathmann. 2004. "The Struggle for Hearts and Minds: Organization, Ideology, and Emotion." *Labor Studies Journal* 29 (3): 1–24.

Brody, David. 1987. *Labor in Crisis: The Steel Strike of 1919.* Urbana: University of Illinois Press.

"Broiler Festival's a Fun Day in the Park." 1992. *Rogers Report* 6 (2): 2.

Bronfenbrenner, Kate. 1994. "Employer Behavior in Certification Elections and First-Contract Campaigns: Implications for Labor Law Reform." In *Restoring the Promise of American Labor Law,* edited by Sheldon Friedman, 75–89. Ithaca, NY: Cornell University Press.

Bronfenbrenner, Kate, Sheldon Friedman, Richard W. Hurd, Rudolph A. Oswald, and Ronald L. Seeber. 1998. *Organizing to Win: New Research on Union Strategies.* Ithaca, NY: Cornell University Press.

Buzby, Jean C., and Hodan A. Farah. 2006. "Chicken Consumption Continues Longrun Rise." *Amber Waves,* April. USDA Economic Research Service. http://ageconsearch.umn.edu/bitstream/126587/2/ChickenConsumption.pdf.

Chang, Grace. 2000. *Disposable Domestics: Immigrant Women Workers in the Global Economy.* Cambridge, MA: South End.

Chatterley, Cedric N., and Alicia J. Rouverol. 2000. *I Was Content and Not Content: The Story of Linda Lord and the Closing of Penobscot Poultry.* With Stephen A. Cole. Carbondale: Southern Illinois University Press.

Chavez, Leo R. 1992. *Shadowed Lives: Undocumented Immigrants in American Society, Case Studies in Cultural Anthropology.* Fort Worth: Harcourt Brace Jovanovich College.

———. 1994. "The Power of the Imagined Community: The Settlement of Undocumented Mexicans and Central Americans in the United States." *American Anthropologist* 96 (1): 52–73.

———. 1997. "Immigration Reform and Nativism: The Nationalist Response to the Transnationalist Challenge." In *Immigrants Out! The New Nativism and the Anti-immigrant Impulse in the United States,* edited by Juan F. Perea, 61–77. New York: New York University Press.

Checker, Melissa. 2005. *Polluted Promises: Environmental Racism and the Search for Justice in a Southern Town.* New York: New York University Press.

Checker, Melissa, Dána-Ain Davis, and Mark Schuller. 2014. "The Conflicts of Crisis: Critical Reflections on Feminist Ethnography and Anthropological Activism." *American Anthropologist* 116 (2): 408–9.

Checker, Melissa, David Vine, and Alaka Wali. 2010. "A Sea Change in Anthropology? Public Anthropology Reviews." *American Anthropologist* 112 (1): 5–6.

Chiem, Linda. 2014. "Miss. Farm Sues NLRB for Pursuing Union-Dropped Charges." *Portfolio Media,* August 12. Law360 (566630).

Cho, Eunice Hyunhye, Francisco Arguelles Paz y Puente, Miriam Ching Yoo Louie, and Sasha Khokha. 2004. *BRIDGE, Building a Race and Immigration Dialogue in the Global Economy: A Popular Education Resource for Immigrant and Refugee Community Organizers.* Oakland: National Network for Immigrant and Refugee Rights.

Ciscel, David H., Barbara Ellen Smith, and Marcela Mendoza. 2003. "Ghosts in the Global Machine: New Immigrants and the Redefinition of Work." *Journal of Economic Issues* 37 (2): 333–41.

Clawson, Dan. 2003. *The Next Upsurge: Labor and the New Social Movements.* Ithaca, NY: ILR.

Clifford, James. 1988. *The Predicament of Culture: Twentieth-Century Ethnography, Literature, and Art.* Cambridge, MA: Harvard University Press.

Clifford, James, and George E. Marcus. 1986. *Writing Culture: The Poetics and Politics of Ethnography.* Berkeley: University of California Press.

Cobb, James C. 1993. *The Selling of the South: The Southern Crusade for Industrial Development, 1936–1990.* 2nd ed. Urbana: University of Illinois Press.

———. 1994. *The Most Southern Place on Earth: The Mississippi Delta and the Roots of Regional Identity.* New York: Oxford University Press.

———. 1999. *Redefining Southern Culture: Mind and Identity in the Modern South.* Athens: University of Georgia Press.

Cobb, James C., and William Whitney Stueck. 2005. *Globalization and the American South.* Athens: University of Georgia Press.

Coclanis, Peter A. 2005. "Globalization before Globalization: The South and the World to 1950." In Cobb and Stueck 2005, 19–35.

Coleman, Mathew, and Angela Stuesse. 2014. "Policing Borders, Policing Bodies: The Territorial and Biopolitical Roots of U.S. Immigration Control." In *Making the Border in Everyday Life,* edited by Reece Jones and Corey Johnson, 33–63. Farnham: Ashgate.

Collins, Patricia Hill. 1998. *Fighting Words: Black Women and the Search for Justice.* Vol. 7, *Contradictions of Modernity.* Minneapolis: University of Minnesota Press.

———. 2000. *Black Feminist Thought: Knowledge, Consciousness, and the Politics of Empowerment.* 2nd ed. Boston: Hyman.

Compa, Lance A. 2004. *Blood, Sweat, and Fear: Workers' Rights in U.S. Meat and Poultry Plants.* New York: Human Rights Watch.

Cook, Christopher D. 1999. "Fowl Trouble: In the Nation's Poultry Plants, Brutality to Worker as Well as to Bird." *Harper's Magazine* 299 (1791): 78–79.

Cordero-Guzmán, Héctor, Pamela A. Izvanariu, and Victor Narro. 2013. "The Development of Sectoral Worker Center Networks." *Annals of the American Academy of Political and Social Science* 647 (1): 102–23.

Cornelius, Wayne. 2001. "Death at the Border: Efficacy and Unintended Consequences of US Immigration Control Policy." *Population and Development Review* 27 (4): 661–85.

Craven, Christa, and Dána-Ain Davis. 2013. *Feminist Activist Ethnography: Counterpoints to Neoliberalism in North America.* Lanham, MD: Lexington Books.

Crenshaw, Kimberlé. 1991. "Mapping the Margins: Intersectionality, Identity Politics, and Violence against Women of Color." *Stanford Law Review* 43 (6): 1241–99.

Crespino, Joseph. 2007. *In Search of Another Country: Mississippi and the Conservative Counterrevolution.* Princeton: Princeton University Press.

Cromer, Linda. 1990. "Plucking Cargill: The RWDSU in Georgia." *Labor Research Review* 1 (16): 14–23.

Cummings, Patricia L. G. 2007. "Collectible Feedsack Cloth and Quilts: The Past Revisited." http://quiltersmuse.com/collectible_feedsack_cloth_and_q.htm.

Davis, Darién J. 2007. *Beyond Slavery: The Multilayered Legacy of Africans in Latin America and the Caribbean.* Lanham, MD: Rowman and Littlefield.

De Genova, Nicholas P. 2002. "Migrant 'Illegality' and Deportability in Everyday Life." *Annual Review of Anthropology,* no. 31: 419–47.

De la Fuente, Alejandro. 2001. *A Nation for All: Race, Inequality, and Politics in Twentieth-Century Cuba.* Envisioning Cuba. Chapel Hill: University of North Carolina Press.

Delgado, Richard. 1995. "The Imperial Scholar: Reflections on a Review of Civil Rights Literature." In *Critical Race Theory: The Key Writings That Formed the Movement,* edited by Kimberlé Crenshaw, Neil Gotanda, Gary Peller, and Kendall Thomas, 46–57. New York: New Press.

Delmarva Poultry Industry. n.d. "Per Capita Consumption of Poultry and Livestock, 1960 to 2001." Accessed September 19, 2006. www.dpichicken.org/index.cfm?content=facts.

Deloria, Vine, Jr. 1969. "Anthropologists and Other Friends." In *Custer Died for Your Sins: An Indian Manifesto,* 78–100. Toronto: Macmillan.

DeRosier, Arthur H., Jr. 1970. *The Removal of the Choctaw Indians.* Knoxville: University of Tennessee Press.

Dittmer, John. 1994. *Local People: The Struggle for Civil Rights in Mississippi.* Urbana: University of Illinois Press.

Doherty, Carroll. 2006. "Attitudes Toward Immigration: In Black and White." Pew Research Center. www.pewresearch.org/2006/04/25/attitudes-toward-immigration-in-black-and-white/.

Duneier, Mitchell. 1999. *Sidewalk*. 1st ed. New York: Farrar, Straus and Giroux.

Dunn, Timothy J. 1996. *The Militarization of the U.S.-Mexico Border, 1978–1992: Low-Intensity Conflict Doctrine Comes Home*. Austin: Center for Mexican American Studies Books, University of Texas at Austin.

Durrenberger, E. Paul, and Suzan Erem. 1999. "The Abstract, the Concrete, the Political, and the Academic: Anthropology and a Labor Union in the United States." *Human Organization* 58 (3): 305–12.

———. 2007. *Anthropology Unbound: A Field Guide to the 21st Century*. Boulder, CO: Paradigm.

Edin, Kathryn. 1993. *There's a Lot of Month Left at the End of the Money: How AFDC Recipients Make Ends Meet in Chicago*. New York: Garland.

Edin, Kathryn, and Laura Lein. 1997. *Making Ends Meet: How Single Mothers Survive Welfare and Low-Wage Work*. New York: Sage Foundation.

Elliott, Debbie. 2004. "Mississippi Choctaws Find Economic Success." *All Things Considered*, July 17. National Public Radio. www.npr.org/templates/story/story.php?storyId=3465024.

Emerson, Robert D. 1984. *Seasonal Agricultural Labor Markets in the United States*. Ames: Iowa University Press.

Enslin, Elizabeth. 1994. "Beyond Writing: Feminist Practice and the Limitations of Ethnography." *Cultural Anthropology* 9 (4): 537–68.

Erenrich, Susie. 1990. *Kent and Jackson State, 1970–1990*. [Silver Spring, MD?]: Vietnam Generation.

Eriksen, Thomas Hylland. 2006. *Engaging Anthropology: The Case for a Public Presence*. New York: Berg.

Fals Borda, Orlando. 1979. "Investigating Reality in Order to Transform It: The Colombian Experience." *Dialectical Anthropology*, no. 4: 33–55.

Feere, Jon. 2012. "An Overview of E-Verify Policies at the State Level." Backgrounder Report. Center for Immigration Studies. http://cis.org/e-verify-at-the-state-level.

Field, Les W., and Richard G. Fox. 2007. *Anthropology Put to Work*. Oxford: Berg.

Fine, Janice. 2006. *Worker Centers: Organizing Communities at the Edge of the Dream*. Ithaca, NY: ILR/Cornell University Press.

Fink, Deborah. 1998. *Cutting into the Meatpacking Line: Workers and Change in the Rural Midwest*. Chapel Hill: University of North Carolina Press.

Fink, Leon. 2003. *The Maya of Morganton: Work and Community in the Nuevo New South*. Durham: University of North Carolina Press.

Fisk, Catherine, Daniel Mitchell, and Christopher Erickson. 2000. "Union Representation of Immigrant Janitors in Southern California: Economic and

Legal Challenges." In *Organizing Immigrants: The Challenge for Unions in Contemporary California,* edited by Ruth Milkman, 199–224. Ithaca, NY: Cornell University Press.

Foley, Douglas E. 1990. *Learning Capitalist Culture: Deep in the Heart of Tejas.* Philadelphia: University of Pennsylvania Press.

———. 1995. *The Heartland Chronicles.* Philadelphia: University of Pennsylvania Press.

———. 1999. "The Fox Project: A Reappraisal (with Replies)." *Current Anthropology* 40 (2): 171–92.

Foner, Eric. 1988. *Reconstruction: America's Unfinished Revolution, 1863–1877.* New York: Harper and Row.

Forest Area Chamber of Commerce. 2015. "Wing Dang Doodle Festival." www .forestareachamber.com/pages/WingDangDoodle.

Foucault, Michel. 1978. *The History of Sexuality: An Introduction.* Vol. I. New York: Vintage Books.

———. 1979. *Discipline and Punish: The Birth of the Prison.* New York: Random House.

Fox, Richard G. 1991. *Recapturing Anthropology: Working in the Present.* Santa Fe, NM: School of American Research Press.

Frank, Reanne, Ilana Redstone Akresh, and Bo Lu. 2010. "Latino Immigrants and the U.S. Racial Order: How and Where Do They Fit In?" *American Sociological Review* 75 (3): 378–401.

Freire, Paulo. 1970. *Pedagogy of the Oppressed.* New York: Herder and Herder.

———. 1982. "Creating Alternative Research Methods: Learning to Do It by Doing It." In *Creating Knowledge: A Monopoly? Participating Research in Development,* edited by Budd L. Hall, Arthur Gillette, and Rajesh Tandon, 29–37. New Delhi: Society for Participatory Research in Asia.

Gabriel, Jackie. 2006. "Organizing *The Jungle:* Industrial Restructuring and Immigrant Unionization in the American Meatpacking Industry." *Working USA: The Journal of Labor and Society,* no. 9: 337–59.

Gans, Herbert J. 2012. "'Whitening' and the American Racial Hierarchy." *Du Bois Review* 9 (2): 267–79.

Gerstle, Gary. 2002. *Working-Class Americanism: The Politics of Labor in a Textile City, 1914–1960.* Princeton: Princeton University Press.

Giddens, Anthony. 1990. *The Consequences of Modernity.* Stanford: Stanford University Press.

Gilbertson, Annie. 2013. "One Mississippi Schools Take of MLK and Robert E. Lee Day." *Mississippi Public Broadcasting.* http://mpbonline.org/News/article /330_mississippi_school_take_off_mlk_and_robert_e_lee_the_takeaway.

Gill, Hannah. 2010. *The Latino Migration Experience in North Carolina.* Chapel Hill: University of North Carolina Press.

Gilmore, Ruth W. 2002. "Race and Globalization." In *Geographies of Global Change: Remapping the World,* edited by Ronald J. Johnston, Peter J. Taylor, and Michael J. Watts, 261–74. London: Blackwell.

Global Exchange. 2008. *The Right to Stay Home: Alternatives to Mass Displacement and Forced Migration in North America.* San Francisco: Global Exchange.

Goldfield, David R. 1990. *Black, White, and Southern: Race Relations and Southern Culture, 1940 to the Present.* Baton Rouge: Louisiana State University Press.

Goldstein, Daniel M. 2014. "Laying the Body on the Line: Activist Anthropology and the Deportation of the Undocumented." *American Anthropologist* 116 (4): 839–42.

Gomberg-Muñoz, Ruth. 2010. *Labor and Legality: An Ethnography of a Mexican Immigrant Network, Issues of Globalization: Case Studies in Contemporary Anthropology.* Oxford: Oxford University Press.

Gordon, Edmund T. 1991. "Anthropology and Liberation." In Harrison 1991, 149–67.

———. 2003. "Rights, Resources, and the Social Memory of Struggle: Reflections on a Study of Indigenous and Black Community Land Rights on Nicaragua's Atlantic Coast." *Participatory Mapping of Indigenous Lands in Latin America* 62 (4): 369–81.

———. 2007. "The Austin School Manifesto: An Approach to the Black or African Diaspora." *Cultural Anthropology,* no. 19: 93–97.

Gordon, Edmund T., and Charles R. Hale. 1997. "Activist Anthropology Concept Statement." University of Texas at Austin. www.utexas.edu/cola/depts/anthropology/activist/concept%20statement.html. Site discontinued.

———. 2002. *Organizaciones indígenas y negras en Centroamérica: Sus luchas por reconocimiento y recursos.* Austin, TX: Caribbean Central American Research Council.

Gordon, Jennifer. 1995. "We Make the Road by Walking: Immigrant Workers, the Workplace Project, and the Struggle for Social Change." *Harvard Civil Rights Civil Liberties Law Review,* no. 30: 407–51.

———. 2005. *Suburban Sweatshops: The Fight for Immigrant Rights.* Cambridge, MA: Harvard University Press.

Gordon, Jennifer, and Robin A. Lenhardt. 2007. *Conflict and Solidarity between African American and Latino Immigrant Workers.* Berkeley: Chief Justice Earl Warren Institute on Race, Ethnicity, and Diversity, University of California, Berkeley Law School.

Grabowski, Anita. 2003. "La Pollera: Latin American Poultry Workers in Morton, Mississippi." Master's thesis, Institute of Latin American Studies, University of Texas at Austin.

Gray, LaGuana. 2014. *We Just Keep Running the Line: Black Southern Women and the Poultry Processing Industry.* Baton Rouge: Louisiana State University Press.

Green, Laurie Beth. 2000. "'A Struggle of the Mind': Black Working-Class Women's Organizing in Memphis and the Mississippi Delta, 1960s to 1990s." In *Frontline Feminisms: Women, War, and Resistance,* edited by Marguerite R. Waller and Jennifer Rycenga, 399–418. New York: Routledge.

———. 2007. *Battling the Plantation Mentality: Memphis and the Black Freedom Struggle.* Edited by Waldo E. Jr. Martin and Patricia Sullivan. John Hope Franklin Series in African American History and Culture. Chapel Hill: University of North Carolina Press.

Greene, Shane. 2007. "Entre lo indio, lo negro, y lo incaico: The Spatial Hierarchies of Difference in Multicultural Peru." *Journal of Latin American and Caribbean Anthropology* 12 (2): 441–74.

Griffith, David C. 1993. *Jones's Minimal: Low-Wage Labor in the United States.* Albany: State University of New York Press.

———. 1995. "*Hay Trabajo:* Poultry Processing, Rural Industrialization, and Latinization of Low-Wage Labor." In Stull, Broadway, and Griffith 1995, 129–51.

Griffith, David, and Ed Kissam. 1995. *Working Poor: Farmworkers in the United States.* Philadelphia: Temple University Press.

Griffith, David, Shao-hua Liu, Michael Paolisso, and Angela Stuesse. 2013. "Enduring Whims and Public Anthropology." *American Anthropologist* 115 (1): 125–26.

Guerrero, Perla M. 2014. "A Tenuous Welcome for Latinas/os and Asians: States' Rights Discourse in Late Twentieth-Century Arkansas." In *Race and Ethnicity in Arkansas: New Perspectives,* edited by John A. Kirk, 141–51. Fayetteville: University of Arkansas Press.

Guggenheim, Charles. 1994. *A Time for Justice: America's Civil Rights Movement.* Directed by Charles Guggenheim. Montgomery, AL: Teaching Tolerance. DVD.

———. 1995. *The Shadow of Hate.* Directed by Charles Guggenheim. Montgomery, AL: Teaching Tolerance. DVD.

Guinier, Lani, and Gerald Torres. 2002. *The Miner's Canary: Enlisting Race, Resisting Power, Transforming Democracy.* Cambridge, MA: Harvard University Press.

Gupta, Akhil, and James Ferguson. 1997. *Anthropological Locations: Boundaries and Grounds of a Field Science.* Berkeley: University of California Press.

Guterl, Matthew Pratt. 2001. *The Color of Race in America, 1900–1940.* Cambridge, MA: Harvard University Press.

Hahamovitch, Cindy. 1997. *The Fruits of Their Labor: Atlantic Coast Farmworkers and the Making of Migrant Poverty, 1870–1945.* Chapel Hill: University of North Carolina Press.

Hale, Charles R. 1997. "Cultural Politics of Identity in Latin America." *Annual Review of Anthropology*, no. 26: 567–90.

———. 2006a. "Activist Research v. Cultural Critique: Indigenous Land Rights and the Contradictions of Politically Engaged Anthropology." *Cultural Anthropology* 21 (1): 96–120.

———. 2006b. *Más que un indio/More Than an Indian: Racial Ambivalence and Neoliberal Multiculturalism in Guatemala*. Santa Fe, NM: School of American Research Press.

———. 2008. *Engaging Contradictions: Theory, Politics, and Methods of Activist Scholarship*. Berkeley: University of California Press.

Hale, Grace Elizabeth. 1998. *Making Whiteness: The Culture of Segregation in the South, 1890–1940*. New York: Pantheon Books.

Hanchard, Michael. 1999. *Racial Politics in Contemporary Brazil*. Durham, NC: Duke University Press.

Haraway, Donna. 1988. "Situated Knowledges: The Science Question in Feminism and the Privilege of Partial Perspective." *Feminist Studies* 14 (3): 575–99.

Harding, Sandra. 1987. *Feminism and Methodology*. Bloomington: Indiana University Press.

———. 1993. "Rethinking Standpoint Epistemology: 'What Is Strong Objectivity?'" In *Feminist Epistemologies*, edited by Linda Alcoff and Elizabeth Potter, 49–82. New York: Routledge.

Hardt, Michael, and Antonio Negri. 2000. *Empire*. Cambridge, MA: Harvard University Press.

Harrison, Faye V. 1991. *Decolonizing Anthropology*. Washington, DC: American Anthropological Association.

Harvey, David. 1990. *The Condition of Postmodernity: An Enquiry into the Origins of Cultural Change*. Cambridge, MA: Blackwell.

———. 1993. "Class Relations, Social Justice and the Politics of Difference." In *Place and the Politics of Identity*, edited by Michael Keith and Steve Pile, 41–66. New York: Routledge.

———. 2005. *A Brief History of Neoliberalism*. New York: Oxford University Press.

Helton, Laura. 2003. "Three Hundred Strangers Next Door: Native Mississippians Respond to Immigration." *A Report of the Poultry Worker Justice Research Project*. Inter-American Policy Studies Occasional 4. Austin, TX: Lyndon B. Johnson School of Public Affairs, Teresa Lozano Long Institute of Latin American Studies, University of Texas at Austin.

Hemment, Julie. 2007. *Empowering Women in Russia: Activism, Aid, and NGOs*. Bloomington: Indiana University Press.

Holland, Dorothy, Dana E. Powell, Eugenia Eng, and Georgina Drew. 2010. "Models of Engaged Scholarship: An Interdisciplinary Discussion." *Collaborative Anthropologies*, no. 3: 1–36.

Holmes, Seth. 2013. *Fresh Fruit, Broken Bodies: Migrant Farmworkers in the United States.* California Series in Public Anthropology. Berkeley: University of California Press.

Holt, Thomas C. 2002. *The Problem of Race in the Twenty-First Century.* Cambridge, MA: Harvard University Press.

Hondagneu-Sotelo, Pierrette. 2001. *Doméstica: Immigrant Workers Cleaning and Caring in the Shadows of Affluence.* Berkeley: University of California Press.

Hood, Ken, Al Myles, David Peebles, and Danny Thornton. 2012. *The Poultry Industry and Its Economic Impact.* Starkville: Mississippi State University.

Hooker, Juliet. 2005. "Indigenous Inclusion/Black Exclusion: Race, Ethnicity, and Multicultural Citizenship in Latin America." *Journal of Latin American Studies,* no. 37: 285–310.

hooks, bell. 1990. *Yearning: Race, Gender, and Cultural Politics.* Cambridge, MA: South End.

Horton, Myles, and Paolo Freire, eds. 1990. *We Make the Road by Walking: Conversations on Education and Social Change.* With Brenda Bell, John Gaventa, and John Peters. Philadelphia: Temple University Press.

Horton, Sarah. Forthcoming. "Ghost Workers: The Implications of Governing Immigration through Crime for Migrant Workplaces." *Anthropology of Work Review.*

Hudson, Winson, and Constance Curry. 2002. *Mississippi Harmony: Memoirs of a Freedom Fighter.* New York: Palgrave MacMillan.

Hyatt, Susan Brin, and Vincent Lyon-Callo. 2003. "Introduction: Anthropology and Political Engagement." *Urban Anthropology* 32 (2): 133–46.

Hymes, Dell. 1972. *Reinventing Anthropology.* New York: Vintage Books.

Inda, Jonathan Xavier, and Renato Rosaldo. 2002. *The Anthropology of Globalization: A Reader.* Malden, MA: Blackwell.

Irons, Jenny. 2010. *Reconstituting Whiteness: The Mississippi State Sovereignty Commission.* Nashville: Vanderbilt University Press.

Jameson, Fredric. 1984. "Postmodernism; or The Cultural Logic of Late Capitalism." *New Left Review,* no. 146: 53–92.

Jayaraman, Saru. 2013. *Behind the Kitchen Door.* Ithaca, NY: Cornell University Press.

Jayaraman, Sarumathi, and Immanuel Ness. 2005. *The New Urban Immigrant Workforce: Innovative Models for Labor Organizing.* Armonk, NY: Sharpe.

Jaynes, Gerald David. 1986. *Branches without Roots: Genesis of the Black Working Class in the American South, 1862–1882.* New York: Oxford University Press.

Johannsson, Hannes, and Steven Shulman. 2003. "Immigration and the Employment of African American Workers." *Review of Black Political Economy* 31 (1–2): 95–110.

Johnson, Emma. 2014. "Obama, USDA Press for Faster Line Speeds in Poultry Plants." *Militant* 78 (15): www.themilitant.com/2014/7815/781503.html.

Johnson, Kevin R., and Bill Ong Hing. 2007. "The Immigrant Rights Marches of 2006 and the Prospects for a New Civil Rights Movement." *Harvard Civil Rights-Civil Liberties Law Review*, no. 42: 99–138.

Johnston, Barbara Rose, and Holly M. Barker. 2008. *Consequential Damages of Nuclear War: The Rongelap Report*. Walnut Creek, CA: Left Coast.

Johnston, Erle. 1990. *Mississippi's Defiant Years, 1953–1973: An Interpretive Documentary with Personal Experiences*. Forest, MS: Lake Harbor.

Jones, Lu Ann. 2006. ""Work Was My Pleasure": An Oral History of Nellie Stancil Langley." In *Work, Family, and Faith: Rural Southern Women in the Twentieth Century*, edited by Melissa Walker and Rebecca Sharpless, 17–41. Columbia: University of Missouri Press.

Jordan, Glenn, and Chris Weedon. 1995. *Cultural Politics: Class, Gender, Race, and the Postmodern World*. Oxford: Blackwell.

Jordan, Winthrop D. 1968. *White over Black: American Attitudes toward the Negro, 1550–1812*. Chapel Hill: University of North Carolina Press.

Juris, Jeffrey S., and Alex Khasnabish. 2013. *Insurgent Encounters: Transnational Activism, Ethnography, and the Political*. Durham, NC: Duke University Press.

Kandel, William. 2006. "Meat-Processing Firms Attract Hispanic Workers to Rural America." *Amber Waves*, June. www.ers.usda.gov/amber-waves/2006-june/meat-processing-firms-attract-hispanic-workers-to-rural-america.aspx#.VeujfOu6_lf.

Kandel, William, and Emilio A. Parrado. 2004. "Hispanics in the American South and the Transformation of the Poultry Industry." In *Hispanic Spaces, Latino Places: Community and Cultural Diversity in Contemporary America*, edited by Daniel D. Arreola, 255–76. Austin: University of Texas Press.

Karianen, David. 2008. "Gender, Race, and Nationality in the Making of Mexican Migrant Labor in the United States." *Latin American Perspectives* 35 (1): 51–63.

Kassam, Yusuf, and Kamal Mustafa. 1982. *Participatory Research: An Emerging Alternative Methodology in Social Science Research*. New Delhi: Society for Participatory Research in Asia.

Katagiri, Yasuhiro. 2001. *The Mississippi State Sovereignty Commission: Civil Rights and States' Rights*. Jackson: University Press of Mississippi.

Katz, Michael B. 1993. "The Urban 'Underclass' as a Metaphor of Social Transformation." In *The "Underclass" Debate, Views from History*, edited by Michael B. Katz, 3–23. Princeton: Princeton University Press.

Kearney, Michael. 1995. "The Local and the Global: The Anthropology of Globalization and Transnationalism." *Annual Review of Anthropology*, no. 24: 547–65.

Keefe, Jeffrey, and Mathias Bolton. 2012. "When Chickens Devoured Cows: The Collapse of National Bargaining in the Red Meat Industry and Union Rebuilding in the Meat and Poultry Industry." Social Science Research Network. http://papers.ssrn.com/sol3/papers.cfm?abstract_id=2168241.

Kelley, Robin D. G. 1993. "The Black Poor and the Politics of Opposition in a New South City, 1929–1970." In *The "Underclass" Debate, Views from History*, edited by Michael B. Katz, 293–333. Princeton: Princeton University Press.

———. 1997. *Yo' Mama's DisFUNKtional! Fighting the Culture Wars in Urban America*. Boston: Beacon.

Khokka, Sasha. 2001. *Uprooted: Refugees of the Global Economy*. Oakland: National Network of Immigrant and Refugee Rights.

Kingsolver, Ann E. 1998. Introduction to *More Than Class: Studying Power in U.S. Workplaces*, edited by Ann E. Kingsolver, 1–20. New York: State University of New York Press.

Kochhar, Rakesh, Roberto Suro, and Sonya Tafoya. 2005. *The New Latino South: The Context and Consequences of Rapid Population Growth*. Washington, DC: Pew Hispanic.

Kousser, J. Morgan. 2000. "Poll Tax." In *The International Encyclopedia of Elections*, edited by Richard Rose, 208–9. Washington, DC: CQ.

Kruse, Kevin M. 2005. *White Flight: Atlanta and the Making of Modern Conservatism*. Princeton: Princeton University Press.

Lassiter, Matthew D. 2007. *The Silent Majority: Suburban Politics in the Sunbelt South*. Princeton: Princeton University Press.

Lawson, James M., Jr., and Andrew Stelzer. 2010. "What's Wrong with the Social Justice Movement?" *Race, Poverty, and the Environment* 17 (2): 79–83.

Leachman, Ida. 2000. "Black Women and Labor Unions in the South: From the 1970s to the 1990s." In *Frontline Feminisms: Women, War, and Resistance*, edited by Marguerite R. Waller and Jennifer Rycenga, 385–94. New York: Routledge.

Lee, Jennifer, and Frank Bean. 2007. "Reinventing the Color Line: Immigration and America's New Racial/Ethnic Divide." *Social Forces* 86 (2): 561–86.

"The Legacy of B. C. Rogers." 1989. *Rogers Report* 3 (3): 7–8.

Lende, Daniel. 2013a. "Anthropology: Growth and Relevance, Not Popularity." *Neuroanthropology PLOS*, September 12. http://blogs.plos.org/neuroanthropology/2013/09/12/anthropology-growth-and-relevance-not-popularity/.

———. 2013b. "Intergroup Resources: Building Social Justice Online and from the Ground Up." *Neuroanthropology PLOS*, February 13. http://blogs.plos.org/neuroanthropology/2013/02/13/intergroup-resources-building-social-justice-online-and-from-the-ground-up/.

Levitt, Peggy. 2000. "Migrants Participate across Borders: Toward an Under-standing of Forms and Consequences." In *Immigration Research for a New Century Multidisciplinary Perspectives,* edited by Nancy Foner, Ruben G. Rumbaut, and Steven J. Gold, 459–80. New York: Sage Foundation.

Lewis, Diane. 1973. "Anthropology and Colonialism." *Current Anthropology* 14 (5): 581–602.

Linder, Marc. 1995a. "'I Gave My Employer a Chicken That Had No Bone: Joint Firm-State Responsibility for Line-Speed-Related Occupational Injuries." *Case Western Reserve Law Review* 46 (1): 33–143.

———. 1995b. "Playing Chicken with People: The Occupational Safety and Health Consequences of Throughput *Uber Alles." International Journal of Health Services* 25 (4): 633–65.

———. 2003. *"Void Where Prohibited" Revisited: The Trickle-Down Effect of OSHA's At-Will Bathroom-Break Regulation.* Iowa City: Fanipihua.

Linder, Marc, and Ingrid Nagaard. 1998. *Void Where Prohibited: Rest Breaks and the Right to Urinate on Company Time.* Ithaca, NY: Cornell University Press.

Lipsitz, George. 1998. *The Possessive Investment in Whiteness: How White People Profit from Identity Politics.* Philadelphia: Temple University Press.

———. 2011. *How Racism Takes Place.* Philadelphia: Temple University Press.

Litwack, Leon F. 1998. *Trouble in Mind: Black Southerners in the Age of Jim Crow.* New York: Knopf.

Lorde, Audre. 1998. "Age, Race, Class, and Sex: Women Redefining Difference." In *Race, Class, and Gender,* edited by Margaret L. Andersen and Patricia Hill Collins, 187–94. Belmont, CA: Wadsworth.

Low, Setha M., and Sally Engle Merry. 2010. "Engaged Anthropology: Diversity and Dilemmas." Supplement, *Current Anthropology* 51 (S2): S203–S226.

Lowe, Lisa, and David Lloyd. 1997. *Politics of Culture in the Shadow of Capital.* Durham, NC: Duke University Press.

Low-Wage Immigrant Worker Coalition. 2009. "Resources." www.lwiw.org/SSA_NM/lwiw_resources.htm. Site discontinued.

Lutz, Christine. 2004. "The Sanderson Strike." Paper presented at Southern Labor Studies Conference, Birmingham, April 15–17.

Mahler, Sarah J. 1995. *American Dreaming: Immigrant Life on the Margins.* Princeton: Princeton University Press.

Mandel-Anthony, David G. 2005. "From Comitancillo to Carthage, Mississippi: Activist Research, Transnationalism, and Racial Formation in a Community of Guatemalan Mam Poultry Workers." Undergraduate honors thesis, University of Texas at Austin.

Marcus, George E., and Michael M. J. Fischer. 1986. *Anthropology as Cultural Critique: An Experimental Moment in the Human Sciences.* Chicago: University of Chicago Press.

Marquardt, Marie Friedmann, Timothy J. Steigenga, Philip J. Williams, and Manuel A. Vásquez. 2013. *Living "Illegal": The Human Face of Unauthorized Immigration*. New York: New Press.

Marrow, Helen B. 2007. "South America." In *The New Americans: A Guide to Immigration since 1965*, edited by Mary C. Waters and Reed Ueda, with Helen B. Marrow, 593–611. Cambridge, MA: Harvard University Press.

———. 2009. "New Immigrant Destinations and the American Colour Line." *Ethnic and Racial Studies* 32 (6): 1037–57.

———. 2011. *New Destination Dreaming: Immigration, Race, and Legal Status in the Rural American South*. Stanford: Stanford University Press.

———. Under review. "The Difference a Decade of Enforcement Makes: Hispanic Racial Incorporation and Changing Intergroup Relations in the American South's Black Belt (2003–2013)." In *Transatlantic Perspectives on New Immigrant Destinations*, edited by Stefanie Chambers, Diana Evans, Anthony M. Messina, and Abigail Fisher. Palo Alto, CA: Stanford University Press.

Martin, Philip L. 1988. *Harvest of Confusion: Migrant Workers in U.S. Agriculture*. Boulder, CO: Westview.

———. 1994. "Good Intentions Gone Awry: IRCA and US Agriculture." *Annals of the Academy of Social Science*, no. 534: 44–57.

Marx, Karl, and Friedrich Engels. 1972. *The Marx-Engels Reader*. Edited by Robert C. Tucker. New York: Norton.

Mauer, Marc, and Ryan S. King. 2007. "Uneven Justice: State Rates of Incarceration by Race and Ethnicity." *Sentencing Project*, July. www.sentencingproject.org/doc/publications/rd_stateratesofincbyraceandethnicity.pdf.

McClain, Paula D., Monique L. Lyle, Niambi M. Carter, Victoria M. DeFrancesco Soto, Gerald F. Lackey, Kendra Davenport Cotton, Shayla C. Nunnally, Thomas J. Scotto, Jeffrey D. Grynaviski, and J. Alan Kendrick. 2007. "Black Americans and Latino Immigrants in a Southern City: Friendly Neighbors or Economic Competitors?" *Du Bois Review* 4 (1): 97–117.

McDermott, Monica. 2011. "Black Attitudes and Hispanic Immigrants in South Carolina." In *Just Neighbors? Research on African American and Latino Relations in the United States*, edited by Edward Telles, Mark Sawyer, and Gaspar Rivera-Salgado, 242–63. New York: Sage Foundation.

McIntosh, Peggy. 1988. "White Privilege and Male Privilege: A Personal Account of Coming to See Correspondences through Work in Women's Studies." Working Paper 189, Wellesley College Center for Research on Women.

McMillen, Neil R. 1990. *Dark Journey: Black Mississippians in the Age of Jim Crow*. Urbana: University of Illinois Press.

Mehta, Chirag, Nik Theodore, and Marielena Hincapié. 2003. *Social Security Administration's No-Match Letter Program: Implications for Immigration*

Enforcement and Workers' Rights. Chicago: Center for Urban Economic Development/Center for Community Change/National Interfaith Committee for Worker Justice/National Immigration Law Center/Jobs with Justice.

Melendez, Barbara. 2013. "Bridging the Immigration Divide." *USF News*, January 17. http://news.usf.edu/article/templates/?a=5106&z=210.

Milkman, Ruth. 2006. *L.A. Story: Immigrant Workers and the Future of the U.S. Labor Movement*. New York: Sage Foundation.

Milkman, Ruth, Joshua Bloom, and Victor Narro. 2010. *Working for Justice: The L.A. Model of Organizing and Advocacy*. Ithaca, NY: Cornell University Press.

Milkman, Ruth, Ana Luz González, and Victor Narro. 2010. *Wage Theft and Workplace Violations in Los Angeles: The Failure of Employment and Labor Law for Low-Wage Workers*. Los Angeles: Institute for Research on Labor and Employment, UCLA. http://kiwa.org/wp-content/uploads/2014/01/LAwagetheft1.pdf.

Milkman, Ruth, and Kim Voss. 2004. *Rebuilding Labor: Organizing and Organizers in the New Union Movement*. Ithaca, NY: Cornell University Press.

Milkman, Ruth, and Kent Wong. 2000. "Organizing the Wicked City: The 1992 Southern California Drywall Strike." In *Organizing Immigrants: The Challenge for Unions in Contemporary California*, edited by Ruth Milkman, 169–98. Ithaca, NY: Cornell University Press.

Mississippi Band of Choctaw Indians. 2007. Official website. www.choctaw.org.

Mississippi Department of Archives and History. 2008. "Sovereignty Commission Online Agency History." http://mdah.state.ms.us/arlib/contents/er/sovcom/scagencycasehistory.php.

Mississippi State University. 2007. *Economic Impact of the Mississippi Poultry Industry*. Starkville: Mississippi Agricultural and Forestry Experiment Station.

Moberg, David. 1980. "Puttin' Down Ol' Massa: Laurel, Mississippi, 1979." In *Working Lives: The Southern Exposure History of Labor in the South*, edited by Marc S. Miller, 291–301. New York: Pantheon Books.

Mohl, Raymond. 1990. "On the Edge: Blacks and Hispanics in Metropolitan Miami since 1959." *Florida Historical Quarterly* 69 (1): 37–56.

———. 2003. "Globalization, Latinization, and the Nuevo New South." *Journal of American Ethnic History* 22 (4): 31–66.

Moody, Anne. 1968. *Coming of Age in Mississippi*. New York: Dell.

Moraga, Cherríe, and Gloria Anzaldúa. 1981. *This Bridge Called My Back: Writings by Radical Women of Color*. Latham: Kitchen Table.

Morales, Rebecca, and Frank Bonilla. 1993. "Restructuring and the New Inequality." In *Latinos in a Changing U.S. Economy: Comparative Perspectives on Growing Inequality*, edited by Rebecca Morales and Frank Bonilla, 1–27. Newbury Park, CA: Sage.

Morrow, Rev. J. H. 1957. *Forest Mississippi: From Pine Grove to Metropolis, A.D. 1860 to A.D. 1957.* MS: Methodist Men, Forest Methodist Church.

MPOWER. 2008. "Ergonomics and OSHA: Prevention of Common Poultry Plant Injuries." In *Solidarity/Solidaridad: Building Cross-Cultural Understanding for Poultry Worker Justice.* In the author's possession.

Murphy, Arthur D., Colleen Blanchard, and Jennifer A. Hill. 2001. *Latino Workers in the Contemporary South.* Edited by Michael V. Angrosino. Southern Anthropological Society Proceedings 34. Athens: University of Georgia Press.

Musolin, Kristin, Jessica G. Ramsey, James T. Wassell, David L. Hard, and Charles Mueller. 2014. "Evaluation of Musculoskeletal Disorders and Traumatic Injuries among Employees at a Poultry Processing Plant: Health Hazard Evaluation Report 2012-0125-3204." U.S. Department of Health and Human Services, Centers for Disease Control and Prevention, National Institute for Occupational Safety and Health. www.cdc.gov/niosh/hhe/reports/pdfs/2012-0125-3204.pdf.

Nabudere, Dani Wadada. 2008. "Research, Activism, and Knowledge Production." In *Engaging Contradictions: Theory, Politics, and Methods of Activist Scholarship,* edited by Charles R. Hale, 62–87. Berkeley: University of California Press.

Nader, Laura. 1972. "Up the Anthropologist—Perspectives Gained from Studying Up." In Hymes 1972, 284–309.

Nagengast, Carole, and Michael Kearney. 1990. "Mixtec Ethnicity: Social Identity, Political Consciousness, and Political Activism." *Latin American Research Review* 25 (2): 61–91.

Narayan, Kirin. 1993. "How Native Is a 'Native Anthropologist'?" *American Anthropologist,* no. 95: 671–86.

Narro, Victor. 2005. "Impacting Next Wave Organizing: Creative Campaign Strategies of the Los Angeles Worker Centers." *New York Law School Law Review,* no. 50: 465–513.

National Conference of State Legislatures. 2012. "E-Verify." December 18. www.ncsl.org/research/immigration/everify-faq.aspx.

National Employment Law Project. 2002. *Reverification: When May Employers Check Work Authorization?* New York: NELP.

———. 2009. "Worksite Immigration Enforcement and No-Match." www.nelp.org/site/issues/category/worksite_immigration_enforcement_and_no_match.

National Immigration Law Center. 2008. "Social Security Administration 'No-Match' Letter Toolkit." 3rd ed. www.nilc.org/immsemplymnt/SSA-NM_Toolkit/index.htm.

Neubeck, Kenneth J., and Noel A. Cazenave. 2001. *Welfare Racism: Playing the Race Card against America's Poor.* New York: Routledge.

O'Brien, Eileen. 2008. *The Racial Middle: Latinos and Asian Americans Living beyond the Racial Divide.* New York: New York University Press.

Odem, Mary, and Elaine Lacy. 2009. *Latino Immigrants and the Transformation of the U.S. South.* Athens: University of Georgia Press.

Ollinger, Michael, James MacDonald, and Milton Madison. 2005. "Technological Change and Economies of Scale in U.S. Poultry Processing." *American Journal of Agricultural Economics* 87 (1): 116–29.

Orey, Byron D'Andra. 2000. "Black Legislative Politics in Mississippi." *Journal of Black Studies* 30 (6): 791–814.

Ortiz, Sutti. 2002. "Laboring in the Factories and in the Fields." *Annual Review of Anthropology,* no. 31: 395–417.

Osterweil, Michal. 2013. "Rethinking Public Anthropology through Epistemic Politics and Theoretical Practice." *Cultural Anthropology* 28 (4): 598–620.

Painter, Joe. 2002. "The Rise of the Workfare State." In *Geographies of Global Change: Remapping the World,* edited by Ronald J. Johnston, Peter J. Taylor, and Michael J. Watts, 158–73. London: Blackwell.

Parrado, Emilio, and William Kandel. 2011. "Industrial Change, Hispanic Immigration, and the Internal Migration of Low-Skilled Native Male Workers in the United States, 1995–2000." *Social Science Research,* no. 40: 626–40.

Passel, Jeffrey A., and D'Vera Cohn. 2011. *Unauthorized Immigrant Population: National and State Trends, 2010.* Washington, DC: Pew Hispanic Center.

Pastor, Manuel, Juan De Lara, and Justin Scoggins. 2011. *All Together Now? African Americans, Immigrants and the Future of California.* Los Angeles: Center for the Study of Immigrant Integration, University of Southern California.

Payne, Charles M. 1996. *I've Got the Light of Freedom: The Organizing Tradition and the Mississippi Freedom Struggle.* Berkeley: University of California Press.

Peacock, James. 2007. *Grounded Globalism: How the U.S. South Embraces the World.* Athens: University of Georgia Press.

Pérez, Emma. 1999. *The Decolonial Imaginary: Writing Chicanas into History.* Bloomington: Indiana University Press.

Perry, Keisha-Khan Y. 2013. *Black Women against the Land Grab: The Fight for Racial Justice in Brazil.* Minneapolis: University of Minnesota Press.

Persaud, Randolph B., and Clarence Lusane. 2000. "The New Economy, Globalisation and the Impact on African Americans." *Race and Class* 42 (1): 21–34.

Petras, James F., and Henry Veltmeyer. 2001. *Globalization Unmasked: Imperialism in the 21st Century.* New York: Zed.

Pitts, Steven. 2007. "The Race Question and Building Labor Power in the Context of the Immigrant Upsurge." *Fall Labor and Working-Class*

History Association Newsletter, Fall. www.lawcha.org/newsletters/fall07
.pdf.

Polgar, Steven. 1979. "Applied, Action, Radical and Committed Anthropology."
In *Currents in Anthropology: Essays in Honor of Sol Tax*, edited by Robert
E. Hinshaw, 409–18. New York: Mouton.

Price, Amy, Emily Timm, and Cristina Tzintzun. 2013. *Build a Better Texas:
Construction and Working Conditions in the Lone Star State*. Austin:
Workers Defense Project in Collaboration with the Division of Diversity and
Community Engagement at the University of Texas at Austin. www
.workersdefense.org/Build%20a%20Better%20Texas_FINAL.pdf.

Quandt, Sara A., Joseph G. Grzywacz, Antonio Marin, Lourdes Carillo, Michael
L. Coates, Bless Burke, and Thomas A. Arcury. 2006. "Illnesses and Injuries
Reported by Latino Poultry Workers in Western North Carolina." *American
Journal of Industrial Medicine* 49 (5): 343–51.

Ramzy, Curtis T. 1984. "Leake County Produce Company." In Spence and
Spence 1984, 179–80.

Rasmussen, Wayne. 1951. "A History of the Emergency Farm Labor Supply
Program: 1943–47." *Agricultural Monograph*, no. 13: 288–98.

Reagan, Ronald. 1987. *Radio Address to the Nation on Welfare Reform*, August
1. www.presidency.ucsb.edu/ws/index.php?pid=34638.

Ribas, Vanesa. 2015. *On the Line: Slaughterhouse Lives and the Making of the
New South*. Berkeley: University of California Press.

Richardson, Riché. 2007. *Black Masculinity and the U.S. South: From Uncle
Tom to Gangsta*. Athens: University of Georgia Press.

Roediger, David R. 1991. *The Wages of Whiteness: Race and the Making of the
American Working Class*. New York: Verso.

"Rogers Wins Tennis Tournament." 1989. *Rogers Report* 3 (3): 3.

"Rogers Wins Title in Southern Open." 1989. *Rogers Report* 3 (2): 2.

Rosaldo, Renato. 1989. *Culture and Truth: The Remaking of Social Analysis*.
Boston: Beacon.

Rose, Mariel. 2008. "South Meets South: Work, Immigration, and Neoliberalism in the Carolina Appalachians." PhD diss., New York University.

Rose, Nikolas S. 1999. *Powers of Freedom: Reframing Political Thought*.
Cambridge: Cambridge University Press.

Rouse, Roger. 1991. "Mexican Migration and the Social Space of Postmodernism." *Diaspora* 1 (1): 8–23.

Rouverol, Alicia J. 2003. "Collaborative Oral History in a Correctional Setting:
Promise and Pitfalls." *Oral History Review* 30 (1): 61–85.

Rowe-Sims, Sarah. 1999. "The Mississippi State Sovereignty Commission: An
Agency History." *Journal of Mississippi History*, no. 61: 29–58.

Rowe-Sims, Sarah, Sandra Boyd, and H. T. Holmes. 2005. "Balancing Privacy
and Access: Opening the Mississippi State Sovereignty Commission

Records." *Privacy and Confidentiality Perspectives: Archivists and Archival Records,* edited by Menzi L. Behrnd-Klodt and Peter J. Wosh, 159–74. Chicago: Society of American Archivists.

RWDSU. 2005. "Bathroom Breaks: A Statement from the RWDSU." www
.rwdsu.info/en/archives/2005/03/bathroom_breaks.html.

Rylko-Bauer, Barbara, Merrill Singer, and John Van Willigen. 2006. "Reclaiming Applied Anthropology: Its Past, Present, and Future." *American Anthropologist* 108 (1): 178–90.

Sampson, Kristin, and Carole Morrison. 2007. *US Poultry in the Global Economy: Impacts on Women, Livelihoods, and the Environment.* Washington, DC: Center of Concern.

Sandoval, Chela. 1991. "U.S. Third World Feminism: The Theory and Method of Oppositional Consciousness in the Postmodern World." *Genders,* no. 10: 1–24.

Sanford, Victoria, and Asale Angel-Ajani. 2006. *Engaged Observer: Anthropology, Advocacy, and Activism.* New Brunswick, NJ: Rutgers University Press.

Sassen, Saskia. 1998. *Globalization and Its Discontents: Essays on the New Mobility of People and Money.* New York: New Press.

Saucedo, Leticia M. 2006. "The Employer Preference for the Subservient Worker and the Making of the Brown Collar Workplace." *Ohio State Law Journal* 67 (5): 961–1021.

Saxton, Dvera. 2013. "Layered Disparities, Layered Vulnerabilities: Farmworker Health and Agricultural Corporate Power on and off the Farm." PhD diss., Department of Anthropology, American University.

Schensul, Jean J., Marlene J. Berg, and Ken M. Williamson. 2008. "Challenging Hegemonies: Advancing Collaboration in Community-Based Participatory Action Research." *Collaborative Anthropologies* 1 (1): 102–37.

Scheper-Hughes, Nancy. 1995. "The Primacy of the Ethical: Propositions for a Militant Anthropology." *Current Anthropology* 36 (3): 409–40.

———. 2009. "Making Anthropology Public." *Anthropology Today* 25 (4): 1–3.

Schlosser, Eric. 2001. *Fast Food Nation: The Dark Side of the All-American Meal.* New York: Houghton Mifflin.

Schwartzman, Kathleen Crowley. 2008. "Lettuce, Segmented Labor Markets, and the Immigration Discourse." *Journal of Black Studies,* no. 39: 129–56.

———. 2013. *The Chicken Trail: Following Workers, Migrants, and Corporations across the Americas.* Ithaca, NY: ILR.

Scott, James. 1985. *Weapons of the Weak: Everyday Forms of Peasant Resistance.* New Haven, CT: Yale University Press.

Sen, Rinku. 2008. *The Accidental American: Immigration and Citizenship in the Age of Globalization.* With Fekkak Mamdouh. San Francisco: Berrett-Koehler.

Sinclair, Upton. 1906. *The Jungle*. New York: Doubleday, Page.

Smith, Barbara. 1983. *Home Girls: A Black Feminist Anthology*. New York: Kitchen Table.

———. 2000. *The Truth That Never Hurts: Writings on Race, Gender, and Freedom*. New Brunswick, NJ: Rutgers University Press.

Smith, Barbara Ellen. 2001. "The New Latino South: An Introduction." In *Across Races and Nations: Building New Communities in the U.S. South*. Center for Research on Women, University of Memphis / Highlander Research and Education Center / Southern Regional Council. http://web0 .memphis.edu/crow/pdfs/new_latino_south.pdf.

Smith, Heather A., and Owen J. Furuseth. 2006. *Latinos in the New South: Transformations of Place*. Aldershot, England: Ashgate.

Smith, Jon. 2004. *Look Away! The U.S. South in New World Studies*. Durham, NC: Duke University Press.

Smith, Rebecca, and Eunice Hyunhye Cho. 2013. *Workers' Rights on ICE: How Immigration Reform Can Stop Retaliation and Advance Labor Rights*. Washington, DC: National Employment Law Project. www.nelp.org /page/-/Justice/2013/Workers-Rights-on-ICE-Retaliation-Report. pdf?nocdn=1.

Sokol, Jason. 2007. *There Goes My Everything: White Southerners in the Age of Civil Rights, 1945–1975*. New York: Vintage.

Sosnick, Stephen H. 1978. *Hired Hands: Seasonal Farmworkers in the United States*. Santa Barbara: McNally and Loftin West.

Speed, Shannon. 2006a. "At the Crossroads of Human Rights and Anthropology: Toward a Critically Engaged Activist Research." *American Anthropologist* 108 (1): 66–76.

———. 2006b. "Indigenous Women and Gendered Resistance in the Wake of Acteal: A Feminist Activist Research Perspective." In *Engaged Observer: Anthropology, Advocacy, and Activism*, edited by Victoria Sanford and Asale Angel-Ajani, 170–88. New Brunswick, NJ: Rutgers University Press.

———. 2008. *Rights in Rebellion: Indigenous Struggle and Human Rights in Chiapas*. Palo Alto, CA: Stanford University Press.

Speer, Lisa K. 1999. "Mississippi's 'Spy Files': The State Sovereignty Commission Records Controversy, 1977–1999." *Provenance: Journal of the Society of Georgia Activists* 17 (1): 101–17.

Spence, Mac, and Louise Spence, eds. *The History of Leake County, Mississippi: Its People and Places*. Dallas: Curtis Media.

Spofford, Tim. 1988. *Lynch Street: The May 1970 Slayings at Jackson State College*. Kent, OH: Kent State University Press.

Staats, Cheryl. 2012. "Furthering the Field of Intergroup Relations." *Race-Talk*, October 8. www.race-talk.org/furthering-the-field-of-intergroup -relations/.

Steinberg, Stephen. 2005. "Immigration, African Americans, and Race Discourse." *New Politics* 10 (3): 42–54.

Striffler, Steve. 2002. "Inside a Poultry Processing Plant: An Ethnographic Portrait." *Labor History*, no. 43 (3): 305–13.

———. 2005. *Chicken: The Dangerous Transformation of America's Favorite Food*. New Haven, CT: Yale University Press.

Stuesse, Angela. 2009. "Race, Migration, and Labor Control: Neoliberal Challenges to Organizing Mississippi's Poultry Workers." In Odem and Lacy 2009, 91–111.

———. 2010. "What's 'Justice and Dignity' Got to Do with It? Migrant Vulnerability, Corporate Complicity, and the State." *Human Organization* 69 (1): 19–30.

———. 2015. "Anthropology for Whom? Challenges and Prospects of Activist Scholarship." In Beck and Maida 2015, 221–46.

Stuesse, Angela, and Mathew Coleman. 2014. "Automobility, Immobility, Altermobility: Surviving and Resisting the Intensification of Immigrant Policing." *City and Society* 26 (1): 105–26.

Stuesse, Angela, and Laura E. Helton. 2013. "Low-Wage Legacies, Race, and the Golden Chicken in Mississippi: Where Contemporary Immigration Meets African American Labor History." *Southern Spaces*, http://southernspaces.org/2013/low-wage-legacies-race-and-golden-chicken-mississippi.

Stuesse, Angela, Cheryl Staats, and Andrew Grant-Thomas. Forthcoming. "As Others Pluck Fruit Off the Tree of Opportunity: Immigration, Racial Hierarchies, and Intergroup Relations Efforts in the United States." *Du Bois Review*.

Stull, Donald D., and Michael J. Broadway. 2003. *Slaughterhouse Blues: The Meat and Poultry Industry in North America*. Belmont, CA: Wadsworth.

Stull, Donald D., Michael J. Broadway, and David Griffith. 1995. *Any Way You Cut It: Meat Processing and Small-Town America*. Lawrence: University Press of Kansas.

Symposium on Inter-Ethnic Conflict in South America. 1973. "The Declaration of Barbados: For the Liberation of the Indians." *Current Anthropology* 14 (3): 267–70.

Tait, Vanessa. 2005. *Poor Workers' Unions: Rebuilding Labor from Below*. Cambridge, MA: South End.

Takaki, Ronald. 1990. *Iron Cages: Race and Culture in 19th-Century America*. New York: Oxford University Press.

Tax, Sol. 1952. "Action Anthropology." *America Indígena* 12 (2): 103–9.

Thomas, Robert J. 1985. *Citizenship, Gender and Work: Social Organization of Industrial Agriculture*. Berkeley: University of California Press.

Tracy, Samuel M. 1895. *Mississippi as It Is: A Handbook of Facts for Immigrants*. Jackson: Messenger.

Trouillot, Michel-Rolph. 1995. *Silencing the Past: Power and the Production of History*. Boston: Beacon.

———. 2001. "The Anthropology of the State in the Age of Globalization: Close Encounters of the Deceptive Kind." *Current Anthropology* 42 (1): 125–38.

Tyson Foods. 2006. "Tyson Today." www.tyson.com/Corporate/AboutTyson /CompanyInformation/.

United Food and Commercial Workers. 2002. "A Voice for Working America: Injury and Injustice-America's Poultry Industry." www.ufcw.org/press_ room/fact_sheets_and_backgrounder/poultryindustry_.cfm.

———. 2005. "UFCW Members and Ergo Injuries." www.ufcw.org/issues_and_ actions/stop_the_pain/how_it_effects_you/index.cfm.

———. 2007. "Bush Administration Immigration Program Would Legalize Racial Discrimination." August 14. www.ufcw.org/2007/08/14/bush-administration-immigration-program-would-legalize-racial-discrimination/.

U.S. Census Bureau. 1990. "Scott County, Mississippi, General Population and Housing Characteristics: 1990." http://factfinder.census.gov/servlet/Basic FactsTable?_lang=en&_vt_name=DEC_1990_STF1_DP1&_geo_id =05000US28123.

———. 2000a. "Forest City, Mississippi, Profile of General Demographic Characteristics, Census 2000 Summary File 1 (SF 1) 100-Percent Data (DP-1)." http://factfinder2.census.gov/faces/tableservices/jsf/pages /productview.xhtml?pid=DEC_00_SF1_DP1&prodType=table.

———. 2000b. "Scott County, Mississippi, Census 2000 Population, Demographic, and Housing Information: General Demographic Characteristics." http://quickfacts.census.gov/qfd/states/28/28123.html.

———. 2005. "2005 American Community Survey." http://factfinder.census .gov/bkmk/table/1.0/en/ACS/05_EST/S2301/0400000US28.

———. 2009. "Mississippi, American Community Survey, Demographic and Housing Estimates." http://factfinder2.census.gov/faces/tableservices/jsf /pages/productview.xhtml?pid=ACS_09_3YR_DP3YR5&prodType=table.

———. 2010a. "Canton City, Mississippi, Profile of General Population and Housing Characteristics." http://factfinder2.census.gov/faces/tableservices /jsf/pages/productview.xhtml?pid=DEC_10_DP_DPDP1&prodType=table.

———. 2010b. "Carthage City, Mississippi, Profile of General Population and Housing Characteristics." http://factfinder2.census.gov/faces/tableservices /jsf/pages/productview.xhtml?pid=DEC_10_DP_DPDP1&prodType=table.

———. 2010c. "Forest City, Mississippi, Profile of General Population and Housing Characteristics." http://factfinder2.census.gov/faces/tableservices /jsf/pages/productview.xhtml?pid=DEC_10_SF1_SF1DP1&prodType= table.

———. 2010d. "Forest City, Mississippi, Selected Economic Characteristics. Universe: 2006–2010 American Community Survey Selected Population

Tables." http://factfinder2.census.gov/faces/tableservices/jsf/pages
/productview.xhtml?pid=ACS_10_SF4_DP03&prodType=table.

———. 2010e. "Morton City, Mississippi, Profile of General Population and
Housing Characteristics." http://factfinder2.census.gov/faces/tableservices
/jsf/pages/productview.xhtml?pid=DEC_10_DP_DPDP1&prodType=
table.

———. 2010f. "Scott County, Mississippi, Profile of General Population and
Housing Characteristics: 2010 Demographic Profile Data (DP-1)." http://
factfinder2.census.gov/faces/tableservices/jsf/pages/productview.
xhtml?pid=DEC_10_DP_DPDP1&prodType=table.

U.S. Department of Agriculture. 2014. "USDA Announces Additional Food
Safety Requirements, New Inspection System for Poultry Products." News
release 0163.14. www.usda.gov/wps/portal/usda/usdahome?contentidonly
=true&contentid=2014/07/0163.xml.

U.S. Department of Health and Human Services. 2014. "2014 Poverty Guidelines." http://aspe.hhs.gov/2014-poverty-guidelines#tresholds.

U.S. Department of Justice. 2002. "Department of Justice Terminates Argentina's Participation in Visa Waiver Program." www.immigrationlinks.com
/news/news1269.htm.

U.S. Department of Labor. 2000. *Year 2000 Poultry Processing Compliance
Report.* Washington, DC: Government Printing Office.

———. 2014. "Occupational Employment Statistics, May 2014." Bureau of Labor
Statistics. www.bls.gov/oes/current/oes513022.htm#st.

U.S. Government Accountability Office. 2005. *Workplace Safety and Health:
Safety in the Meat and Poultry Industry, While Improving, Could Be Further
Strengthened.* www.gao.gov/assets/250/245042.pdf.

U.S. Social Security Administration. 2008. Mission Statement. www.ssa.gov
/aboutus.

Valenzuela, Abel, Jr., Nik Theodore, Edwin Meléndez, and Ana Luz Gonzalez.
2006. "On the Corner: Day Labor in the United States." www.sscnet.ucla
.edu/issr/csup/uploaded_files/Natl_DayLabor-On_the_Corner1.pdf.

Vargas, João H. Costa. 2006. *Catching Hell in the City of Angels: Life and
Meanings of Blackness in South Central Los Angeles.* Critical American
Studies Series. Minneapolis: University of Minnesota Press.

Vélez-Ibañez, Carlos. 1996. *Border Visions: Mexican Cultures of the Southwest
United States.* Tucson: University of Arizona Press.

Vine, David. 2009. *Island of Shame: The Secret History of the U.S. Military Base
on Diego Garcia.* Princeton: Princeton University Press.

Vinson, Ben, and Bobby Vaughn. 2004. *Afroméxico: El pulso de la población
negra en México; Una historia recordada, olvidada y vuelta a recordar.*
Mexico City: Centro de Investigación y Docencia Económicas/Fondo de
Cultura Económica.

Visweswaran, Kamala. 1994. *Fictions of Feminist Ethnography*. Minneapolis: University of Minnesota Press.

Waldinger, Roger. 2001. *Strangers at the Gates: New Immigrants in Urban America*. Berkeley: University of California Press.

Waldinger, Roger David, and Michael Ira Lichter. 2003. *How the Other Half Works: Immigration and the Social Organization of Labor*. Berkeley: University of California Press.

WAPT. 2003. "Some Immigrants at Odds with Scott County Circuit Court: Marriage Licenses for Undocumented Residents Spark Controversy." August 14. Channel 16. Jackson, MS.

Warren, Henry W. 1914. *Reminiscences of a Mississippi Carpet-Bagger*. Holden, MA: Davis.

Warren, Jonathan W., and France Winddance Twine. 1997. "White Americans, the New Minority? Non-Blacks and the Ever-Expanding Boundaries of Whiteness." *Journal of Black Studies* 28 (2): 200–218.

Waterston, Alisse. 2006. "Are Latinos Becoming 'White' Folk? And What That Still Says about Race in America." *Transforming Anthropology* 14 (2): 133–50.

Watkins, Joe. 2008. "Nanih Waiya and Chata: Remembering Ourselves." In *Voices from the Mound: Contemporary Choctaw*. Exhibit brochure. Santa Fe, NM: Institute of American Indian Arts Museum.

Weinbaum, Eve S. 2001. "From Plant Closing to Political Movement: Challenging the Logic of Economic Destruction in Tennessee." In *The New Poverty Studies: The Ethnography of Power, Politics, and Impoverished People in the United States*, edited by Judith Goode and Jeff Makovsky, 399–431. New York: New York University Press.

Weise, Julie M. 2015. *Corazon de Dixie: Mexico and Mexicans in the U.S. South since 1910*. Chapel Hill: University of North Carolina Press.

Wells, Miriam J. 1996. *Strawberry Fields: Politics, Class, and Work in California Agriculture*. Ithaca, NY: Cornell University Press.

White, Sarah. 1996. "Organizing the Mississippi Delta Catfish Industry: An Autobiographical Work-in-Progress." Paper presented at the North American Labor History Conference, Detroit, Michigan, October 17–19.

Wickham, Allissa. 2014. "NLRB Asks Court to Pluck Poultry Co.'s Labor Probe Suit." *Portfolio Media*, October 17. Law360 (587955).

Williams, Kim M. and Lonnie Hannon III. Forthcoming. "Immigrant Rights in a Deep South City: The Effects of Anti-immigrant Legislation on Black Elite Opinion in Birmingham, Alabama." *Du Bois Review*.

Willis, William S., Jr. 1972. "Skeletons in the Anthropological Closet." In Hymes 1972, 121–53.

Winders, Jamie. 2013. *Nashville in the New Millennium: Immigrant Settlement, Urban Transformation, and Social Belonging*. New York: Sage Foundation.

Wolf, Eric. 1982. *Europe and the People without History.* Berkeley: University of California Press.

Wong, Kent, and Janna Shadduck-Hernández. 2008. "Immigrant Workers and the New American Labor Movement." In *New Directions in the Study of Work and Employment: Revitalizing Industrial Relations as an Academic Enterprise,* edited by Charles J. Whalen, 211–24. Cheltenham, UK: Elgar.

Woodruff, Nan Elizabeth. 2003. *American Congo: The African American Freedom Struggle in the Delta.* Cambridge, MA: Harvard University Press.

"Workers Come from Near and Far." 1995. *Rogers Report* 7 (3): 1, 8.

Yancey, George. 2003. *Who Is White? Latinos, Asians, and the New Black/ Nonblack Divide.* Boulder, CO: Rienner.

Yezbak, Charles. 2007. "Koch Foods Agrees to Pay Unpaid Overtime Wages to Poultry Workers." Wage and Hour Law Blog, May 31. http://wageandhour .yezbaklaw.com/2007/05/articles/overtime-violations/ koch-foods-agrees-to-pay-unpaid-overtime-wages-to-poultry-workers/.

Zamudio, Margaret M. 2001. "Organizing Labor among Difference: The Impact of Race/Ethnicity, Citizenship, and Gender on Working-Class Solidarity." In *Places and Politics in an Age of Globalization,* edited by Roxann Prazniak and Arif Dirlik, 111–38. Lanham, MD: Rowman and Littlefield.

Zlolniski, Christian. 2006. *Janitors, Street Vendors, and Activists: The Lives of Mexican Immigrants in Silicon Valley.* Berkeley: University of California Press.

Zúñiga, Víctor, and Rubén Hernández-León. 2006. *New Destinations: Mexican Immigration in the United States.* New York: Sage Foundation.

Index

Page references followed by *fig.* indicate an illustration.

accidents. *See* injuries/accidents
action anthropology, 234
activist research, 227–47; anthropology
   decolonized via, 17, 228–29, 240, 245,
   247; anthropology influenced by, 245–47;
   collaborative, 17–20, 240–43, 274n34;
   fieldwork/data collection, 16–20, 233,
   239–42; genealogies of, 234–37; goals of,
   17, 23–24, 228–29, 236, 247; identity
   politics of fieldwork, 20–21, 227–34;
   methodologies of, 19, 208, 236, 245, 247;
   multiple roles of researchers, 17–20, 239,
   274n28; and an organized collective,
   241–42; research questions/design, 17,
   237–39; and the struggle for liberation,
   245–47; successes of, 246–47; in theory
   vs. practice, 24, 240–41, 244–45, 271n15;
   and the unperceived observer, 24;
   validating findings/writing up, 242–45,
   274n34
AFL-CIO, 66
African Americans: displacement by immigrant workers, 113–15, 128, 158; Great
   Migration of, 33–34; job discrimination
   against, 128; migration to the South, 4;
   perceived as lazy, 75–77, 110–13, 117–18,

136, 157–58, 221; population growth in
   the South, 28–29; unemployment among,
   182, 269n22; use of term "Black," 249n3;
   violence by whites against, 29, 33 (*see also*
   cross burning; lynching); voting rights of,
   30; wartime leaders among, 39. *See also*
   Black struggles for civil and labor rights;
   racial segregation
agriculture industry's fair labor exemptions,
   34–35
Alabama and Vicksburg Railroad, 29–30
Algood, Tonny, 63–66
Alicante, Tutu, 231–32
American Anthropologist, 235
American Civil Liberties Union, 256n7
American Community Survey, 269n22
American Poultry International, 74–75
American Revolution, 27
anthropology: activist (*see* activist research);
   alternative products of, 245–47; applied,
   235; authority of, 235; critical turn in,
   234–35; and cultural critique, 235;
   decolonization of, 17, 228–29, 240, 245,
   247; engaged, 235; public, 235; radical,
   235; relevance of, 244
antidiscrimination laws, 104

CALIFORNIA SERIES IN PUBLIC ANTHROPOLOGY

The California Series in Public Anthropology emphasizes the anthropologist's role as an engaged intellectual. It continues anthropology's commitment to being an ethnographic witness, to describing, in human terms, how life is lived beyond the borders of many readers' experiences. But it also adds a commitment, through ethnography, to reframing the terms of public debate—transforming received, accepted understandings of social issues with new insights, new framings.

Series Editor: Robert Borofsky (Hawaii Pacific University)

Contributing Editors: Philippe Bourgois (University of Pennsylvania), Paul Farmer (Partners in Health), Alex Hinton (Rutgers University), Carolyn Nordstrom (University of Notre Dame), and Nancy Scheper-Hughes (UC Berkeley)

University of California Press Editor: Naomi Schneider

1. *Twice Dead: Organ Transplants and the Reinvention of Death,* by Margaret Lock

2. *Birthing the Nation: Strategies of Palestinian Women in Israel,* by Rhoda Ann Kanaaneh (with a foreword by Hanan Ashrawi)

3. *Annihilating Difference: The Anthropology of Genocide,* edited by Alexander Laban Hinton (with a foreword by Kenneth Roth)

4. *Pathologies of Power: Health, Human Rights, and the New War on the Poor,* by Paul Farmer (with a foreword by Amartya Sen)

5. *Buddha Is Hiding: Refugees, Citizenship, the New America,* by Aihwa Ong

6. *Chechnya: Life in a War-Torn Society,* by Valery Tishkov (with a foreword by Mikhail S. Gorbachev)

7. *Total Confinement: Madness and Reason in the Maximum Security Prison,* by Lorna A. Rhodes

8. *Paradise in Ashes: A Guatemalan Journey of Courage, Terror, and Hope,* by Beatriz Manz (with a foreword by Aryeh Neier)

9. *Laughter Out of Place: Race, Class, Violence, and Sexuality in a Rio Shantytown,* by Donna M. Goldstein

10. *Shadows of War: Violence, Power, and International Profiteering in the Twenty-First Century,* by Carolyn Nordstrom

11. *Why Did They Kill? Cambodia in the Shadow of Genocide,* by Alexander Laban Hinton (with a foreword by Robert Jay Lifton)